Tommy McGinty's Northern Tutchone
Story of Crow

A First Nation Elder
Recounts the Creation
of the World

Dominique Legros

Mercury Series
Canadian Ethnology Service
Paper 133

Published by
Canadian Museum of Civilization

CANADIAN CATALOGUING IN PUBLICATION DATA

Legros, Dominique, 1946-
legrosd@total.net

Tommy McGinty's Northern Tutchone story of crow:
a First Nation elder recounts the creation of the world

(Mercury series)
(Paper/Canadian Ethnology Service; 133)
Includes bibliographical references.
Includes a summary in French.
ISBN 0-660-17506-1

1. Tutchone Indians — Folklore.
2. Indians of North America —
Yukon Territory — Folklore.
3. Ravens — Yukon Territory — Folklore.
4. Tales — Yukon Territory.
I. Title. II. Series. III. Series: Paper (Canadian
Ethnology Service); 133.

E96.A86L43 1999   398.2'09719'104528864   C98-901363-4

PRINTED IN CANADA

Published by
Canadian Museum of Civilization
100 Laurier Street
P.O. Box 3100, Station B
Hull, Quebec
J8X 4H2

Senior production officer: Deborah Brownrigg

Cover design: Expression Communications Inc.

Cover illustration:
The cover, conceived by Dominique Legros, is a pas-
tiche of the turn-of-century book illustrations by the
great Russian theatre decorator, illustrator, and painter,
Ivan Iakovlevitch Bilibine. It integrates Alexander
Murray's drawings of the Kutchin Indians (Richardson
1851), who are said to have been dressed like the
Tutchone by Robert Campbell in 1850 (Wilson 1970).
The illustration was executed by Fabrice Descurninges,
a Montreal designer.
fdescurninges@netscape.net

Canadä

OBJECT OF THE MERCURY SERIES

The Mercury Series is designed to permit the rapid
dissemination of information pertaining to the disciplines in which the Canada Museum of Civilization is
active. Considered an important reference by the
scientific community, the Mercury Series comprises
over three hundred specialized publications on
Canada's history and prehistory.

Because of its specialized audience, the series consists
largely of monographs published in the language of
the author.

In the interest of making information available quickly,
normal production procedures have been abbreviated.
As a result, grammatical and typographical errors
may occur. Your indulgence is requested.

Titles in the Mercury Series can be obtained
by calling 1-800-555-5621;
by e-mail to < publications@civilization.ca > ;
by internet to cyberboutique.civilizations.ca
or by writing to:

Mail Order Services
Canadian Museum of Civilization
100 Laurier Street
P.O. Box 3100, Station B
Hull, Quebec
J8X 4H2

BUT DE LA COLLECTION

La collection Mercure vise à diffuser rapidement le
résultat de travaux dans les disciplines qui relèvent
des sphères d'activités du Musée canadien des civilisations. Considérée comme un apport important dans
la communauté scientifique, la collection Mercure
présente plus de trois cents publications spécialisées
portant sur l'héritage canadien préhistorique et his-
torique.

Comme la collection s'adresse à un public spécialisé,
celle-ci est constituée essentiellement de monogra-
phies publiées dans la langue des auteurs.

Pour assurer la prompte distribution des exemplaires
imprimés, les étapes de l'édition ont été abrégées. En
conséquence, certaines coquilles ou fautes de gram-
maire peuvent subsister : c'est pourquoi nous réclam-
ons votre indulgence.

Vous pouvez vous procurer les titres parus dans
la collection Mercure par téléphone, en appelant
1-800-555-5621, par courriel, en adressant votre
demande à < publications@civilisations.ca >,
par internet à cyberboutique.civilisations.ca
ou par la poste, en écrivant au :

Service des commandes postales
Musée canadien des civilisations
100, rue Laurier
C.P. 3100, succursale B
Hull (Québec)
J8X 4H2

Abstract

This book "tells" in writing the Northern Tutchone story of crow, which up until now and since time immemorial has been narrated orally. The text of this sacred story is based on several original versions told by Mr. Tommy McGinty, a Canadian Northern Tutchone Athapaskan elder from the village of Pelly Crossing in the central Yukon Territory, a few hundred kilometres east of the north/south Alaskan border. Pelly Crossing is the present-day hometown of the Northern Tutchone Fort Selkirk First Nation.

The story begins with an account of how crow rebuilds the world after it has been flooded. It continues with numerous other deeds, including the theft of the sun and the creation of daylight, the theft of water and fish, the loss of crow's beak, his dwelling inside a fish where he feasts on the animal's fat, various stratagems to steal food, and episodes in which he is a dupe himself or alternatively duping others.

This revered and sacred narrative bears on the origins of our present world. It is shared by diverse and numerous First Nations inhabiting the Northwest Territories, the Yukon, Alaska, northern Alberta and British Columbia, the northern part of the northwest coast of North America, and farther afield, eastern Siberia. Mr. McGinty also includes supplements developed to account for an earthshaking event – the exposure of the Tutchone universe to Western culture and the colonization of the Tutchone world by Euro-Canadians.

The volume simply reports this aboriginal Genesis and deliberately refuses to subject it to any particular anthropological theory. Equally, it refuses to speak of mythology and instead makes this oral text coeval with Christian sacred books. A foreword and an introduction explain why. A long postscript describes the meaning that the Northern Tutchone attach to the story and to the context of its oral production – whether told in full or in part. The postscript also examines the constraints that emerged when the move from the oral to the written was undertaken and suggests how the oral could be rekindled on the basis of the written. Those who wish to keep crow's heroic deeds alive and remember what they are honouring will easily recapture the greater malleability allowed by the oral.

Broadly speaking, the approach falls within what is known as new ethnography. The book's main task, however, is to pay tribute to the knowledge and wisdom of the people of the Tutchone First Nations.

Résumé

Cet ouvrage raconte par écrit l'histoire du corbeau des Tutchones septentrionaux qui, jusqu'ici et depuis des temps immémoriaux, ne s'était communiquée que de bouche à oreille. Ce texte sacré est fondé sur plusieurs narrations offertes par M. McGinty, un vieil Amérindien appartenant à la Première Nation des Athapaskans Tutchones de Fort Selkirk maintenant installée dans le village de Pelly Crossing, au centre du Territoire du Yukon, à quelques centaines de kilomètres de la frontière séparant le Yukon de l'Alaska.

Le récit rapporte d'abord comment le corbeau a reconstruit le monde après qu'il eut été submergé par un déluge. Il se poursuit par les nombreux hauts faits du corbeau. Ceux-ci comprennent le vol du Soleil et la création de la lumière, le vol de l'eau et des poissons, la perte de son bec, son séjour dans le ventre d'un poisson où il se gorge de la graisse de l'animal, de nombreux stratagèmes pour voler de la nourriture aux autres, et des épisodes où tantôt il se ridiculise et tantôt il ridiculise les autres.

Cet récit sacré relate l'origine de notre monde contemporain. De nombreuses Premières Nations y croient, notamment celles des Territoires du Nord-Ouest, du Yukon, de l'Alaska, du nord de l'Alberta et de la Colombie-Britannique, du nord de la côte ouest et, plus loin, celles de la Sibérie orientale. Le récit de M. McGinty comprend certains suppléments visant à expliquer un événement récent sans précédent, la découverte de l'univers culturel occidental par les Tutchones et la colonisation du monde des Tutchones par les Euro-Canadiens.

L'ouvrage ne fait que raconter cette Genèse autochtone et refuse délibérément de la soumettre à quelque interprétation anthropologique que ce soit. Il se refuse même à parler de mythologie, préférant donner à ce texte un statut religieux égal à celui des textes sacrés chrétiens. Un avant-propos et une introduction expliquent pourquoi. Une longue postface explique le sens que les Amérindiens attachent à ce récit, comment on le raconte, par morceaux ou en entier. Finalement, la postface porte sur les difficultés rencontrées lors du passage de l'oral à l'écrit et comment faire revivre l'oral à partir de l'écrit. Ceux qui voudront témoigner des hauts faits du corbeau et se souvenir de ce qu'ils honorent et font revivre retrouveront ainsi aisément la plus grande malléabilité de l'oral.

En gros, l'approche appartient à ce que l'on nomme la nouvelle ethnographie. Il s'agit ici avant tout de rendre hommage au savoir et à la sagesse des gens des Premières Nations Tutchones.

ACKNOWLEGMENTS

Off and on, I have visited and worked with the Northern Tutchone Athapaskan Indians of the Yukon Territory since the summer of 1972. Over the years, I have had the chance to share the lives of many elders, in a few cases for too short a time but in most for long periods.

In Carmacks my main exchanges were with George and Eva Billy; Johnny Mack and Ellen Silverfox; Stanley and Kitty Jonathan; Sam and Jessie Jonathan; Peter Johnny (Little Peter), Cathro and Margaret Peter; Suzie Skookum together with May and Jimmy Robert; Roddy and Bessie Blackjack; Peter and Sally Silverfox; Selina O'-Brien; Lily Washpan; Sam, Bert and Edward Charlie; Taylor McGunty, his wife Mary-Luke and his mother Violet together with David and Irene Johnson; George and Emma Shorty; George and Sarah Charlie; Jack and Rachel Tom; David and Gertie Tom; Jackson and Kitty Bill.

In Pelly Crossing my main teaching came from Mary and Jack Sam; Edward and Margaret Simon together with Harry Baum; David and Martha Silas; Dany and Betty Joe together with Julia Joe; John and Jessie Alfred; Fred Blanchard; Harry and Magdeline McGinty; Sam and Tom Isaac; Johnson and Victoria Edwards; David and Rachel Tom Tom. Tommy and Annie McGinty and Lizie Hager.

Other important conversations I have had were with Bessie John from Kluane Lake; David and Edwin Hager, Peter and Betty Lucas, David Moses, and Lucy and Sam Peter from Mayo on the Stewart river; John and Polly Fraser from Champagne in the southern Yukon. All my knowledge of Tutchone "law-ways" and culture comes from these people. But they gave me something more enduring. The lives they shared with me transformed my own life, my conceptions of right and wrong, of honoring life, my most fundamental ideas about what constitutes a viable social organization, my way of relating to people, the weak and the strong, and more crucial, the ordinary people; what I disliked and liked in my own French cultural universe, my way of loving a woman or a man, of sleeping, of relating to wild animals, who toward the end, even came to visit me at night in my dreams.

Thanks to the research assistants who have helped a great deal in transcribing the field-research tapes from 1984 and 1990-91: Andrew Conway, Cornelia Howell, Fabrice Rouah, Paul Schwartz and Larry Taman and the students of my seminar on fieldwork.

Lynn Hart, John Leavitt, David Mofford, Mark Paulse, and Anthony Synnott have proofread the manuscript, in parts or in whole. They are good friends and have done their best to give me a hand. But feel free to hold them responsible for any oddities left in my English syntax. English is their native language, not mine. While it is true that they worked for free, this is no excuse. Be that as it may, great thanks to all.

À Leïla-Tsäntch'ia qui connaît l'histoire du corbeau depuis toujours.

In memory of Linda Joe and Robert Alfred, two Tutchone friends who died in 1990-91 at the peak of their youth.

There was one old man... who... had answers in the form of stories for nearly every question... asked, and he told stories unasked because they came to him to tell. They were unexpected visitors, those stories, he explained..., and they stood outside his door until they were asked to come in. He did not know why they called upon him and did not call on many others. They tortured him at times, these people and events who came unasked and walked about in his mind. They always seemed to want to get out where people could see them. They had puzzled the old man a great deal because they were not always beautiful nor their behavior pleasant. Nevertheless one and all wanted to get out as soon as ever they could to show themselves. They always departed about their own business once they had been given outside life by his lips -- for he could not write at all. So they had no home in the papyrus rolls like others who spring from the minds of scribes. These, his images and happenings of the mind, scramble from his lips and entertained the listeners for a day, then went to join the thousands of other dreams where they dwelt. Where did they hide? He did not know. But he believed that they did not die. They were stronger and more enduring than men.

Zora Neale Hurston
Moses, Man of the Mountain, 1939

CONTENT

LINGUISTIC NOTE

Use of Northern Tutchone words has been kept to a minimum. In some cases such words are present because English cannot adequately translate some Tutchone ideas. However, in many instances, Tutchone phrases are here simply to remind the reader that Mr. McGinty's first language was not English and that the story he narrates was originally conceived in a First Nation language.

The Northern Tutchone alphabet used is adapted from the phonemic chart developed by The Yukon Native Language Centre. It counts 43 consonant sounds (including glottal stop graphically represented by an apostrophe (')); third line at the end, and 9 vowel sounds. When vowels are nasalized or lengthened, the meaning changes. Nazalized vowels are underlined (example *a* versus *a̲* like *ts'at* (hat) or *nalat* (boat) versus *dek'a̲* (man in Pelly Crossing) *a̲ sounds like an* in French). Long vowels are repeated (example *a* versus *aa*). Northern Tutchone language has four tones: high, mid, low-rise, and low tone (these are not indicated).

CONSONANT SOUNDS

Plain			d	dl	ddh	dz	j	g	gw	
Aspirated			t	tl	tth	ts	ch	k	kw	
Glottalized			t'	tl'	tth'	ts'	ch'	k'	k'w	'
Voiceless fricative				ł	th	s	sh	kh	khw	h
Voiced fricative				l	dh	z	zh	gh	ghw	
Nasals	m	n							
Nasal + stop	mb	nd				nj			
Others						r	y		(w)	

VOWELS SOUNDS

High	i		u	
Mid	e	ä	o	
Low	ae		a	
Diphthongs	ay		aw	

FOREWORD

This book is to "tell," in writing, *The Northern Tutchone Story of Crow* which thus far, and since time immemorial, has only been narrated orally. The text of this sacred story is based on several original versions told by Mr. Tommy McGinty, a Canadian Northern Tutchone Athapaskan Indian elder from the village of Pelly Crossing in the central Yukon Territory, a few hundred kilometers east of the north/south Alaskan border. Pelly Crossing is the present day hometown of the Northern Tutchone Fort Selkirk First Nation.

***

In writing the book I have taken some unusual positions which undoubtedly ought to be outlined and explained in its very first pages. Yet what follows in the next few pages will be foremost of interest to my colleagues in anthropology and, among general readers, to those who are curious about some of the problems which have recently faced anthropologists doing fieldwork and reporting their findings mainly for academic audiences -- not so much to serve the needs of the people they have worked with. A reader not involved in these debates may very well choose to move on directly to the story of crow itself, or to its introduction.

First, the singularity of the volume: although it is the result of a cooperative effort between Mr. McGinty and an anthropologist, myself, it does not constitute a traditional anthropological work for it focuses on reporting the story and deliberately refuses to subject it to any particular anthropological theory. In other words, the story is not given a meaning by resorting to techniques such as the structural analysis of myths or any other Western so-called scholarly approaches. The text is limited to the meaning that Northern Tutchone themselves attach to the story, to its full narration, to the context of its oral production, and finally to an examination of the constraints that emerged when the move from the oral to the written was undertaken. Broadly speaking, the approach falls within what is now known as new ethnography. To be sure, some may rightly argue that, somehow, I interpret the story for I select it for publication. If this is so, and it is, I do so, however, only in as much as I *celebrate* the cultural production of a First Nation and in as much as the activity of appreciating it is already in part interpreting. But this is quite distinct from *dissecting* for theoretical purpose, which is altogether an entirely different manner of interpreting. My hope is that in this theory-free format the story may keep its sacred character and have as large a readership as feasible, among First-Nation Canadians as well as among other Canadians, among non-specialists and specialists.

Second, a narrative such as *The Story of Crow* is usually categorized by anthropologists as a creation *myth*. However, here, the use of this epithet is avoided altogether, and the story is more commonly referred to as the Tutchone charter *sacred narrative,* as the *Tutchone Genesis*, or more generally as a *religious oral text.*

Third, normally, a creation myth has no known author. Nevertheless, as must have been noticed, the title of the book is **Tommy McGinty's** *Northern Tutchone Story of Crow.*

Finally, North American Indian creation narratives are supposed to refer to the beginning of time and not to realities which have obviously been brought about in the last few centuries by the coming of Europeans to America. However, Mr. McGinty's version of the *Tutchone Genesis* does address issues linked to the arrival of Europeans, to their settling on a New Continent (that is, into a universe new to them but obviously not to peoples such as the Tutchone), to the objects the outsiders have brought with them or developed at a later time – submarines included.

Such a series of limitations, restrictions, and proviso, cannot fail to lead some readers to beg at the onset for a corresponding series of questions.

First, why should *The Story of Crow* <u>not</u> be subjected to, say, among other techniques, a structural analysis? Why speak of a religious narrative rather than of a creation *myth*? Why make the story

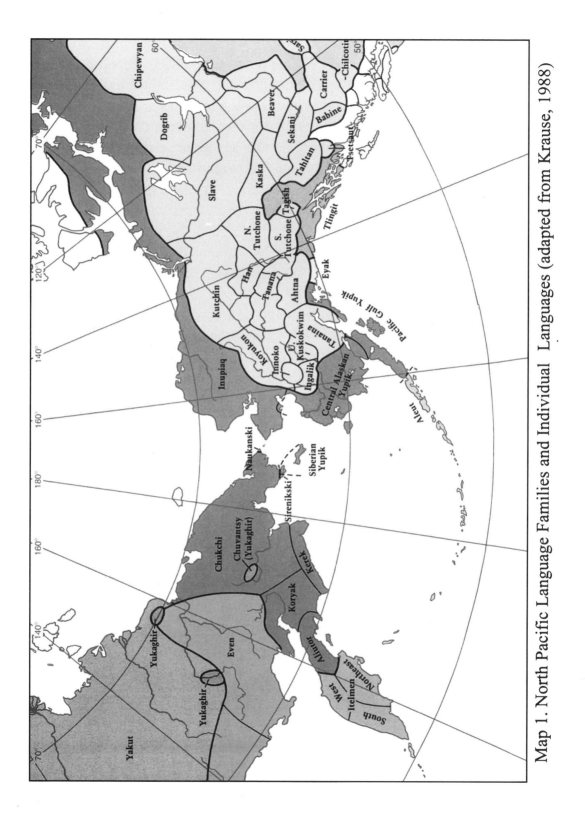

Map 1. North Pacific Language Families and Individual Languages (adapted from Krause, 1988)

someone's story? Are not such 'oral texts' always a collective heritage? In what respect this particular story may be said to have an author?

Second, why keep, in a supposedly very ancient story, obvious recent indigenous supplements which have been designed to explain the presence of a late phenomenon: the Euro-Caucasian contemporary world? Will it not make the story appear as lacking authenticity? In contrast, could this not make non-Indian religious texts (the *New Testament* for example) sound more authentic? Or could it be that even religious narratives based on the apostles do also innovate as they process and reprocess information through time? Finally, given the dominance of Christianity in the Western Hemisphere, can someone really find solace and a deep religious meaning in a story like that of crow? Who? Why?

These two sets of questions should be answered at once. Anthropologists will rush to raise the first series as preliminary questions of methodology. General readers, among whom many will be of Christian background, will inevitably have the second set coming to their minds as they discover the content of the story.

***

The reason why *The Story of Crow* is left unanalyzed comes from the contemporary relationship between observing-participating anthropologists and the people they are observing. Renato Rosaldo describes this new dimension with rare pointedness:

> Social analysts must now grapple with the realization that its objects of analysis are also analyzing subjects who critically interrogate ethnographers -- their writings, their ethics, and their politics (Rosaldo, 1989: 21).

My present a-theoretical position is entirely rooted in this new socio-political reality, which I welcome. It also validates one of Fabian's intuitions (1983: xi): such change cannot originate from an initial personal theoretical reflection but from imposed "changes in the praxis and politics of anthropological research and writing" (Fabian, *ibid.*). In my case, this change clearly comes from a demand made to me by the band council of one of the Northern Tutchone First Nations I have worked with, on and off, for over twenty years.

At the beginning of my last long fieldwork (1990-91), their band council requested as a condition to my planned study that I now research and write *for* Them, not *on* Them for *Them* in the outside world, "down South." Although worded less abruptly, in short, it requested that I become a scribe to Mr. Tommy McGinty, one of the most learned elders in Tutchone culture and a long-time friend and ethnographic consultant. After discussion, part of Mr. Tommy McGinty's project became taping in English all the sacred Tutchone narratives he knew and having me write them down as well as getting them published.

However, to have to change praxis, to move from studies *on* the Other to research *for* the Other makes one realize how much classic anthropological discourses are, to say the very least, unbecoming when addressed to this Other. Am I to present Mr. McGinty's material in the usual anthropological way, summarized and embedded in an anthropological analysis, dissected through one of the existing approaches to the study of myth? Are not these the present academic canons to conform to for anthropological work to qualify as scholarly? But, to refer only to the dominant school in the domain, may I really transform his narratives into shortened texts and tell Tutchone:

here is a scholarly and scientific account of your elder's narrative X -- its meaning is best understood by, say, an equation such as

$$\frac{[\text{overestimated kinship relations}]}{[\text{underestimated kinship relations}]} \cong \frac{[\text{man's autochtony}]}{[\text{negation of man's autochtony}]}$$

Am I to venture more such equations, which seems to convince some among Us, Western scholars, but are hardly falsifiable in spite of their mathematical appearances? Can I also do so knowing full well that the structural analysis of myths can also be construed as a mere re-mythologization of myths at another level *and a re-mythologization for Us* (see Lyotard, 1971 and Jameson, 1972)?

Linda Charnes writes that the academic studies of culture:

[…] run the risk of functioning like the AIDS opportunistic infection, to the extent that it isolates a host culture, moves in, and injects its own theoretical RNA, and then replicates its own structures from the inside out. And in particular it tends to look for host cultures and host communities that have typically been immune to these kinds of analysis, if only by virtue of their marginality. This is not to suggest that we should not engage in a certain kind of theoretical approach […] but that we should be aware of our own potential for parasitism (1992: 256).

Although the conceit conveyed by this metaphor is as elegantly expressed as risky to make, I can follow it in as much as successful parasitism implies a full "understanding" of and a "perfect match" with the host -- e.g. theories are not vacuous even though they might have nothing to do with the representation of the host *in itself and for itself.*

Nevertheless, be that as it may, clearly, for Tutchone readers, an academic study would destroy the whole allure of their narratives, the authority of their storytellers, betray their band council's aims, and even more so Mr. McGinty's. As Thomas (1994: 185) writes, at best most Western anthropological interpretations construe all Others primarily in terms of their difference from Us and thus reduce Them to the terms that complement White societies' absences: the Other's identity is talked about in as much as it allows thinking through the uprooting that modernity imposes on the settlers' dominant community. Hence, if our texts are to address at once readers in both the observed and observer's societies we cannot escape giving up on standard anthropological discourses and having to speak of the observed as our contemporary and coeval and of our societies as no less and no more than coeval to those of the Others.

This is why to use words like *myth* for an Other's creation narrative is as crude, coarse and unacceptable as to address a Christian audience on the *myth* of Jesus or a faithful Jewish assembly on its *myth* of *Exodus*. To a common reader, a myth is at once categorized, by the very word that is being used, among other things, as a fabricated story. And anthropologists do understand and use the word in this meaning too. For example, Derek Freeman (1983), who attacked as a total fabrication Margaret Mead's analysis of Samoan youth, subtitled his book: "The Making and Unmaking of an Anthropological Myth." To make things worse, he discusses at length why Mead's story functions like a myth by blending historical fact and significant fiction in such a way that it 'rings true' to an area or an era (*ibid.*: 95-109). Even if, with Lévi-Strauss (1958: 232-235), I believe that oral sacred texts such as *The Story of Crow* radically differ from the form of sacred texts in written traditions, to keep conveying this difference by applying the term *myth* to the former and not to the latter is somehow to betray the admiration that one has for the cultural achievements of smaller civilizations and, unwillingly, to keep oneself locked into the arrogant vocabulary developed by civilizations (with writing systems) which have colonized other peoples (without any). And to refer to all religious texts (oral or written; theirs' or ours') as myths does not solve the difficulty either for it introduces another bias. When They read Us, they also read in our choice of the word "myth" the arrogance of the so-called enlightened scholar -- of the unbeliever towards the believers. Thus my opting for more neutral terms such as sacred narrative.

The world over, anthropologists are now confronted with similar dilemmas (see Abu-Lughod, 1991: 159-160 for Egyptian Bedouins' negative reactions to her first book and Caroline Brettell (ed.) for what happens *When They Read What We Write* or *The Politics of Ethnography* (1993)). In other words, the informant, the field consultant, cannot be considered anymore as means to ends, but could be regarded as a possible direct, unmediated, conversational partner between *There* and *Here*.

To stay in North America, today's First Nation peoples are now publicly taking strong exception to academic "representation" of their histories or cultures (cf. Sioui, 1992). Conflicts over similar issues are such that researchers as prominent and respected by First Nation peoples as the Canadian archaeologist and ethnohistorian Bruce Trigger now wonders:

> *Can Non-Native Scholars Write a History of the Native Peoples of North America? Will the Cambridge History of the Native Peoples of North America be the Last Scholarly Account of Native Peoples by Non-Aboriginal Scholars* (Trigger, 1995)?

As soon as such questions are raised by the observed, the observer realizes that ethics or simple decency dictates that the insider material be published, at the least initially, with few comments on its meanings other than those made by indigenous consultants -- a solution bravely adopted by Julie Cruikshank in a prize-winning book (1990) much acclaimed by First Nation peoples, perhaps indicating a return to the wealth of minimally structured Boasian monographs, and one venue for the future of ethnographies.

***

Our version of *The Story of Crow* is thus published as it was orally kept alive by Mr. McGinty a few years before his death in 1993. Mr. McGinty was recognized by his people as the best narrator of his time, and also certainly as a man of great wit. This is why I have entitled the book *Mr. McGinty's Northern Tutchone Story of Crow*. Attributing the story to Mr. McGinty or evoking a personal version does not mean that Mr. McGinty has created the story. The story is first and foremost a collective Tutchone heritage. Behind McGinty's erudition stands in particular that of his grandfather Copper Joe -- a man born in the 1850's -- and that of earlier unknown generations of Tutchone. Nevertheless, and even if as Lévi-Strauss wrote (1958: 232), the substance of such a type of story lies neither in its style nor in its narrative form, nor in its syntax but in the story that is actually told in it, Mr. McGinty is certainly creative in relationship to the story's 'oral' script he has been handed down-- no less than a great pianist playing the score of one of Chopin's sonatas, but also, no more than any interpreter may ever be. He creates just as a great pianist does, that is within the bounds of a pre-given script. Tradition and creation are not antinomic or opposed. That the substance of a story lies in the story itself, and in a story with no known author, does not entail that the way of telling it should have no style. To reverse a famous metaphor made by Walter Benjamin ([1955], 1969: 91-92), the telling of a story clings to its storyteller the way the clay of a handcrafted vessel takes its last form, which singularizes it among all similar vessels, from the hands of its own singular potter.

Mr. McGinty's version of *The Story of Crow* was taped in English on three occasions (in 1984 and twice in 1990-91), twice for research purpose alone, once for Tutchone students in the context of a three-month Yukon College course on Tutchone culture delivered in Pelly Crossing. In the last case, in 1991, Mr. McGinty attracted young native men and women from three different Tutchone villages. His audience's response was enthusiastic. Every week, many of these First Nation students drove some hundred kilometers to listen to him and a few other elders.

Mr. McGinty's wish to have the narrative taped and written down in English came from a fear that failure to do so might lead to its definitive demise. Somehow, his worry was in part justified. For the last decades, all Tutchone children, teenagers and young adults had been educated in the Euro-Canadian school system which made almost no room for Tutchone culture beyond rudimentary lip service, if any. As may be expected, Tutchone language was loosing ground. In the 1980's, out of a total of 1120 Northern Tutchone people living in Mayo, Pelly Crossing, Carmacks and the White River area, only 180 were excellent speakers but they were all above the age of 50. There were only about 45 good speakers between the ages of 16 and 50. The vast majority of the younger generations were only poor speakers and about 200 were non-speakers at all (Anonymous report, no date; 27-31). In Pelly Crossing, proportions of excellent, good, poor and non-speakers were very similar to the various percentages for the overall Northern Tutchone national figure.

As Mr. McGinty could not read or write, his aim was to have a scribe (myself) who could provide public schools in Tutchone villages with a written version of this narrative. His hope was that Euro-Canadian teachers could thus pass it down for generations to come, especially to indigenous children, teenagers, native young men and women who no longer had any grandpa knowledgeable in indigenous oral literature and language.

***

Publication of this story in English will provide literate monolingual English-speaking Tutchone with a readier access to the story. However, to move from the oral to the written presents a manifest social hazard. It will also inevitably make the story known to Euro-Canadians living around them. This will most likely expose the Tutchone sacred narrative to expressions of disbelief and the faith Tutchone still have in their own *Genesis* to unflattering judgements on the part of many Christians who, thus far, could still think that Tutchone had been thoroughly Christianized and who had no inkling of the existence of this aboriginal version of *Genesis*, much less of its continuing importance among their First Nation neighbors.

Yet, discussing such narratives in the field with elders, my experience is that what Caucasians normally pass off as "myth," as "traditional," "static," and perhaps "non-reflexive," may indeed be as flexible and open-ended as postmodernity and in this sense more open-ended than religious beliefs based on "scriptures." During the last three or four generations, Northern Tutchone have made this Athapaskan sacred chronicle speak anew. Thus, its contemporary version addresses in the form of logical supplements issues such as the invention of submarines and motor boats or the connection between crow, Virgin Mary, and Jesus-Christ -- the last being the reincarnation through Mary of the first.

In the case at hand what seems clear is that the supplements given to the story are in response to the Caucasian cultural universe that has surrounded all Tutchone for close to one-hundred years. This competing reality gradually introduced new objects, social facts, and symbolic configurations that were obviously unknown and thus unaccounted for in the earlier versions of the Tutchone chronicle of the creation of the world. However, over time, hiatuses appeared between the world evoked in the older Tutchone narrative and today's transfigured Tutchone universe. To bridge these gaps, Tutchone embedded new components in their narrative. Yet, as will be seen, these supplements neither dilute the Tutchone content of the religious narrative nor adapt their tradition to make it fit the ideas lying behind the new Euro-American technologies, commodities and Christian mythology. On the contrary, the additions reveal how *The Story of Crow* already includes all Euro-American ideas and concepts (submarines, motor boats, Jesus, Virgin Mary, socio-cultural changes). In so doing, the inserts consolidate the relevance of the Tutchone account of the genesis of the world and thus prevent its otherwise certain demise from the contemporary Tutchone universe.

Caucasian Christian readers, unlike Tutchone (Christian and not so Christian), could enter into such a text with strong negative prejudices. How can "an old myth" still summon meaning or any form of faith today? Reading the standard episodes will no doubt help them feel or even understand why, for they will inevitably realize that they are not dealing with some inconsequential story but with a world treasure. But the answer also lies in the very supplements that have just been discussed and which, obviously, are now an integral part of the story for it is through them that it is kept breathing.

At this juncture, some may utter words to the effect that the story now lacks authenticity. How can the true narrative of crow truly speak of Western social facts, beliefs and commodities? This, however, can only be asked if one holds a naive view of tradition for any legacy is at any given time made of multi-layered, composite, heterogeneous discourses struggling for homogeneity. Europe may serve as a case in point. Since the Renaissance, it claims that its comes directly from Ancient Greece and Rome. But this is not exactly so. Europe forgot about most of Rome and Greece for close to a millennium. What is exact is that starting with the Renaissance, while Europe was threatened by Islam, some Christians unearthed discourses from long-forgotten pagan past cultures and reclaimed them in the context of a Christian civilization with, at that time, extremely deep historical roots. They did so to subvert the then monolithic discourse of Christianity, to alter the civilization which initially went with it, and they eventually did develop a new humanism through the process of reclaiming the past within a cultural context which had irremediably diverged from that of fifteen hundred years earlier. But there is no doubt that during such historical transplants, Roman and Greek discourses were mobilized to account for phenomena and developments which no Roman or Greek could ever have anticipated. Does this make the European tradition inauthentic? Absolutely not for it is now truly informed by the Greek and Roman past. Thus claims of inauthenticity in the case of contemporary First Nation narratives may very well simply be the application of double standards of judgement. As Sahlins reminds us (1994: 381):

> When Europeans invent their traditions -- with the Turks at their gates -- it is a genuine cultural rebirth, the beginnings of a progressive future. When other peoples do it, it is a sign of cultural decadence, a factitious recuperation, which can only bring forth the simulacra of a dead past.

Here, it may also be useful to evoke what Walter J. Ong, a brilliant Jesuit father and intellectual, concedes about Christianity.

> Memory lives. It lives in real time. It constantly reinterprets itself, relates itself to the present. Otherwise it is no more [...]. [The] continued proclamation of what Jesus said and did, based on memory coming from the direct witness to his life *through their successors,* is a *continued* historical event in the preaching and liturgy of the church. As stages of consciousness succeed one another, [such a proclamation] reflects the changes. In a highly mythological era, it speaks to the mythologically tuned mind. In our historicist age, it attends to its own historicity, and even "demythologizes." But throughout, memory must keep itself straight: must remember and keep alive what it is remembering (Ong, 1981: 168, italics supplied).

Thus, religion, which is always challenged by time and the reconfiguration of life, may well be a discourse to be continually "retold" if it is to be "heard afresh." And if this is true of Christianity, why should it be different for a First Nation religion?

In the Tutchone case, Western stories, social facts or objects have been decoded as other human beings' expressions of ideas which were already present in the ancient and sacred Tutchone oral narrative. Thus, Christian lore was not heard as bringing new "Good News" but, rather, *as incorporating some Athapaskan truth -- a truth content somehow twisted or distorted by Euro-Canadians who never knew crow before his reincarnation as Jesus.* Western technological thought as embodied in engines, motor boats, submarines, was similarly recognized as the implementation by foreigners of some of the ideas and concepts that the Athapaskan maker of the world we all live in had already set forth at creation time. Even the socio-cultural changes induced by being subjected to the power of Euro-Canadians were accounted for in Athapaskan terms. Through trials, errors or plain mischief, crow had given the example of breaking Indian laws in much earlier times.

This is why Jean Pouillon (1991) is right in insisting that tradition in an oral form can be faithful not by repeating itself word for word but by fostering creativity. In the Tutchone case, the incorporation of new episodes and new ancillary comments has been feasible without destroying the "overall structure" of the story and thus people's faith in it. But, if we follow Father Ong, is it not true of Christianity too?

Younger Tutchone might uphold Athapaskan tradition for other reasons than Mr. McGinty and the men and women of the older generations. Had I, like them, been raised since early childhood in their culture, I would certainly take a vantage point different from the one I have thus far adopted, and which consists in assuming my status of stranger among the Tutchone.

This different perspective would be very close to the one taken by a Tlingit ethnographer Nora Marks Dauenhauer and her husband, Richard Dauenhauer (1987: ix-x). I would simply paraphrase these two authors. Thus, would I have reiterated after them, we, like many other aboriginal peoples, are involved in our oral literature because we believe it has value in the modern world, that it is a treasury of spiritual gifts from which we can draw in times of need, and that we may find comfort and reward in seeing how our children's ancestors faced the puzzles of their lives. These are stories to make us adult, deliberately disguised as something else. But in fact, they do address in their own arcane way, which is a mark of maturity, the ambiguities of the human condition with which we all must come to grips: coming of age as adults, alienation, identity and self concept, conflict of loyalty, pride and arrogance, separation and loss -- and many other experiences that are part of being human. These stories offer an alternative, or rather an antidote, to the glorification of suffering prevalent among our Christian colonizers. They make us see the actual human condition from afar, from a distance which allows us to recognize in ourselves and in everyone else some lesser or greater degree of morality and immorality, but without having us wallowing in guilt before having acted in an evil way. They anticipate on a stage different from our own and in a time that antedates us by far, our contemporary dilemmas and our own unconscious wicked sides as well as those of everyone else's. Then, they make us smile or laugh at these aspects of ourselves and others. They are pre-emptive measures striking us back from both the past and the far away, or, rather, from when "everywhere" was also "everywhen," when there was not nights and no days and only a dull light. They will inspire generations to come, both Tutchone and non-Tutchone, as they have enlightened older generations, Mr. McGinty's and earlier ones. As we shall see in one episode of *The Story of Crow*, they even go as far as admitting, through a humorous plot, that a man is prone to extend his desire for his wife to his wife's mother -- and that for this reason the relationship between son-in-law and mother-in-law is in constant need to be policed. So these stories are truly more than for everyone to listen to and laugh at. Even though they may and should be told to children, children will make sense of their full potential only later on, when they will have become adults and when they will reflect on the stories told to them in childhood, as they narrate them to their own children and grandchildren. Ultimately, these stories are for those who wish to know who they are (whoever they are). It is in our reactions of rejection or closeness for this or that episode that we *begin to learn* who we are, (no matter who we are). It is in those reactions that we keep most secret, even to ourselves, that we *truly find out* our own truth.

Younger Tutchone's confidence in the *Tutchone Genesis* may also come from the *socially and culturally integrative character* of the contemporary form of the story in that it makes Christianity and Athapaskan sacred traditions coeval -- existing in the same age of the world. In contrast, Caucasian Christians are still extremely parochial in as much as they see their version of *Genesis* as closed (leaving no room and unable to integrate a different people's knowledge and understanding of the beginning of the world), and are incapable of recognizing and making sense of the sacred when it is expressed in a way that differs from theirs. A recent case may serve to substantiate the point. Sometime in the eighties, a group of First Nation students from a high school in the Yukon learned the epic of the crow and planned to perform it on stage for an end of term school celebration. However, at the last moment, the bishop responsible for this teaching institution got wind of the project and refused to allow this show to be part of the festivities. The performance of *The Story of Crow* was cancelled, pure and simple. Obviously, First Nation persons claiming to have access to the sacred through crow is still perceived by some Euro-Canadian religious leaders as a profanity.

Will the circulation of a written version of *The Story of Crow* as requested by Mr. McGinty help in fostering more mutual respect? We may only hope. However, will not having this tradition written down destroy the creativity that its oral aboriginal form allowed? In other words, will the book of *The Story of Crow* betray its actual storytelling? Pouillon would say so (1991: 711), but I am not as certain. Quite often, what its narration brings to an audience are bursts of laughter, not devotion to some god or gods (see also Clastres, 1974). Even written, a sacred narrative that somehow makes one laugh about its heroes can never confer to the sacred the rigidity of a written tradition which takes its protagonists and itself for the final word the world over.

Be that as it may, *The Story of Crow* is followed by a postscript -- *From the Oral to the Written and Back to the Oral* – in which are detailed the Tutchone cultural context, the recent history of this First Nation, how *The Story of Crow* was and is normally told, how the constraints of writing alter or transfix its regular oral narration and how the inconveniences of the written may be transcended by future storytellers. Those who wish to keep the memory of crow straight and thus remember what they are keeping alive will then easily recapture the obvious greater malleableness allowed by the oral format, of which *verbatim* extracts from Mr. McGinty 's 1984 and 1991 tapes are provided.

INTRODUCTION

Crow? Actually, the accurate English name for the crow of this North American Indian charter story should be the raven. But most aboriginal people use the word 'crow' instead of 'raven' and, here, I follow their usage.

The story starts with an account of how crow rebuilds the world after it has been flooded. It continues with numerous other deeds, some exemplary and some not so good. This revered and sacred narrative bears on the origins of our present world. It is shared by diverse and numerous First Nations inhabiting the Northwest Territories, the Yukon, Alaska, Northern Alberta and British Columbia, the northern part of the Northwest Coast of North America and further away, Eastern Siberia.

Needless to say, the account varies from Nation to Nation -- time and the oral transmission of the story across such a huge expanse of land and diversity of peoples is enough to explain why! Yet, in spite of this variety, the story is always easily recognizable.

Almost everywhere, crow combines the attributes and abilities of a male human being and of a raven. He is also characterized by an insatiable appetite and acts in very funny ways. Certain episodes are shared among most of the recorded versions. These include, among others, the theft of the sun and the creation of daylight, the theft of water and fish, the loss of his beak, the crow's dwelling inside a fish or a whale where he feasts on the animal fat, various stratagems to steal food from others, and episodes in which he is a dupe or alternatively duping somebody. In some versions, other special feats are attributed to him. Originally, they may have concerned other characters or they may simply be recent local elaboration (Chowning, 1962).

Mr. Tommy McGinty's rendition of *The Story of Crow* is one such version. It includes the central elements of the standard narrative as well as a number of supplements which must have been developed over the last three or four generations for they account for an earth-shaking event which took place only in 1898 (during and after the Klondike gold rush) -- the exposure of the Tutchone universe to the Whiteman's world and the colonization of the Tutchone world by Euro-Canadians.

The reason why Tutchone people talk of 'crow' instead of the 'raven' is simply that the word 'crow' was used to designate the raven among the early White settlers from whom they initially learned English, three or four generations ago. Today, some younger First Nation people who have been schooled in English prefer to translate the Indian word (*ts'ehk'i* in Northern Tutchone) by the "raven." Others would also like the name of the bird preceded by an article and no capital letter used for the name of the bird. The late Bill Reid, the great Haida artist, argued that,

> [...] dropping the article 'the', somehow diminishes the great figures of myth to imagined characters in quaint folk tales of unsophisticated simple people [...] (Reid, 1984: 64-65).

He also stated that to speak of "Crow" rather than of "the crow" obscures the fact that, in First Nation sacred narratives, animal protagonists are the actual animals called the 'crow', and not some hero or deity or god having the form of an animal (*ibid.*). In Tommy McGinty's account of the story I have adopted a compromise. I write crow and not Crow for it is clear that the nature of crow is that of a live being (with the characteristics of an animal as well as of a human being) and not of a deity as will be detailed below. However, I follow the elder's long established omission of the definite article. This omission is most likely due to their Athapaskan linguistic *substratum* and in this sense not intended to convey a special meaning. However, maintaining the omission in an English written version will serve to remind monolingual English readers that people like Mr. McGinty do not conceive of animals as Western people do and that his notion of the sacred differs markedly from that of, let us say, the Judeo-Christian worldview.

The Story of Crow is often characterized as a sacred and religious narrative. And so it is, but Mr. McGinty would certainly agree with Bill Reid: even though crow made the world, crow never was, nor is, a god, nor God. In as much as one must transpose the concept of "crow" into the closest English equivalent one may speak in a loose sense of crow as "God" and many Tutchone, Mr. McGinty included, do make this parallel. But, paradoxically, this proposition shatters the very Western concept of God for the crow never was, nor is, worshiped.

The crow, which is responsible for the genesis of the world, is the actual bird. But as elders put it, at the beginning of times it was not simply a bird -- "crow was both *human being* and *bird,* either way, back and forth." The crow of immemorial times is still present today in the form of the actual birds. When encountered in the bush, it may be saluted like a person, usually by an expression like "hello, grandfather" ("after all," elders say, "it is he who made this world") or it may not be. But other animals, which do not have any significant place in Tutchone religious narratives, are also talked to. When crows bother people by stealing and eating too many eggs from food species such as ducks or grouses, they may be shot at and killed like any other animals. The crow plays a role in shamanism by offering in secret, and through dreams, some individuals with its *zhäak* (its spiritual power as well as its ready-made medicine-songs), but it does so as an animal and as any other animal may do, not as a special entity. Here, the most important thing is that the general position of actual animal species in relationship to human beings has no true equivalent in European and Euro-American cultures. Within the Tutchone worldview, animal species are never simply animals in the Western sense for they are conceived of as endowed with *zhäak* -- a form of spirit and power *that no human being is born with,* but a type of soul or rather of poise or aplomb that some human beings long for. They can acquire it, not through prayers, but only through the unsolicited good will of a concerned animal species (or of several for the most powerful medicinemen or women). Conversely, the Western concepts of gods and deities or of God, and of the relationship that human beings establish with such distant entities through sacrifices or prayers, have no real equivalent in the Tutchone worldview.

The same may be said about the notion of sacredness. Sacred among the ancient Tutchone were the stories that were simply deemed to have actually happened in primordial times. To be sacred, stories did not need to refer to some transcendental realities or have their various plots conclude with some moral lesson. They did not need to be awesome, overwhelming, or towering and monumental. For example *The Story of Crow* provides examples of cunning for people to borrow from in their own life, and yet it is a sacred story to be highly respected because it tells something which is believed to have actually happened at the beginning of time. Upon hearing it men reflect on how to achieve their own ends through some new tricks (to seduce a woman for example, as we shall see in Mr. McGinty's account). Meanwhile, when between themselves, older women comment on the behavior of men, and the tone is anything but sacred (in the Western sense of the term) with lots of speculations about crow's nature and what it tells about men in general (Julie Cruikshank, personal communication). Could it be that this form of sacredness is antithetic to sacredness in the Judeo-Christian tradition? Perhaps! But then there exists here material for Caucasian readers to broaden their understanding of what constitutes religious behavior.

***

In the Western Far North, quite a few individuals still know and tell their respective account of *The Story of Crow* around camp fires or alternatively, but more recently, around wood or oil stoves in Western style homes. Yet it is still largely unknown to the outside world, even in Canada or in the United States, countries into which most of these First Nations have now been absorbed. This unfortunate state of affairs is obviously in great part the result of the hostility of Christian missionaries to Indian aboriginal religions, hostility that has forced the latter to go underground. However, several other determinants have played a role.

First, until recently, this indigenous counterpart of the Judeo-Christian *Genesis* has always been transmitted orally only and in unwritten languages which are very difficult for European language speakers to master. Second, it is composed of a number of episodes that may each be told independently and in fact, often are. The result is that non-native anthropologists who could have acted as culture brokers between these First Nations and the rest of the world have mostly heard only a few segments of the whole story and so only some episodes have found their way into publications. Fortunately, there exists an exception: Frederica de Laguna's work (1972) on several Tlingit versions of the story, and other work. However, de Laguna's versions are from a Northwest Coast ranked society which was entirely different from interior Yukon societies such as the Tutchone's. Third, whatever has now been published has found its way into print through university or specialized presses. Most often, in these publications, the story is not told for itself but is rather used in summarized form for Western anthropological and other theoretical concerns. To be fair, the phenomenon is not particular to First Nation cultural material. As Grover (1992) writes in a landmark volume on Cultural Studies:

> The bulk of writing on culture [...] that acknowledges culture as being produced by people other than artists, intellectuals, and academics seems directed to other academics rather than to the people whom they describe as producing it (1992: 228).

Such forms of publications have rendered the "texts" of these First Nations' sacred oral tradition not only quite inaccessible but also unpalatable to most First Nation and Caucasian readers alike; but particularly to younger natives who have been estranged from their forefathers' culture and who could otherwise use published materials to keep their tradition alive.

Who, but an scholarly academic would enjoy the dissection of a tradition for what it may eventually tell about the human condition over the pleasure given by listening to what this tradition actually narrates? Especially when it is witty!

Although I am an anthropologist with a keen interest in theoretical considerations, the written version of *The Story of Crow* here offered tries to avoid such pitfalls. To this end, I let what was narrated stand on its own, without unwieldy theoretical considerations, trying to keep as close to its oral format as feasible. Several factors convinced me that it is not only possible to tell such stories without cumbersome professional comments but that it is the best (if not the only) way to tell them in order to heighten interest in a printed version among indigenous readers and entice North American non-natives to hear the aboriginal religious traditions of their fellow citizens expressed in their own terms. By remaining within the Athapaskan narrative tone, it will also make the latter realize how much another civilization may express itself about the spiritual without the overbearing gravity the West usually confers upon the sacred.

The first factor that encourages publishing in as unmediated a fashion as possible is that narratives such as *The Story of Crow* seem to be fundamentally transcultural in nature. Could I be forgiven for providing a personal observation? For the last four years I have been cornered into telling bedtime stories to my six-year-old daughter Leïla. Many evenings, short on my own lore, I have narrated, among other things, episodes of *The Story of Crow*. The dynamics of children in regard to storytelling is particular. The same episode has to be narrated over and over, including the details that seem unimportant. Then, when the potential of the segment has been exhausted, but only then, the child requests a new episode; the order does not count much, just as in the original storytelling. However, in no case is there ever any request concerning cultural context. How could there be one from a two or three or four-year-old child? The story captivates readers or listeners without mediation. Most children ask for it over and over -- natives and non-indigenous alike. As will be witnessed by the thoughtful reader, the way the story plays with core dimensions of the unconscious may be part of its capacity for transcultural success among young children, native as well as non-native.

To say that the story is transcultural does not mean, however, that it addresses itself to the listeners or to the readers with a selection of some universal themes, if such rootless ideas ever existed. Quite the contrary! For example, most of this epic's plots (and their purports) have no true correspondence in the European lore, or, to take other examples from elsewhere in the world, in the Hindu tradition or in that of the Muslims. If *The Story of Crow* is as universal as, say, *Exodus* in the *Old Testament*, or the *Bhagavad Gita*, it is also just as local as these two great written traditions are. The story as narrated by Mr. McGinty occurred along the Yukon River just as *Exodus* is rooted in Egypt, the Sinai and Palestine, and as the *Bhagavad Gita* unfolds in the context of the battlefield of Kuruksetra in ancient India. And, if these three local stories are universal it may be because the universal reality of each and every human individual life is that it is always locally determined and contextual -- in contrast to what the French philosophers of the Enlightenment believed and wrote on the matter.

Another reason for the fortune these stories encounter with children may be that they belong to the category of hopeful tales as opposed to tragic myths. The distinction between these two kinds of stories was made by the psychologist and psychoanalyst Bruno Bettelheim in *The Use of Enchantment...* (1975). Bettelheim points out that in many cultures supernatural characters are not powerful beings but plants, animals, human, and nature spirits who use intelligence, physical prowess, or cunning to accomplish their ends. This clearly is the case in Tutchone stories. In doing so, argues Bettelheim, this kind of story offers hope and suggests the possibility of growth and self-realization. They are crucial for the healthy development of children in that they allow them to identify with human-like heroes who win out in the end and in that they give them confidence that no matter how bad things may seem now they might be improved in the future. In telling such hopeful tales parents pass on to their offspring the deep conviction that they too will achieve self-reliance and independence. In contrast, tragic myths foster the idea of human powerlessness and submissiveness -- these stories include many biblical accounts (*The Book of Job* for example) and Greco-Roman myths in which powerful or awesome or capricious supernatural entities confront human beings with all their might, too often making them lose confidence in themselves.

While it is true that stories such as that of crow make quite explicit and sometimes crude references to sexuality which may embarrass some Christian parents, they should still be encouraged to tell them to children the way they are normally narrated, like Tutchone do with their grandchildren, that is, by adapting the language to the children's age but without censuring these parts. To be truthful, everything is relative in these matters. In the case of children who have already been rendered too shy about the sexual dimension of human life, it is hoped that parents will be able to rephrase the episodes concerned in a way that reflects their own values on how and to what extent one may talk about actual sexual activities.

Or is it that words should never be uttered about such fundamental matters as sex in the presence of little ones?

In the same moment, parents will realize that Western culture, even in its secular version, does not let them approach the domain of sexuality in the same matter-of-fact manner as the Athapaskan. And this may make them wonder why different civilizations hold such different views on what is a proper education for children -- this would be an interesting intercultural exchange between Indian and Caucasian fellow citizens in Canada and the U.S. who usually do not have very much opportunity to talk to each other. Yet, I have to admit that when telling the story to an Euro-Canadian audience I have myself to tone down the directness of some of its language. As the old saying goes "When in Rome, act as a Roman."

All this in no way means that the story is for children only. On the contrary, the story is for adults to narrate; and while narrating, to marvel at its effects on the audience, to witness its obvious reverberations among listeners, young and old alike, and to, perhaps unwittingly, grasp that they, the storytellers, have been handed a masterpiece to tell without the tale making them understand in what precise respect it is so. Then, the adult narrator is also swept away by the breadth of the story's claims and questions herself or himself about its intended meanings -- especially for these events that are subtly surrealistic or deliberately playing with the constitution of the unconscious (without revealing how in any way).

Here, I cannot resist evoking Walter Benjamin's famous essay on *The Storyteller* ([1955], 1969: 83-109). Actually written more than half a century ago, this short text anticipated Bettelheim's analysis as well as what has been gleaned through field observations in many parts of the world. Thus, wrote Benjamin:

> The wisest thing -- so the fairy tale taught mankind in olden times, and teaches children to this day -- is to meet the forces of the mythical world with cunning and high spirits (*ibid.*: 102). [Today,] almost everything benefits information. Actually, it is half of the art of storytelling to keep a story free from explanation

as one reproduces it (*ibid.*: 89). [A story] does not expend itself. It preserves and concentrates its strength and is capable of releasing it even after a long time (*ibid.*: 90). It resembles the seeds of grain which have lain for centuries in the chambers of the pyramids shut up air-tight and have retained their germinative power to this day (*ibid.*: 90). It does not aim to convey the pure essence of the thing, like information or a report. It sinks the thing into the life of the storyteller, in order to bring it out of him again. Thus traces of the storyteller cling to the story the way in which the handprints of the potter cling to the clay vessel (*ibid.*: 91-92). There is nothing that commends a story to memory more effectively than that chaste compactness which precludes psychological analysis. And the more natural the process by which the storyteller forgoes psychological shading, the greater becomes the story's claim to a place in the memory of the listener, the more completely is it integrated into his own experience, the greater will be his inclination to repeat it to someone else someday, sooner or later [...]. The more self-forgetful the listener is, the more deeply is what he listens to impressed upon his memory. When the rhythm of the work has seized him, he listens to the tales in such a way that the gift of retelling them comes to him all by itself (*ibid.*: 91). And among those who have written down the tales, it is the great ones whose written version differs least from the speech of the many nameless storytellers (*ibid.*: 84).

To stick as much as feasible to the spoken word is what I aimed for when in 1993 I did my own first rough transposition of the *verbatim* transcripts of Mr. McGinty's audio-tapes into a flowing *written* text. As an economic anthropologist, my field of specialization, I was at that time aware neither of Dennis Tedlock's work (1978, 1983) on transforming "audible texts" into "visible and performable texts" nor of that of Jaime de Angulo (1953, 1973, 1976a, 1976b) -- nor even of Benjamin's essay on the storyteller. The informed reader will find that my idiosyncratic approach to transposing the oral into the written is probably closer to the spirit of de Angulo's approach to writing what was once only oral than to Tedlock's attempts at creating permanent readable/performable texts out of ephemeral oral performances enacted from memory alone. Although obviously my project was never meant to make a theoretical contribution in the field of oral literature, I will nevertheless make a very modest one in the postscript on the basis of my experience in the field and of my experiments in writing up the oral. From this personal vantage point I will briefly outline what a "performable text" can do and what it cannot pretend to do. My point will be on where the *gift of retelling* comes from and what the consequences may be for "textual" narration.

***

North American publishers have not yet shown much interest in giving a direct and unmediated voice to such people with such oral traditions. But this does not mean that their stories could not have a broad readership. France's most prestigious publishing house -- Les Éditions Gallimard -- has a special collection devoted to them. Under the editorship of the great French novelist and storyteller Jean-Marie Le Clézio, it has now successfully published some twenty volumes, quite a few from South American Indian narrators. As Le Clézio reminds us in a pamphlet for the *Québec Festival Présence Autochtone 1998*:

> Whatever our cultural origins, our responsibility for the survival of such people is involved. Ameridians are no strangers to us.
> They are a part of ourselves, of our own destiny (my translation).

In what local cultural context was, and is told the story that Le Clézio could have published? How was the transition from Mr. McGinty's oral versions to a written one made? What difficulties were encountered? What were the philosophical quandaries linked to these hurdles? If, as Benjamin writes, and as I also know it to be true, "half of the art of storytelling [is] to keep a story free from explanation as one reproduces it" (*ibid.*: 89), let us postpone answering. Let us first enter into Mr. McGinty's Athapaskan world by the front door! By his narrating of what crow really did for people at the dawn of time; for people from all walks of life! First Nation or Others.

TOMMY McGINTY'S

NORTHERN TUTCHONE STORY OF CROW

THE WORLD IS FLOODED, BUT CROW SAVES HIS LIFE

Crow is the one who put up the world -- first time. And in the early days, way back, crow could turn into man and back into bird and fly around -- either way, back and forth.

Crow means *ts'ehk'i* in our language. But *ts'ehk'i* has got to have two names, Whiteman's way. Sometimes you have to call him God because that's God who made the world. And sometimes you have to call him crow too, because that's him, the crow, who really made the world we live on. You call him God or crow, either way, back and forth.

And way back, in the real early days, crow knows that there is going to be a big flood. Water's going to come up and up all the way. Somebody talks to him. Somebody tells him there is going to be a flood and that he's got to do something to get away. His mind is the one who tells him what's coming up.

And as he knows, he goes to look for two birds: one *yaazok* and one *chät tadjia. Yaazok*, that's the gray bird with yellow legs and a real sharp beak like a pencil, about seven or eight inches long. The Whiteman doesn't know this bird's true name. So he calls it the great yellow-leg sandpiper. This bird hangs around lakeshores and marshes in the evening. His grub is way down in the mud. He's got to shove his whole beak down there to get it out. he eats, eats, and when he's got enough eat, he goes some place else. He flies way high in the sky, saying: "*tigidigi- digidigidigidi...*"

That's why they call him *yaazok*. And nighttime, you can hear him all the way through: "*tuguduguduguk...*" he whistles.

Crow catches one of these *yaazok* birds and kills him.

"*Chät,*" that means any kind of duck but all the big ducks have their own names on top. "*Chät tadjia,*" that's any kind of small duck and that's the only name a small duck gets: it means "big duck's fart." If he is a really small little duck, you can say "*chät tadjia zra*" too:

"big duck's little fart." When people want to be nice to a small duck they can call him *chät tadjiara*. Indian way, it sounds like "duck's fart darling" and it sure looks better.

So crow grabs one of those "duck's fart" ducks and kills him too. Some old Indians think that he took the little one with a black and brown body, a white shirt in front, and a big black head, except for big white paint on each side. That's the *tadjiara uh tthi' dek'aw*, the white-head little duck. When he flies he talks. He says: *chän, chän, chän, chän*. Not too many of this kind of duck comes to this Yukon country, but he shows up once in a while... That's a real fancy little duck. Whiteman's got a name for it. He calls it the hooded merganser be-cause it's got a big head like a parka hood. The Whiteman doesn't know about "duck's fart darling's" duck business.

And crow kills these two birds and skins them. He makes sure he's got everything: each skin with legs and beak, wings and head -- the whole bird's outfit in one piece with feathers on. After that, wher-ever he goes, he keeps these skins with him.

And it starts to rain. Rain, rain, rain, rain. It rains. Water is going up all the time. Crow flies around all over the place. He watches eve-rything. But after a while, he gets tired staying up in the air all the time. He looks around and sees one high hilltop still sticking out above the flood. He lands there to take a rest. He looks out...The water is still coming up. And it comes up more and more. Soon enough there will be no country left at all. So crow grabs his *yaazok* skin, the sandpiper's one with the long beak. He jumps inside, just like if he puts on a snowsuit, and he lets himself float way up to the sky. Pretty soon he's going to reach the place where the stars are. Star, that means *then* in our language... Old timer Indians say that a star is some kind of small hole in the sky. Crow sees one of the holes and sticks the *yaazok* long beak right up through that hole. Somehow, he knows what's coming ahead of time. And as soon he has got his nose up in the crack, the water hits him right clean up. And that water never comes down. So he keeps his nose up in the hole. That's the only way he can breathe. He waits, he waits, he waits, and he waits... He is stuck. Old timers heard that he stayed there a really long, long time.

Many days later, the water starts to go down. Crow feels it. His pants are getting dry. He jumps out of his sandpiper skin suit. Sandpiper that means *yaazok*: you remember now! Then he grabs his duck skin suit -- the *chät tadjia*'s skin, you know the "duck's fart" duck's clothes. He puts them on. The water comes down and he lets himself float around all over the place. He goes about just like a duck. But he doesn't see no land. Nothing there. He can't find no place where to land and rest. There is water all right around. As it gets pretty stuffy in that duck's suit, he gets out and takes off for the air. He flies around. He flies around all over the place. Nothing. No land. He can't find no place where to stay yet. And then he starts to worry:

"It must be I made a mistake," he says. "I came out of that duck's skin! What for I left it behind? How am I going to swim now? I don't know at all how to do that on my own. Damn it!"

He doesn't really swear but that's what he means. So he keeps on paddling through the air with his wings.

CROW BUILDS THE WORLD ANEW

And soon enough, he spots one small little piece of land sticking out of the water. It's so little tiny that you can't even say it's an island. Old Indians call it *nonga ddhaw*. It sounds like it means "there is something on top." Crow thinks to himself:

"What's that now? Let's fly down closer to have a better look." After a while he can see real good.

"That must be bare rock," he says. "It must have come from under the water. Let's go land there and see that."

As Crow gets down closer and closer, he also spots two black things on the rock.

"Hey, that's a woman and her young one lying down there on top!"

Old timers call these two guys *tsye*. Maybe that's the kind the Whiteman calls seal. To me it sounds pretty close to *tse* and *tse* means beaver. But I don't think these two guys were beavers.

And crow is coming in, flying downward from behind. These two animals look the other way. Crow thinks in his own mind what he is going to do. He medicine-thinks. He reaches inside that mamma seal's mind. He says:

"Mamma seal, I hope you don't look at me. Don't look back! Look one way!"

He keeps medicine-thinking while he rushes down from the air. Mamma seal never sees anything, and he lands right in between her and her kid, turns around, and, quick, grabs the kid away.

He knows what he is doing. He says:

"Mamma seal, I'm going to take this baby away from you, I'm going to fly away with it."

And that woman tells him:

"No, you can't do that, it's my baby, I don't want to lose it."

Crow keeps talking:

"No, I want to take it away from you for sure, you know."
And pretty soon both are arguing back and forth. As they are talking away, crow knocks on the rock, and asks her a question:

"Anyway, where does this one comes from? The one you sit on. Can you tell me?"

"It's from under the water," she says. "There is lots of it down there. Are you going to take my kid away from me if I swim down and get some for you?"
Crow says:

"Right on... That's land I need -- get it!"
That mamma seal wants her baby back real bad. So she dives into the water and down she goes. Soon enough, she swims back up carrying a great big piece of land. She pushes it right against the rock. Crow looks at it and says:

"What about this side here? Bring some more all the way right around the rock."
And the woman seal brings another piece and another piece... Then crow asks:

"Some more yet? Bring up another piece with some little trees on top! You know, with brush like that. Look here, I'll show you."
The seal goes back in and takes out one piece just like he said. Then, crow tells her:

"Take another piece! Keep going doing that."
The seal woman keeps going, doing just as he asks her. She dives in, she comes out... She dives in, she comes out... She dives in, she comes out... Pretty soon, she brings up a sandbar with some driftwood on top. Crow says:

"Where does this sandbar come from? Bring some more."
And she brings back a whole big piece. Crow walks around on the rock still holding the baby.

"What about this kid here?" he says. "I want to see more of that land. There is lots of room here yet."
She comes out, comes out, comes out... She brings everything back up on top of the water. She wants to pay crow to get her kid back.

Now a lot of land is piled up all around the rock. Crow looks and thinks about it. He figures that maybe it's going to work out good. The whole thing has come back again. He's got everything, trees on top, everything...

He looks at that mamma seal:

"O.K.! Here! Take your baby back."

That mother grabs her little one and dives right back into the water. Old timers say that she and her kid swam back to where they came from...

And this crow here, he goes to work on the land the seal brought back out for him. He pulls this piece in here. He brings another one there. He drags that other piece close by. He throws another one in... Pretty soon, all the sections he's got fit in with each other. Crow looks at his job. He sees lots of cracks left in between the sections. He goes around and plugs them up with a little driftwood and a little bit of sand on top. He medicine-thinks as he goes along:

"Glue together," he tells them pieces.

"Se dun ts'ao dye," he says.

"Inh ts'a e dye
Inh ts'a e dye
Sana do otl'e do."

See: he talks about the world. He says:

"This way, you pieces are going to come apart real easy when there're going to be earthquakes. This way, the world will not get destroyed."

He keeps going and fixes up all the sections with his driftwood and sand.

Then, beginning around the rock, he starts jumping with his two feet all over his ground. He wants to spread the land, to make it bigger: way out here, way out there, and out everywhere. The same way a White woman makes her dough flat with a roller. See that: crow's done everything way before Indian or Whiteman started doing it too! Crow knows everything.

And all along he medicine-sings as he jumps and jumps on his ground:

"Nuu-k'yeh, k'yeh, k'yeh! Nuu-k'yeh, nuu-k'yeh," he sings.

"Naanin-k'yeh," he means. "Spread away all right around and join together": that's what he means

"When I jump on you, listen to me," he says.

"Come right around and join together.

That's what I mean," he says.

And crow keeps making his circles bigger and bigger, further and further away from the rock, jumping and medicine-singing all over his land. He keeps them sections going, going around, and going around. They're all spreading out now -- out, out, all. Pretty soon they come right back around and crow's got the whole world made back, and it looks like a ball.

And it's not a bullshit story, I tell you. Them sections are still here today. Go down any place on the Yukon or on the Pelly Rivers. Wherever the water has cut out a big bluff, you can see that the earth is made of sections of sand mixed in between layers of dry mud... All over the place you see that. That comes from crow. And here and there, you find some old driftwood crow put in between his sections of land. Sometimes it has turned into rock. That's because of the way crow made the world -- how he covered up the flood water with the pieces he got back from the seal.

AN OSPREY DOES NOT WANT TO SHARE WATER

But after that:

"Darn, no water!"

And crow's thirsty, and he's getting hungry too.

"*Inhe mät sedetle*!" he says. By that he means "yes, I am hungry!"

He walks around, he flies around and he looks all over the place. Nothing to eat... no game. Nothing

Pretty soon, though, he finds one guy's camp. That's *tuundye*'s -- the eagle's friend's camp. Crow sees it and lands there.

Don't ask who made *tuundye* and where he came from. The old timers didn't say. But at that time this was the only other person in the world beside crow.

Whiteman's way, *tuundye* that's the osprey hawk. But his true name is *tuundye*. *Tuundye* is a big man -- about two feet from head to tail with six feet wide wings to fly with. He looks pretty much like an eagle but he eats different. What he really likes is fish. And *tuundye* is a pretty good fisherman. He sits down on top of a tree by the riverbank, watching the water. When a fish comes by, he sees it right away. It doesn't matter how deep down the fish is swimming... *Tuundye* flies off and catches up to wherever that thing is swimming. He dives in and disappears right clean through the water. After a little while, he comes back up with a fish in his beak and flies away with it. It must be that *tuundye*'s got special eyes, or else, that he's really good at finding out the little waves a fish makes on top of the water while it swims way at the bottom.

Anyway, the way the story goes, crow meets *tuundye* and finds out that he's the only man who's got water left. It's in a hole, about ten inches wide and about half a foot down in the ground. Under there, water is running all over and there are plenty of fish. *Tuundye*'s just got to shove his head in his hole. He can drink all he wants and eat plenty good too. He's got everything he needs there. But he's a pretty stingy man. He doesn't want anybody to get close to the hole.

So crow walks to him and says:

"Oh gee, my brother-in-law, I am pretty dry. Give me something to eat... Maybe just give me a little bit of water to swallow."

Indian way, when you call someone brother-in-law, that's really nice because brothers-in-law always help each other. And you can call brother-in-law any guy who is about the same age as you, but who belongs to the clan across from your own. That's because your sisters or yourself must always get your husbands or wife from that other clan.

But *tuundye* doesn't care about the brother-in-law business. He looks at crow and says:

"No, I won't give you nothing."

He shoves his head back down in his hole, eats some fish, drinks some water -- everything right to crow's face... *Tuundye* wants to save that hole for himself alone. He's real stingy for it.

Crow walks around -- round and round around *tuundye*. He doesn't know what to do. He thinks:

"Gee, I am dry, and that *tuundye* is never going to give me anything."

And crow thinks in his mind about what to do. Pretty soon he finds out. He says to himself:

"I chase that *tuundye* man away. I make like a war to him. When he hears an army is coming, he's going to get scared and run away. Then we steal his water and we steal his fish too. I made the land. I love it so much... It's better I chase him away. I take those fish and the water away from him and the country is going to be better."

Then crow takes a rest. He sleeps. When he wakes up, *tuundye* is still watching his water hole. Crow walks to him.

"Gee, my brother in-law," he says, "I had a real bad dream. I dreamt of a big war coming in to us. I think it's over this water here. Me, I die, but you, you run away. It's a bad dream. It's a big war. Run for you life. Don't come back to your hole. Otherwise, they're going to kill you."

And crow flies out over the bush. He looks around from the air. He looks for some water to drink but sees nothing...

"Gee, I'm dry," he says. "Let's land some place."

He flies down. And he already knows what he's going to do. He walks through the bush looking around for some tree leaves he wants -- some real fancy leaves. Pretty soon, he finds what he needs and he grabs a whole bunch of them. He sits down and starts to work on these leaves. He puts them together into some kind of shape. Then he talks to the shape he's made. It must be he medicine-talks to those leaves. Pretty soon this thing walks around. Then, crow says:

"You're going to be a bird. Fly, I want to see it."

So this thing flies around. That's a *t'ots'ya'* bird. Then crow makes a whole bunch of them *t'ots'ya'* birds.

T'ots'ya' is a pretty hard word for a Whiteman to say. When he tries it, his tongue gets stuck all over inside his mouth. So he calls that kind of bird hawks -- rough-legged hawks. That's easier to say. But he's got it wrong again because that's not the name crow gave him for sure. Anyway, the *t'ots'ya'* is pretty much as big as *tuundye* except for his wings which are a little bit shorter -- about four feet only. And the *t'ots'ya'*, that's mainly a mouse-eater even though he eats some fish too. He flies over open fields where it's easy to see any kind of small four-legged animals running around.

Pretty soon, crow is finished with the *t'ots'ya'* birds. They're going to be his soldiers. He keeps working, though. He takes more leaves and this time he puts the *etthedzaat* bird together. He makes only one of that kind. And he tells him:

"*Etthedzaat* bird you're going to be called *etthedzaat* or *atthiili'*; but me, I'm going to call you *Kushekok*. That's going to be your nickname and you're going to be like my own sister's son to me -- my true nephew. Any time I get stuck or I get a hard job, I'm going to call you to back me up, to help me."

It must be that later on the *etthedzaat* bird made many kids, and these kids many more kids themselves, because there are still a few of this kind flying around in the bush today. The *etthedzaat* man is a really small owl, about seven to eight inches tall from tail to head. He lives on mice. His head can go right around his neck. That's one owl that not scared at all. He never flies away when he sees you. You walk up to him, wave your hand half a foot away from his face, talk to him... anything. He doesn't take off. Maybe that's the one the White-man calls the boreal owl.

Once the leaf-birds are all finished, crow calls them back. The *Kushekok* and the other birds come in and crow talks to them all:

"This *tuundye* man there has got lots of fish and lots of water. Now this world's got nothing yet. No water, no grub yet. We try to get something from *tuundye*. That's the only way we're going to eat. You birds, there's going to be lots to eat for you. And after that your grub's going to grow for you. We also need water to drink. So we're going to make some water for the world and we'll try to make it good for all kinds of people to live in it. You give me a hand. We're going to scare this *tuundye* away from his fish and water. We take that water, we take all his fish, and we'll spread them all out on the land -- all of them."

That's what crow said first! And he added:

"I'm going to go back alone to *tuundye* and there I'm going to do like I die. And *Kushekok,* he's going to come a little later. He's going to find me dead and he's going to cry -- he's going to holler -- a really loud voice. And you *t'ots'ya'* fellows, you're going to come and make noise like if a war was coming. But don't kill *tuundye*, just chase him away..."

The *t'ots'ya'* birds say, "O.K." And *etthedzaat* says "O.K." too. The three kinds of them are going to go now do their things. And those leaves crow has made into birds to fly, he send them around. They fly around. Then crow says: "come back into men again now." They all come back to men.

"Now," crow says, "you take a club, and I'm going to see this *tuundye* man there."

So crow goes back to *tuundye* again. He gets to his camp and asks him again for water. *Tuundye* says:

"No!"

He doesn't want to give him any. Crow walks around for a while and then starts to stagger. It looks like he is real sick. He just pretends, though. Then he falls down in front of *tuundye*'s home. It looks like crow's going to die.

"Rhaa, rhaaaaaa, rhaaaaaaaaaaaaaaa," he croaks.

"Nothiiiiing tooo driiiiink, I staaaart dyiiiing now," he says.

Tuundye just watches him. And pretty soon it looks like crow is dead: he doesn't move, nothing there, no breathing, nothing! It seems he is real dead. So his helper, his nephew, the *Kushekok*, comes in. He sees his uncle lying down there, right across from *tuundye*:

"Aaaaaah! My uncle is dead," he hollers.

The *Kushekok* just pretends. He knows crow's not dead for good. But just the same, he cries:

"My uncle!" He means *ih ndoa,* my mother's brother.

"*Ih ndoaa, aaaah, aaah, aah, ah, aah, aaah*; My mother's brother, *ih ndoaaa, aaaah, aaah, aah, ah...*" My dear mother's brother.

From there, the *t'ots'ya'* birds hear *Kushekok* crying louder and louder. *Kushekok* sure can sound pretty sad when he wants to. They rush in through the bush. They break everything down there.

"Boom, boom, boom... Crack, crack, crack..."

It sounds like a big war party is coming in. The *tuundye* man can't miss the racket. He listens. He figures out some kind of army is marching on. But he can't see nothing. Boy, he's really scared now -- it shows all over his face. Pretty soon, he runs away for his life...

But he's sure too stingy for his water:

"What about my hole?" he thinks... "I'm going to lose it!"

So he comes back. He gets a few drinks and some fish. Anyway, that's what old timer Indians said... Then he runs away in the bush again. Not for long, though. He still worries about his fish and water. He sneaks back to his hole again. He eats more and rushes to hide back into the bush. Yet he still worries... He runs back again. But this time the *t'ots'ya'* soldiers make a hell of a racket and scare the shit out of him. *Tuundye* takes off for good. Run, run, run, run... Nobody can stop him now. The *t'ots'ya'* men chased him way out.

And that crow jumps up from where he had laid down dead. He's sure alive now. He looks around, walks straight to *tuundye*'s water hole, sticks his head down inside, and swallows fish and water and everything he can get. And he swallows and he drinks... He drinks... All you can see is his ass sticking out up in the air. And he keeps drinking... After a while, it looks like his tail's going to come right off his mouth. His stomach is so full that he's got no more room in there. So he pulls off. He nephew sees that. He gets his head down in the hole too. And after him, the *t'ots'ya'* gets in there too. When all everybody is finished, *tuundye*'s hole is just about empty -- crow and the other fellows have pretty near cleaned up the whole thing.

Now crow's team is ready and all of them birds fly off. Crow carries a little stick. He turns around and talks to his *etthedzaat* nephew (*Kushekok,* the little boreal owl) and to the *t'ots'ya'*. He says:

"Come behind me, follow me."

Now, wherever crow wants to make a lake, he shakes his beak and drops some water from his mouth. When the water hits the ground, it makes a lake. When a lake's going to be a fish lake, he drops fish in there -- one woman and one man; one of each in every lake, in every place. He also drops some fish out over the ocean. And everywhere he goes, he says:

"Your kind of people is going to stay in there forever."
He does that with every kind of fish-lake and fish.

That's a real true story, and you can prove it. You know, in this country some lakes have no creek coming out and no way for any fish to get in? Yet many of them have got fish anyway. So it must be from when crow put them in there long times ago -- way back!

And in some places where crow needs to make some water channels, he scratches the ground with his stick and says:

"Channel you're going to go this way. And lake here, water's going to go from here to there. It's going to bring in fresh water for these fish. This way they'll stay alive."

And where he makes a lake with a river going right down from it, he brings some fish up and tells them:

"You go up this way and you spawn. After that, you're going to go for your life; you're going to die. And your kids are going to go back down home to where you come from. When they're grown up, they're going to come back where you died to make more kids. You'll do that until the end of this world. Keep it going. Another thing too: you fish will have to watch for your heads. Don't let people handle them the wrong way. It's going to bring bad luck to them if they do so: you'll have to keep away from anybody who does that. You'll watch too for anyone who doesn't take good care of his fish grub, for any kid who plays around with your eyes. If they do that, you must never come back to their mom's and dad's nets, you must never give yourselves away to them anymore."

And in some places, crow makes a little channel between a lake and a river or maybe another creek. And he tells them whitefish, *tehzra* whitefish, and all the same kinds of lake-fish:

"You spawn this way here in the creek. You keep it full all the time, forever, each time you spawn."

That's why the *tehzra* whitefish comes down out of his lakes to spawn in small creeks. They spawn and maybe some of them go back to the lakes. They sure do that, here around Pelly Crossing, between Tatlaman Lake and Mica Creek.

The Whiteman has no name for the *tehzra* whitefish. So he calls it *tehzra* too or broad whitefish. Since he can't say *tehzra*, he says *tezra*, though. Someone read it to me from a Fisheries Department book. But that's because the Whiteman has no *tehzra* in his own country. And that's funny. Because this time, he's got the right word for the kind he's talking about.

Anyhow, crow does the same thing in every place, all right along the country. Soon enough though, he has nothing left in his stomach. So he calls in his crew. The *Kushekok* and the *t'ots'ya'* birds catch up with him. Crow keeps flying and tells them:

"Now, you do just like I did."

His men get to work. They go everywhere, up and down in the country. And pretty soon they're all finished. In a few years time, there is lots of rivers, lots of water, and lots of fish everywhere. And that's how all the rivers and lakes you can see today were first made.

After that, crow's crew split up. *Kushekok* stuck around with crow. But the other fellows -- the *t'ots'ya'* -- went away from crow for good; they went to make their living on their own as they still now do. And trees, grass and more animals started to come about. Some were good people, but some of them were pretty bad.

A SECOND FLOOD COMES

And after crow made everything back, another flood happened. But not much is known about this one story. It looks like too many things turned out bad. Lots of animals grew up. All kinds of animals. Old timer Indians said that giant snakes walked around. Indian way, they called them *gu*. There were elephants too. Everything like you see on TV nowadays -- like in Africa. Indian people killed some of the bad animals. Some days, I'll tell you the stories... How Indians save their lives from *gu*.

So by that time crow didn't like what was going on. He thought about it. He said to himself:

"This world is getting bad. It's going to be flooded again. I mean that. *Daji dachande*. It's going to go. It's going to be flooded. All the bad things are going to go."

Then somebody talked from the air. Maybe it was Moses. He said:

"You build a big boat."

Crow did that and put the moose, the bear, the caribou, the lion and everything in it. But he left out the giant snakes and the elephants, and all the bad animals. He left them to be drowned. He also left the sheep and the goats. And after that, it rained through the whole country. Pretty soon, the land got pretty near all flooded again, but not as high as the first time around. The sheep and the goats climbed up to high places and were saved. But the *gu* and the elephants got drowned. They had no place to go. Same thing for the *t'ots'ya'* birds. They didn't come in the boat and didn't find any place where to rest. They all died.

Then crow made the flood to go down. He medicine-dreamed about it and that drained the water back to where it was before. That way the rivers and the ocean came back and ran the same way. But it must be that this new flood was pretty rough. Right here, in the middle of the Pelly River, you can see lots of big rocks all piled up in one place -- right in the middle of the river. Some of them are bigger than a house. It must be that the waters were so strong that they pushed them down there.

Some old Indian told that story to the minister at Fort Selkirk, the first mission man who came to our country. He said that it was real true, that it was the Bible story.

Anyway, there are proofs for it. Down in Dawson City, gold miners have dug up the ground pretty deep, and they've found all kind of old animal bones in it. Same thing around Pelly or Carmacks. Almost any place in the Yukon. When I was a young man, Frankie Goulter, a Whiteman, found an elephant underground around Carmacks village where he was looking for gold. It was buried fifty feet deep in the ground and stuck inside a glacier. It was all frozen up and still in one piece: hair, skin, meat and bones together. The hair was about eight inches long. It looked like the bear's. But it was soft, not stiff -- it was like my hair on the side of my head here. The meat was red like the king salmon's meat. George Fairclough, the other miner with Frankie, ate one big piece from the leg bone and gave the rest to his dogs. They ate that old meat all right. And then these two miners could dig no more. So they drilled the frozen ground, put dynamite in the hole and blew the whole thing out. They let the ice and everything thaw out, took the rest of the meat for George's dogs, and Frankie said to shove the bones in the mineshaft.

That elephant must have died when crow flooded the world the second time. It must have drowned when the water came up and then sand covered it. When the water went down it drained through the sand and that elephant got left underground. Then it froze and a glacier grew around it. And that's why its meat and skin never rotted.

And the world we now live on came after that one story. That's why I always say that this world is the second one.

CROW THROWS HIS OLD BLANKET AWAY

Now, crow is somewhere by a big lake. From the way old timers told the story, I guess it could also be the ocean. Either way. He walks along the shore. The *Kushekok*, his owl nephew, is sneaking around behind him, so that crow can call him if he needs him. There are some other birds too. I don't know what kind. But they whistle all over the place. Crow is happy. He feels good. He walks down.

"Yeah," he says. "I have done pretty good. I'm pretty good now. I made lots of fish to eat and I made a good land. I made lots of animals and got rid of the bad ones. And the birds keep me happy. I love my land."

He is walking with his gopher skin blanket on his back. Blanket that means *ts'ät*. You know about the gopher? Down South people call it the prairie dog. I don't know why. Us we eat it. It doesn't look like a dog at all. It's not a squirrel but it's more like it. We call it *tsaw* and the squirrel *dläk*. And it digs tunnels underground. The skin is pretty small -- about six or seven inches by five. And it is not too thick at all. But in the old days it didn't matter: Indians made blankets with it because it was really warm and light. I should know. My grandma made one for me when I was a kid. I remember that. She took lots of those skins and cut long straps out of each one. Then she knitted these straps together. Just like you make a basket with a tree's fine roots!

So crow walks around with that kind of blanket on his back. It's an old one and it always comes apart. But soon enough he gets lucky: he finds a good fancy one hung on some little tree. He drops his old one and tries the new one on. It feels and looks much better. He says:

"This new blanket, this *ts'ät* here, is the best -- the best kind to have. I'm tired of what I wear. It's no good. From now on, I'm going to use this new blanket. That's the one I should keep! A darn good warm blanket!"

He wraps the old one around a rock and throws it way out on the water. After that, he walks around with the new one.

But soon as he walks a little way in the bush, the branches get caught in it, and it gets all torn off. He has got no blanket no more. He feels bad.

"Well," he says, "I have to go back get my old blanket."
He walks back to where he had thrown it in the water. He looks. It's far from the shore and too deep down there. So he takes a long pole and he makes some kind of hook at the end -- you know, with a little branch sticking out. He walks into the water. He tries his pole. He shoots it around, shoots it around toward that blanket. It's not long enough. He walks in some more. But he gets a hard time. The water reaches just about to his nose. And some of it gets in. Half of the time the waves cover him. He gets mad.

"I should not have thrown that away," he says. "I'm just a tight
asshole. *Tthaw' tthole etije.*"
That's a real Indian swear word that one.

Anyway, after a while, he manages to reach his old blanket, to hook it, and to bring it back. He wrings it with his two hands. He unties it from the hook. He dries it and puts it on again.

"My god," he says. "I nearly drowned over my old blanket. That
fancy blanket fooled me. It breaks too easy."
And he walks along the shore for a little way. He finds a new blanket again. It's got a different color this time. It's real fancy. He looks at it and says to himself:

"That's the kind you got to put on your back. That's what you
should use for a blanket. You old one here, you're no good."
He picks up the new one. He puts a rock in the old one and throws it in the water again. Not too far, though. Maybe about ten feet away. It's going to be easy to grab it back if needs be. Crow gets smart fast, you know. From there, he walks. And his new blanket get caught everywhere again. It breaks apart. He takes it off and tears it into pieces.

"Now I break you up, I'm finished with you," he says. "That's
what I should have done in the first place. No more will I pick
you up."

He goes back to his old blanket, picks it up, wrings it out and packs it up again. And he walks along the shore.

And you know what, all along crow made a big mistake. These fancy blankets he founded were no blankets at all but just big flat pieces of leaves mixed up in lake-mud that were hanging from trees by the shore. See: the lake water had gone up, flooded the little bush close by. Then it had gone down and left over them a blanket of mud all mixed up with other stuff. You find this kind of mud cover on small trees all around any big lake (but not along rivers). It's a little less than a quarter of an inch thick and it really looks like a colorful *ts'ät,* you know, a blanket.

So that's the kind of blanket crow liked so much.

CROW WISHES SOMETHING HE DOES NOT WANT

Pretty soon after he left his fancy blankets for good, crow gets hungry.

"I don't know what I'm going to do now," he says. "How am I going to eat?"

He looks at the lake and he sees a big fish swimming around. But there's no way for him to catch him in the water. So he sits down and thinks. Then he gets an idea. He stands up, looks on the ground, and picks up a little white rock. He holds it in his hand, between his thumb and first finger, right in front of his chest. He holds it for the fish to see.

"Fish," he says, "look over here."

The fish hears him and jumps around:

"What?"

"Look at this little white thing here," says crow, "this is good fat. I wish you eat it. It's real good. Me, I'm going to eat some of it."

The fish takes a big jump out of the water and hits crow right in the chest. Crow falls flat on his back. He's knocked out. Maybe he gets like a heart attack.

Gee, he always makes you laugh this crow.

And the fish rolls round and round on the ground. He bucks around, bucks around. Pretty soon he crawls back into the water. At about that time, crow manages to get up. He looks around. No fish! He hollers:

"Fish, come back up here. It's an order."

He's a funny guy, hey! But you can bet all your fur catch that the fish stays where he belongs. Crow thinks about the whole thing:

"Well," he says, "what's been going on anyway? How did he get away from me? I'm going to try again. I'll call him back."

He calls him out, but this time he walks some feet away from the shore and takes a stick. The fish jumps and hits him in the chest again. Crow falls backward. But he gets up right away. The fish is rolling around, rolling around. Crow grabs his stick and clubs him down.

"Now," he says, "that's the way to get food. I fooled him good this time."

Gee, he makes you laugh this man: he boasts about everything.

"I brought him in out," he tells. "I'm going to eat it now..."

On and on... I don't know what kind of fish he got. The old timers didn't say. Must be salmon or trout, maybe some kind of jackfish or something else.

But the trick with the little white stone, that's crow that has done it first. And, it's because of him that fish always bite at hooks. That's why you can pull them out now. Old timers used to make their hooks with white bone. Sometimes, they didn't use bait. It didn't matter. The fish bit just the same. And under ice too. They used to put their hooks down, jiggle them. The fish would see them from a long way. They would come out and bite at them. Yeah, all this is because of crow. That's why fish always go this way. All everything in this crow story, everything that crow has done, he has done it for this land.

Anyhow, after that, crow packs his fish up in the bush. He is thinking.

"I want to build a fire. I'll look for a good tree stump with roots."

After a little while, he finds the right tree. It has been uprooted by the wind. Maybe a storm went by. The trunk is lying down on some other tree. When it was alive, the roots had spread all around; just a few inches underground. Maybe it was frozen under there and there had been no way for them to go any deeper. Anyway, now, half of these roots are sticking out in the air, hanging over the place where the trunk used to be.

Crow builds a fire right under there. He hangs his fish on the end of a stick and drives its other end into the ground, close to the blaze. The fish starts to roast on its side facing the fire. One big root is hanging over it. Crow sits down and waits for his lunch to be ready. After a while, he flips the fish over to roast its other side. He sits down again and waits. Pretty soon, the fish is cooked all right. But, by this time, crow thinks about what the big hanging root has got on its mind.

"*Shraa!*. Root," he says, "you wish for that fish I cooked here? O.K., I wish you eat it."

So the root falls right over the fish and down into the ashes. The only thing crow's got left is the fish tail sticking out from under the root.

"Root," he hollers, "I'm sorry I said that. Leave me a little bit of the fish, leave me some."

The root shakes the fish tail. Crow pulls on it. It comes out but the fish stays under. He lifts the root. The fish is all covered with ashes. Now the only thing crow can do is lick his mouth. So that's what he does. And that's all he's got left to do, I guess.

Boy, is he not a funny guy this crow!

And you know lots of people still go the same way. They're pretty sure something cannot happen. They wouldn't want it to happen at all. And then, they speak from the other side of their mouth:

CROW MARRIES A GOOD WOMAN

So for now crow is just walking hungry. He is going along a river. He walks, he walks, and pretty soon he finds some woman living alone in a camp. There're lots of dried fish hanging on her racks. And this woman is really nice looking: you know, nice tits sticking out... And nice fat legs too. Crow sees all that.

"Oh gosh," he thinks. "Jeez..."

He comes into the woman's camp. He sits down some way from her.

"Gee," he says. "You got real nice legs and nice tits. And you made lots of dried fish too. My God, where're you coming from, anyway?"

She tells him:

"I've been living here all my life. Drying fish is what I do. That's how I make my living. Yeah, I sure work hard for it."

"Are you married? You got a man?" says crow.

"No, I got no man, nothing."

"Do you need one?"

"Yeah, I need a man but where am I going to get him from?"

"Well," crow says, "I'm here. Can I get married to you? What kind are you?"

"Wolf side, wolf clan," she answers.

"Me, I'm crow clan," he tells her. "So we are just right for one another."

He raises his two hands and grabs one of her thighs.

"Please, you got such nice soft legs! How about me staying with you?"

"I don't know for sure," she says. "But I guess it's all right. You can come in and stay. Bring your stuff inside here."

He moves inside her brush-camp. She cooks some fish and feeds him.

After that, crow lies down and starts to think all kinds of crooked ways:

"My gosh," he tells himself. "I wish it gets dark real quick. I can't wait."

Nighttime comes at last. He calls his new woman:

"What about making love right away?"

"Myself," she says, "I don't know what kind of thing you're talking about."

"I'll show you, I'll show you how to do it."

He throws his blanket on top of hers.

"We use my blanket on top. It's nice and warm. It's for sleeping under it. Your blanket, we use it as a mattress."

But that's just because he wants to keep his own one nice and tidy. And he says:

"Take all your clothes off. I take out all my clothes too."

Pretty soon they're are bare naked and they go inside their blankets. Crow fools around with her. Then the woman complains:

"What for you do that? What's that you shoot up inside me? What for you pee in there?"

"That's the way," he says, "that's the way you do it. When men come to you, they got to use you this way. That's what men do with women. You'll see, next time I make it again to you, you're going to go after me for more. You're going to love me real hard then."

He sucks at her tits and everything and they make real good love.

After that, they stay together like husband and wife. The woman has got a good boat. She goes fishing with that.

"Gosh," says crow. "Where did you get that boat? What kind is this, this *nalat*?"

In English, boat means *nalat*.

"Where did you get it from?"

"I made it myself," she answers.

"Gee!" he says. "I've never seen such a good job done on a boat in my whole life, ever since I was born on this earth. You've done a pretty good job. I'm going to make one too. Show me which way you make it."

She teaches him:

"This is how I do the work here. Then I do like that. And then
this way and then that..."
She tells him everything.

After that, crow's got a boat too and they both go around on the
water. They go fishing. They get lots of salmon and stay in camp to
dry them up for the winter. They cut them up open, clean them, and
slice them out in thin strips. And then, they go hang them on a fish-
rack to dry up. It's summer time. It's really hot. It's hard work. Crow
wipes his face:

"I sweat too much," he says. "I am tired now. Maybe you should
go turn over the fish on the rack. They are not dried on the other
side yet."
She walks by him and crow smells something. He calls her back.

"Pull your dress a little higher up," he tells her. "Right above your
knees. This way you can get a cold draft, some cold air between
your legs. The other way, you sweat too much and you smell too
hard, you know..."
She does it and walks back to the fish-rack. She wears some kind of
shirt with short sleeves. She reaches for the salmons above her head
and turns them over. She raises her arms way up and crow sees hair
in her armpits. It's got a yellow-brown color. Not a black one. Crow
finds this real funny. He starts to laugh, and he laughs...

"Yah, yah, yah, yah," he chuckles. "Yah, yah, yah, yah, yah," he
says.
He's going to choke himself, laughing.

"What for are you laughing?" his wife asks him from the fish-
rack.

"I laugh at you, I laugh at you..."

"What's the matter with me?" she asks.

"Ah, I just saw lots of hair in your armpits. And it's got a yellow-
brown color. That's the first time I see this kind of color there."

"Oh yeah," she snaps back. "It makes you laugh. O.K., I'm leaving you then. I'm going away for good."
She runs down to the river shore. Crow gets up and runs after her. He
grabs her by the shoulder. But right at that time, she turns herself into
fog, into some kind of haze drifting through the air. Crow loses his

grip. His hand goes right clean through her. And the fog starts to float away above the water. It sprawls over the river and reaches its other side. Nobody can stop her no more.

Crow stands up all baffled. He just looks. There is not much else he can do.

Pretty soon, though, he hears lots of noise coming from the fish-rack. He turns around and sees all the fish coming back alive: those still hanging on the drying rack and those that have already been bundled up for the winter. They're bucking like hell, trying to get back into the river, trying to go behind crow's wife. Some of them are already leaping toward the shore. They're jumping up with all their strength. It's going to take another second for them to be back into the river. So crow opens his mouth as big as he can and tries to get as many of them to jump inside. But these fish he swallows go right through his throat, stomach, guts, and, out through his asshole. It looks like he is shooting fish from down there. They spring right clean through his body. He can't do nothing. He can't stop them -- nothing. So he runs up to the rack. Two bundles are still tied up. The fish in there are bucking... One fish-roll is starting to break open. Pretty soon, they're all going to jump away... Crow grabs a club and kills them all. He saves these two fish-bundles, but that's all.

And after that, he runs to his boat. He goes behind his wife. She is way out, floating over the water. He follows her. He tries to grab her. But he just falls through the fog.

"My wife..." he says. "Come on, come back, come back, come back."

No answer! Nothing!

"This woman," he says. "This good-love-making woman is getting away from me. That's my fault. I shouldn't have said something like that. I should have talked good. I make good love with her, very good. Now she runs away from me. I don't know what to do."

He keeps following her. He tries to talk to her again. No answer. Nothing. He's just paddling through a fog. And pretty soon, he starts to get mad, real mad.

"You, foggy woman," he hollers, "you, *ats'ow' inja,* I look under your arms and you got lots of yellow-brown hair -- and between your legs too. Lice laid their young ones there -- white ones. That's why your hair is kind of brown and not black. You've got too many lice there. You smell bad too. And now get mad at me. Don't think of me no more. No more will I think of you."

And crow paddles back to the shore and walks up to the camp. He feeds on the fish he's got left. And after that he goes out again.

INSIDE A SUCKERFISH

He walks. Soon enough, he's back to the big lake where he found the fancy blankets -- you remember the mud *ts'ät*. He feels hungry.

"*Mät sedetle,*" he says, and by this he means "I'm hungry."

He wants to eat. But he doesn't know what to do yet. He walks for a while. He thinks… He is thinking… And then, some place, he stops. He's just found out how he's going to make food. He looks around all over the shore. He spots a birch tree. He goes there, peels the bark down and cuts it out into some kind of flat shape. He corners it up. It becomes a birch bark pan. He tries that one. It works all right. That's a good pot. Then, he picks up a rock -- the kind that can go into a hot fire without cracking up. He washes it good. He puts some water in his pan. After that, he gathers some pieces of dried driftwood, ties them together with a willow branch, and loads this bundle of firewood on his back. He looks down at the ground. He sees a little white rock -- no bigger than a small candy. He picks it up.

Way out on the lake, a big fish is swimming toward him. It's real big -- about a hundred feet long, maybe more. Crow sees him. He raises one hand and shows the white rock to the fish.

"*Łyok cho,* big fish, way over here," he hollers. "Look here at that little bird in my hand. He only wants to see your throat -- down to near your tonsils. That's what this little bird wants to see."
The big fish opens his mouth halfway.

"Fish, he can't see them yet. Look here, see this white thing."
Crow waves his hand. The fish gets closer to the shore. Crow gets ready. He grabs his pan and his other stuff.

"This little bird doesn't see your tonsils good, yet," he says. "Your mouth is still half full with water. Open it up more."
The fish opens it up. Crow shouts:
"Gawkk…"

And he jumps into the fish's mouth, flies right through his throat, and gets inside his stomach. Down there, he walks to the opening for the guts. He cuts a hole and gets inside the fish's body. Lots of fresh air gets in through the fish's breathing. Crow can breathe pretty good.

And this, crow did it for everybody to follow his tracks. That's why the Whiteman can make submarines and work in mines. Crow's big fish, that's just the same idea as the submarine. Same thing with the mine: when the guys go down five hundred feet, they bring in air with pipes and they breathe good all the same. The Whiteman didn't find all this by himself. He just went the same way as crow went with the big fish.

Anyhow, crow is in there and he builds a fire with his driftwood. It makes some smoke, but now he can see good enough. He looks around at the guts and the heart.

"Oh my God," he says, "there is nothing but fat in there. It's just full of good grub. I sure fooled him, hey. Now I'm going to eat all of it."

He puts his stone in the fire, and waits until it's real hot. He throws it in the pan and the water starts boiling. He cuts the fish guts out and cleans them in the hot water. He gets lots of fat and makes lots of fish grease.

Then he eats fat, eats fat, eats fat... Pretty soon, he gets a stomach ache. He's already eaten too much grease. He has to go to the bathroom. He looks around. He sees the fish asshole. That's the only place he can use in there. He runs there and makes it his own shit-house, his own toilet hole. After that, he goes back to eat fat and drink grease. His stomachache gets worse. Now he spends half the time eating, and the other half running to his bathroom at the end of the fish, shooting greasy water out. You sure can laugh! This fish must have looked funny with this long trail of grease behind it. It must have looked like a submarine hit by a mine and leaving a trail of oil behind.

This big fish story is real true, you know. The fish crow went in is the suckerfish. Well, even today, he's got lots of black skins left inside his body. That's from the smoke of crow's fire. And on top of his guts there is no fat at all. Nothing. It doesn't matter how fat the rest of the body is; there is never any of it on the guts, never. All this, because crow ate it all. And this fish smells bad too -- some kind of hard smell. When you gut it out, you got to cut his asshole and throw it away first thing or else your fish is gonna stink. And this also comes from the time crow used it as his back house.

Now, crow has cleaned up all the fat from the guts. The fish didn't notice anything yet. He swims around. Crow can still breathe pretty good in there. But then he looks at the heart. There is still a lot of fat on it. Crow gets his water boiling again. He grabs the heart and cuts it out. He cooks it and eats all the fat that's left. (That's also why there's never any fat on the sucker's heart).

Finally, the fish is going to die. But he fights like hell for his life. He jumps one way, then another one, then to some other place. Now he goes as fast as a bullet. Right inside, crow flies all over the place, just like a loose piece of cargo. He tries to hold on something but it's too slippery in there. He falls down in the fish's asshole, just where he went to the bathroom. He gets stuck in his own shit up to his neck. Finally he manages to grab a piece of gut hanging around. He grabs this one, holds on to it and hollers:

"*Łyok cho*, big fish, *khezi uch'i zuli tat'i ghun ungliaadye*. Big fish, if you're starting to die, head down to a big town near by. Go to a big country where lots of people stay. Go to this kind of place."

The fish says O.K. He swims by a big village on the shore and heads for it. He paddles full speed, slides right clean off the water and lands on dry ground, right on top of the bank where the people are staying.

Again, crow did that to make the world better, to improve it. Today, that's the way a jackfish jumps out of the water and lands at your feet when you shoot it. It's no bullshit story. Some White guy from outside didn't believe it. So I took him to Laggar Lake where there are lots of big jackfish. Some of them were swimming by the shore, facing us. I shot a big one in the head. It jumped right out, right out on dry land. Gosh, that Whiteman got scared. He thought I did some kind of witchcraft. But that's not true. When a big jackfish faces you and you shoot it, it always jumps out of the water. You just have to pick it up. That's the way crow's big fish landed right in the middle of the town.

Now the fish is dead. No more fresh air is getting in. So crow is starting to choke. He worries about how he's going to come out. But pretty soon he hears lots of people hollering outside. They use their spears to cut meat off the fish's ribs. He listens. It sounds like they are making fish grease and filling their pans with it. Crow figures out he's going to lose his fish to them. He listens. Now some guy is poking his spear through the skin and pushing it through between two ribs. Maybe the guy does not know there's got to be a lot of pressure in a big fish like that. The guy pushes through and it makes a hole:

"Pssssssssseeeeeeeeeeuuuuuuuhhh..."

The air comes out full blast. And:

"Zoooooooooouuuuuuuuuuuummmmmmmm..."

The people see something flying out like a rocket -- a little black thing. That was crow, but they didn't realize... Crow lands way down, way out in the bush. Right away he worries again about his fish. He doesn't want to lose it to these people. He thinks about it... And he figures out how he's going to get fed anyway. He calls his sister's son, the small owl, the *Kushekok*. His nephew flies back to him. Then, he takes some fancy leaves, he fiddles around with them, and he brings the *t'ots'ya'* birds back alive. He talks to them birds:

"There's going to be another war. These people there are going to take this big fish away from me. I want to make war on them. I want to get my fish back."

"It's all right," they tell him, "we'll help you."

Crow makes more *t'ots'ya'* soldiers. Then he speaks again:

"You wait for me. I want to meet these fellows first. I want to ask them about it. The *Kushekok* comes with me. Tonight, I pretend I'm going to get sick. Tomorrow I'll be like I died. I'll be all stiff. I'm not going to move one bit. And the *Kushekok* is going to cry. When you hear that, you *t'ots'ya'* fellows will come in. Make lots of noise. You chase them away. And I get my fish back."

And crow walks toward these people. Everybody hollers:

"We have found a big fish. We have found a big fish."

Crow walks through them. Everybody is making fish grease. There are birch pans here, and there, and all over the camp. But nobody feeds him. Crow sees an old fellow. He walks up to him, sits down and talks with him. The old fellow says:

"Did you hear the story about the big fish we found?"

"No," answers crow.

"Well, we found this big dead fish right in the middle of our camp. That's the one all everybody is getting grease from, lots of it."

Crow looks at him and says:

"Gee whiz... Do you know that this kind of fish is supposed to bring bad luck."

The old man:

"I don't know. How come? How come?"

Crow explains:

"See, I've been going around all over the world and me and my nephew are the only one left now. My nephew, that's the *Kushe-kok* right here. My younger brothers, my older brothers, my father, my mother, all my relations used to live in a kind of big town like yours. They found a big fish like you guys, but a big a war came on top with it. They all got killed. I don't know why in the hell I came in to your place. The way the story goes is that some stranger showed up after the dead fish landed there. That's what the old timers said. The stranger came in and he died. Then the war started. Me and the *Kushekok* were going around in another country. That's why we got saved. And now this big fish dies in your camp. It's going to be the same for you. I don't know what I'm going to do."

The old fellow feeds him. He gives him lots of grease. Crow drinks all of it.

"*U khi,*" he says. "*U khi nye...*" He tells himself that it is his own grease.

Nighttime comes. The old fellow lies down and falls asleep. Crow sings away throughout the evening. He medicine-sing. Then, right in the middle of the night, he pretends he feels like he's being shot at, that he's real sick.

"*Ah baa, ah baa, ah baa, ah baa...*" he hollers.

Whiteman way, he means:

"Ouch, ouch, ouch, ouch..."

He rolls around and get to the fireside. He lies there. He doesn't move but he still breathes. All everybody looks at him. The old man tells his people:

"Maybe he told a true story about that fish and the war..."

And next morning, somehow, it looks like crow is real dead. The *Kushekok* comes in. He starts to cry:

"My maternal uncle," he hollers, "*ahhh, haaa, ahhh, haaa.* My mother's brother died. *Ih ndo ah-ah-ah-ah.*"

"*Ih ndo,*" that means "my mother's brother.

All the people get scared. Crow was right, they all think. And soon enough the big war starts:

"*Gu, gu, gu, gu, gu.*"

The *t'ots'ya'* soldiers walk through the bush. Sticks get broken everywhere. Everybody in the village runs around all over the place. Pretty soon they all take off for the bush. The *t'ots'ya'* soldiers push on through the town. They chase the people all the way out. Crow still pretends he's dead. The *Kushekok* runs to him and ties him up with a rope. Then he goes through all the pans of fish grease. He drinks grease, he drinks grease, and he keeps going.

Crow hollers to him:

"Untie me out, untie me, untie me..."

Finally, the *Kushekok* has drunk enough grease. He's full. He walks back to crow and unties him. Crow looks around, looks around. He sees some pans left there, and here... He runs up to them. He looks. A little bit of grease is left in this one. He licks the bottom of the pan with his tongue. In this one, the grease has already hardened: frozen grease, you know. He leaves the pan there. He runs to another one. It's got a little bit left. He licks it up too. And he runs around throughout the whole camp, licking what he can there, here, and everywhere. And pretty soon there's no grease left to drink. He sees the *Kushekok* sitting down on the top of a tree. He screams at him.

"*Kushekok,* you're a bad man. You drank all my grease. You drank it all. I wish you fall down from the top of the tree and break your neck."

And what he wishes happens. The *Kushekok* falls down, hits the ground and breaks his neck. He's in two pieces now: his head here and his body there.

Crow takes the pans where the grease is already "frozen" solid and starts to pack them away in the bush. He is going to drink all that later on, somewhere else. And he packs, back and forth, back and forth. It's hard work and he sweats. He stops to wipe his face.

"By God, I need some help," he says. "But who's going to be my helper now? Why did I medicine-wish that my nephew breaks his neck? Why did I say that? I need some help. I'll fix him back."

He walks where the *Kushekok* fell down. He picks up the head and the body. He puts some of his spit on one piece. All around where the neck broke off. Then he brings the two pieces together.

"You pieces," he says, "you join together."

And the *Kushekok* gets glued back with crow's words and spit.

"Now," says crow, "move your head this side and back to this side. See, now you can wind it up right around this way, and back right around the other way again."

That's why this kind of little owl can turn around his head full circle one way and back full circle the other way. That's because of what crow's done to him, through his nephew. Maybe you never saw any. They aren't too many of them in the bush. It's too bad. It's real funny to watch how he does it.

Anyway, crow tells the *Kushekok* to walk again. He walks. Again, what crow does to his nephew is to show how to fix people for everybody to follow. Everything that crow has been doing in the early days is still going on today. That's where the Indian doctor comes from. And that's the same for the Whiteman doctor.

So the *Kushekok* is back alive and crow explains something to him:

"You know, you should be thankful for what I'm doing. I fooled these people and they all ran away. I got my fish back. Now we got to go drink more grease. We're going to pack it all up in the bush."

Crow and the *Kushekok* pack the fish grease off, pack it off -- back and forth, back and forth. Then they drink all they got. And when they're finished they split apart again. The *Kushekok* goes one way. Crow walks to another place. Now crow is going around to fool people, to see which ones are good, which ones are bad.

CROW MEETS WITH THE OTTER PEOPLE

He walks along a river and comes into a village. Lots of people are staying in this camp. They're fishing. This time crow is getting into the otter people. They are bad luck animals. Crow walks through them.

"Hello! Hello! Hello! Hello!" they tell him.

"You fellows know me?" he asks. "I'm named crow and you can call me crow."

"Us," they say, "we're named the otters." Indian way it means *krodyeh.*

But nobody feeds him. The otters give him nothing, nothing. Well, maybe they feed him a little fish grease. But that's all they give him. Crow looks around and asks them:

"Where does all this fish come from? What kind of place?"

"It comes from lots of places," they answer.

"Well," he says, "they're not much fat. Where I come from, there're lots and lots of fat fish. It must be that right where you're fishing the fish are too skinny."

"How much more fat should they be?" they ask him. "What's fat enough for you?"

"Well," he says, "I know fish a lot fatter than that. In my country, there're the fattest ones you'll ever see. Me here, I eat just one and it makes my stomach ache. It makes me sick. It's too fat, too rich."

So the otter people tell him to come up in their camp. He says "O.K.," and he stays with them for a while. They go out fishing everyday. Crow tries to think them through. He wants to fool them too. He sees there's a lot of fish grease in the camp and he wants to drink it all. So, one day, after eating, he tells them:

"Ah, I drank too much grease. I want to take a shit."

He just pretends, though. That's because the otters don't feed him too good. He steps out and walks through the bush. He looks for something. Then he finds it. It's some little pieces of lynx shit: it's all dried up and white. (It's got to be the lynx's shit but I don't know for sure, though. It could also be some mouse's shit, or the marten's.) Anyway, crow puts some pieces in his pocket. He walks by the shore and goes to the place where the people gut their fish out. Nobody's back there at work yet. He throws these pieces of shit down on the ground.

He walks back up to the camp and sits down. Soon enough an otter man gets up and walks to the fish-gutting spot. He wants to check how many more fish they still have to go through. By gosh, as soon as he sees the shit, he runs up right clean back and he hollers:

"Some kind of animal came down around our fish-gutting place. I saw his shit."

They all look at him.

"It's all white. It must be a bad animal," he says.

They all get scared. They run away and dive in the river. Crow goes down by the shore and takes the shit back. He hides it. He walks up to the camp and sits down. The otters are swimming around. They look at their fish-gutting place. The pieces of white shit are all gone. They all come back.

Now, crow knows how he can steal from them. He found out: they're scared of this kind of white shit. He thought them through. So he stays around with them and waits. One day they tell him:

"Why don't we go where you say there're lots of fat fish? Let's go there!"

"That's fine with me," he says. "I'll show you fellows."

They all go up there with him. One man says that he's going to try.

"You use your fish-spear," crow tells him. "You hook the fish up and you bring it back."

The man goes in the water. He spots a big king salmon. No, I mean some kind of fat fish: the *tehzra* whitefish, or the grayling, or the trout, or the jackfish. You know... Whatever otter people eat. The man aims at the head and hooks the fish in there. He brings it back to the shore. He takes his knife and cuts it open. Everybody watches. The guts come out. They're all covered up with fat.

"Gee," they say. "This fish is pretty fat. Crow sure knows about fat fish places. What everybody knows, he knows it through crow, through *ts'ehk'i*! Crow says things right all the way through."

"Yeah," crow tells them, "me, I don't lie. And right now I'm going in the bush to look for a pole to make myself a fish-spear."

He goes out. The otter people keep pulling fat fish out. Crow knows he has got some time ahead of him. He rustles around to get some more white lynx shit. He picks up all he can get. Down where the otters have their home, he throws some in each house. He puts one white shit here, another one there, and there, all over the place inside these guys' camps. He also throws some back where they gut their fish. He cuts a pole and he runs back to the fat fish place. The otter people look worried:

"What were you doing?" they ask him. "You have been gone too long..."

"Gee whiz," crow says, "this pole here gave me a hard time. I wanted a good straight one. And I got the best one. Fish will never break it. But I had to walk a long way to get it. You see this big hill behind here? That's where I found it."

And everybody starts fishing again. Crow too. He takes his fishing pole and steps in the water. It looks like he's working, but he just fools around with the pole. He doesn't kill any fish. He's doing that just for show. Pretty soon it gets dark. The otters build a makeshift camp. Crow stays with them. Everybody goes to sleep. Crow stays awake, though. He keeps thinking for a long time. And then, right in the middle of the night he starts to make medicine. He sings. Everybody gets up.

"Oh gosh, you fellows..." he says, "two of your young people should run back to your other camp and check it. I had a bad dream. That's why I am making medicine with my songs. I dreamed about some people's camp. I saw that there were lots of bad things there -- something wrong. From there, these people take off. And me too I'm taking off. We're running away from something. I sure dreamed about something bad."

That story is all bullshit, though. That's him who put lynx shit there in the afternoon. But the otter people don't know that. So they send two guys down to their main camp, two young fellows. Soon enough they come back, running full speed. They pant, but they manage to speak:

"The 'big eye' one came back..."

I guess they mean the lynx.

"We've never seen this kind of animal before; he went inside all our houses. Where we cut fish too! That's a dangerous animal -- a real danger."

Everybody hollers:

"Let's go back, let's go back down and check inside our houses. We'll find a new place after."

All the otter people line up in Indian line and walk back to the main camp. Crow goes with them. He walks in the middle of the line. He looks like he's real scared.

"ME, here, MYSELF", he says, "I sure will run away if it's a true story. But I don't swim like you fellows. I jump in the river only one way: down. Then, I walk on the bottom for a long, long way -- as far you can see, maybe more, and then I come out."

He picks up a big rock and packs it with him. That's how he's going to stay at the bottom. Pretty soon, they are back at the main camp. Everybody looks at his house. The "big eye" has shitted everywhere. The otters get real scared. They all dive in the river. Crow runs behind them. He throws his big rock out in the water. It sounds like he's dived too. But him, he just jumps to the foot of the bank. Down there, the river has eaten up into the bank. He hides himself in the kind of little cave the water has made. He sits down in the dark. He is there, all black in a dark place under the bank, and there is no way you can see him. The otters come out to catch their breaths. They look back. Nothing! Crow must be walking under water, they think. They dive back in the water. They come out again. Nothing! They dive back in. On and on. Crow is under the bank, watching them coming out and swimming back in. And pretty soon he can't see them no more. They're all way out.

I guess they went down all the way to the ocean. And it's just as well that crow found out about what scares them. That animal is real bad luck. It's the worst one. If you come across its path you get *nedlu* after. *Nedlu*, that means "convulsion" I think. It makes you die. Or you go crazy. Crow scared them away with the lynx white shit. He found out and that's why this kind of shit is still the best medicine against the otter. That's what old Indians used to save people from *nedlu* fits.

Anyway, the way the story goes, crow is still under the bank. He comes out. He looks around. He doesn't see anybody left.

"Well," he says to himself, "I sure fooled all these people out. Now I'm going to take away all their fish grease and grub. I'm going to eat all I want."

The *Kushekok* comes back in. He gives a hand to crow. They go inside the otters' houses and pack all their grease and grub away.

"My nephew," says crow, "I fooled these people for you. You help yourself. Eat fat. Drink lots of grease."

They both live on that for a while. They clean up everything. And from there they split "out" again. Crow goes to a new place.

CROW STEALS THE SUN FROM THE LAKE TROUT

And this crow is walking again along some lakeshore. There he finds another woman. This girl swims around on top of the water. He calls her and she comes to him. It's a muskrat woman. Crow asks her:

"What're you doing?"

"I'm looking around," she says. "I'm looking for food to eat."

"That's easy," he tells her. "Look at these big flat leaves floating here, right where the water is shallow. It is called *ihtthya*."

He goes into the water to show her. He kicks in the mud with his foot, right under the leaves. One plant gets loose. He pulls on it. It's got two roots, about five inches long. He kicks into another one and pulls it out. It's got one root this time. It's about six or seven inches long. That kind of root is just like carrots, but they are white, not red like the Whiteman carrots. And crow tells the rat girl:

"They're good to eat, you know. Swim down and look in the mud. Do this and do that and you get a lot out. Then you break the branch off, wash the roots and we eat them."

The rat girl dives into the water for him. She brings back a whole bunch of these white carrots. And crow and the girl eat together. Pretty soon, they live on them.

That's why the muskrat still feeds on these roots. They're good. Moose also eat them. People can eat them too, raw or cooked. They taste a little bit like bear roots. The *Tzän Huch'än* (Muskrat Indian people) from the White river, around Snag, used to eat lots. They had a big lake full of them. My grandpa Copper Joe came from there and he was crazy about them. He used to eat them raw. It sounded just like chewing on carrots:

"Chomp, chomp, chomp, chomp, chomp, chomp..."

Anyway, right here in the story, that's what crow and the rat girl are now eating. They're staying together, having a good life.

One day, they're walking along the lakeshore. After a while, they get tired and sit down to take a rest. Crow sees something on the lake.

"Hey," he says, "that's a fish over there."

He's talking about the lake trout -- *mbyaat,* you know. (Some people say it's *gyo*, the king salmon, but I'm not sure.) I guess he sees him jumping on top of the water for his food. He calls him.

"Come over here," he says.

"What?" answers the fish.

Crow explains:

"Fish, see this woman who's here with me. I wish that she were your wife. But she's mine, she's a good looking woman."

Crow and the rat girl get up and watch the fish.

"Yeah..." says the trout before diving in.

From there, crow and the rat woman walk away, down along the shore. Crow leads the way. He's thinking by himself. He never looks behind. Some place, though, he turns around to check how his wife is doing. She's not there any more. He looks around for where she could have gone. Nothing.

Then, he hears somebody calling him. It comes from the lake. He looks. It's the trout.

"*Ts'ehk'i,* crow," hollers the fish, "look at my wife here."

The rat woman is sitting on top of him fish, way out on the water.

"Oh God," says crow, "give her back. Don't do that to me. Give her back to me."

"No," says the trout. "You made me wish to take her away from you."

Crow sits down. He cries. He doesn't know what to do. Then he starts walking again. He thinks, thinks...

A big fat woman is staying around by the shore. Crow sees her. It's a frog old woman. He walks to her. She sees he's crying; water is running down from his eyes.

"What are you crying for?" she asks him.

"Oh," he says, "I've lost a good woman. Somebody kidnapped her from me."

"Oh yeah..." she replies. "Do you want to see her again?"

"Yeah!" he says.

The frog woman sits down. She picks up a stick close by and puts one side into the water. She raises it slowly and lifts the water -- just like if she was lifting her blanket to look inside her bed. Crow peeps in and sees everything that is going on under water. His wife is over there, walking around on the bottom of the lake. And way down, he also sees something like a big fire, something shining real strong. The light it makes comes outside and brightens the day. All that time it was the sun. Right away, crow knows he wants to steal that. Without it, his land is going to keep its dull daylight. That's all.

Anyhow, the good looking muskrat girl is still walking down there. Crow turns around and asks the frog:

"Are you sure that's her?"

"Oh, yeah, that's her," she tells him.

Then, she drops the water blanket down. The daylight turns back to its dull color. Crow doesn't know how he's going to get under there. He talks to the frog woman:

"Can you hold the water up the same way again? I want to go under. I want to see this muskrat girl."

"Well," she says, "give me something, pay me. You're not going to get your wife back, unless you pay for it."

"What kind of thing do you want?" he asks her.

"Anything... Look around for me. The thing that suits me, the one I like, you give it to me, and you get your wife back."

Crow goes in the bush. He sees a balsam tree. The last branch goes straight up and it's all bushy. He flies there and breaks off the very top. He brings it down and gives it to the frog woman.

"No," she says, "it's not what I want."

Crow goes back into the bush. He sees a little spruce tree. That's the kind we call *udji sok'*. It's got a really thick bushy branch at the end. Crow brings the top of that one to the frog. She looks at it but she does not want it.

"No, not this kind," she says. "I don't want it. Leave it, throw it here."

After that, crow brings back the top of the birch tree. But she doesn't want it either. So he goes out again. He thinks.

"I don't know what kind of thing she wants..."

Finally, as he walks around, he finds some pussy willow -- I think it means *k'alatr'o*, you know. It's got a thick bushy top with white things hanging at the end. That's what you call buds or catkins. When they're dried up they turn into some kind of down feathers. If you need a lot of this fluff, you just roll them buds between your hands. They get bigger and bigger. Crow sees this little willow tree all covered with this kind of buds. He breaks it off and brings it to the frog old woman.

Gee, he looks happy. He knows she wants this kind of feathers. He found out. His mind told him so.

"Whew," he tells her, "me, the crow here, I'm tired."
The frog woman looks at him and asks:

"Where does it come from this thing? The white stuff here? This kind of cotton? That's the kind I was looking for."

"Oh," says crow, "I had to go a long way out to find it. I ran over those two hills there. This stuff was in a high place."

"Well," the woman tells him, "you can bring this kind in for me. Get lots of it, though. Then you'll have your wife back."

Gee, crow starts to run like hell. He goes into the bush close by where there are willow patches. He spreads his blanket on the ground. He picks lots of these feathers and piles them up in it. He gathers the blanket's corners and takes the bundle to the frog old woman. He puts it down.

"That's the kind you want, isn't it?"
He knows the answer but he asks anyway:

"Holy smoke," she says. "Yeah, gosh, I sure want this. You know what I want it for? For my bedding -- wintertime, you know. It's going to be real good for me. That's the kind I was looking for all along."

This one little story is another one that makes the crow story come true. In this Yukon country, right up to this day frogs make nests in holes underground with this kind of willow cotton. Wintertime comes; they go on top of their bed. When it gets down to sixty, seventy or eighty below, they freeze. Springtime comes, they thaw out and come back alive. The same thing as with bears.

So that day, crow sure makes this old frog is happy. She tells him:

"O.K., you can go under the lake and get your wife back. But take with you what you brought in to me: the balsam top branch, the spruce's, the birch's, and the willow's. You'll need them."
She also gives him a rope and a big chunk of ice to pack with him.

"Now," she says, "you take that. You keep it with you and you go. When you come back you'll pull on the rope."

That's why old timers said that the frog is a good animal -- a good luck animal. It must come from the time crow fixed her bed, you see.

"All right," crow tells her.
She lifts the water again. And crow walks under there. He sets the rope so that he'll be able to pull on it on his way back. He moves on, packing the tree tops he had cut off and the ice. Inside, under the water, he walks through lots of animals: graylings and all kinds of big fish. But they're all asleep. Pretty soon, he spots the lake trout's camp. He hides away and watches what's going on in there. The trout man has got a wife and a daughter. Crow sees that they are big shot people. They never do a thing. They just sit on their soft beds. Indian way you call this kind of family bunch *dän nozhi'*. That means, "people with a lot of stuff." After that crow sees his wife. He watches what she does from behind his tree branches. Oh, this trout makes her work real hard. She's got to cook and do everything for them. That's why he kidnapped her. He made her a slave, a *händye*.

You know, long time ago some big shot Indians used to have *händye* too. They work for them. These workers would be some kids with no parents and relations or some people they would have grabbed away from someone else. And that too comes from crow's time. All everything that happened after with people, later on, crow did it for them ahead of time. You see, he's the one who told the trout about kidnapping his wife.

Crow is sitting outdoors. He's watching and pretty soon he sees his rat woman coming out of the camp. She's going to chop wood in the bush nearby. Crow doesn't know what to do. He thinks about it. He looks at her splitting up a piece of wood. Then he figures out something:

"I wish that her axe handle breaks," he thinks to himself.

His wife hits the log with her axe and the handle breaks into two pieces. Crow had only been watching, though, just thinking about it, that's all. And somehow it happened just like that. That's the way it's going with him. He just thinks about something, anything, and that makes it happen.

The rat girl starts to cry. She knows her boss is going to bawl the shit, the hell out of her. Crow medicine-thinks.

"Sit down," he says, "and look the other way."

He walks to the axe, picks up the pieces and joins them together. It's fixed. He goes to hide again behind his tree branches... The rat woman turns around. Gee, that axe handle is back in one piece. She's sure happier now. She takes the axe and starts to chop wood again. Crow is still thinking, though. He's telling the axe: "I wish you break again." His wife hits the log and the handle breaks again. She sits down and cries, and cries... Crow walks to her.

"What're you crying for?" he asks her.

She looks up.

"Hello, hello, my boyfriend, hello my husband," she says.

"What are you crying for? Tell me," he asks her again.

"Ah," she says, "these trout people sure make me work hard. I got to get away from here but I can't find any way to do it. They keep their eyes on me all the time. And you know, they're real mean to me too."

"But right now, what're you crying for?"

"Ah, my boss is a real bad one and I just broke his axe. Now he is going to kill me over it. That's why I'm crying."

"Let me see it," says crow.

He picks up the pieces, joins them, and makes them glue to each other.

"Try it again now," he tells his wife. "I fixed it back for you."

She does it and it works all right. You can't see anymore where it had been broken.

"Tell me," he says, "where does this 'shining up' thing come from?"

(He is talking about the sun.)

"That's my boss' own," she replies. "He keeps it inside his house. He uses it for light. And he sure wants to hold onto it."

"Tell me, what kind of things is he scared of?"

"Well, he's sure scared of camp-fire steam. When I spill some water in the fire, he runs into his hole with his wife and daughter."

"Tell me about his daughter too. What's she like?"

"Oh, she's a real big shot girl. She is a real *dän nozhi'*. Her dad doesn't want her to do a thing. He has some slaves and they all work for her. He does not let her eat on her own. Somebody else has to handle the food. That's what I do. I cook, I get a spoon and I feed her. And, on top of that, she's not allowed to go to the bathroom herself. Some woman has to carry her there and handle the whole thing -- clean her up and everything, you know."

"Oh yeah..." crow says sounding kind of surprised.

"Well," he adds, "I know what we're going to do. For now you're going to stay with them and wait for me. When the time is ready, I'll come back and get you out of this place. You'll wait until they start to eat. You'll throw some water on the fire. They'll run away into their hole and then you'll run to me. I'll take you back."

The rat woman agrees.

"Yeah, you'll come back with me," says crow. "And when we'll get back on the land, I'm going to give you a good place to live in. I'll show you a lot of things and after that you're going to go on with your own living. Nobody is going to boss you no more.

Well, anyhow, that's for when I've done what I got to do now." The muskrat girl agrees again. Crow stays behind in the bush and his wife goes back to her boss' camp...

"Gee," crow says, "I want to get this light. I want to get it real bad. I need it for my world."

Pretty soon, he sees the big shot girl coming out in an open place by her dad's camp. He looks at her and he thinks to himself -- he medicine-thinks. He knows what to do. He wants to do something to her to think about getting some water.

"Ah, you girl, I wish you get dry. I wish you take your cup, go down to the river and drink water there."

Right then, the girl feels thirsty and asks for some water. She goes back home and sits down on her soft bedding. The muskrat slave brings her a cup of water.

"I don't want this water," the girl bitches. "Mom, give some to me."

Her mother fills another cup and gives it to her.

"No... I don't want it," she whines again. "I want to get it myself."

Her father gives her water from another birch-bark pot.

"No," the girl says, "I don't want it either. I want to go for it. I want to get my water at the river myself."

Everybody gives her water but she never wants to drink any of it. She wants to walk down to the water herself. She repeats it over and over. They have to let her go.

So her dad makes some people break a good trail for her. They make it fancy. They cover the ground with her dad's best blankets and everything he's got, all the way down to the river. That's for her to walk on. She steps on it but somebody starts to follow her.

"No," she says, "I'll go alone. There'll be nothing wrong. I'll come back right away."

Crow's hanging somewhere around the camp. That's him who makes her think that way. Pretty soon she dips her cup in the water. She fills it up. She brings the cup to her lips. She stops. She's seen a little piece of black dirt floating in it. Oh, it's no bigger than a needle head. But she dumps it anyway. She fills her cup again. The same little piece of dirt is still inside. She dumps the water again. The river is all crystal clear but every time she fills her cup up the little dirt is right inside. She sits down: she fills the cup up, she dumps it; she fills it up, she dumps it; she fills it up, she dumps it... The dirt is still inside there.

Finally, crow gets through to the woman's thinking again.

"You girl," he thinks, "just drink it down like that, with the dirt inside."

So the girl gets tired of dumping out her water. She lifts her cup up and drinks the whole thing -- the little piece of black dirt and all. Now she's swallowed crow's spirit. All along, the little dirt was crow's spirit.

And that's him, crow, who was putting it back again and again in her cup.

After she has drunk she walks back to her camp. Her mother ask her:

"Why is it that you've been gone for so long?"

"I don't know," she answers. "Something happened. I filled my cup with water and a black little piece of dirt got inside. I spilled it, filled it again and another piece got inside -- the same kind of piece. Finally, I got tired of it, and I swallowed it. I drank the water with the thing inside."

Soon enough, her stomach gets growing. She's going to have a baby. Soon this baby comes out between her legs. It's a little boy.

That's the same kind of story as with the Virgin Mary's. She didn't make the little Jesus through a man. A bird talked to her too. That's how she got her boy too. That's how God was born again. And all this happened because crow did it first, when he put his spirit in the girl's cup. Crow has done everything ahead of everybody. He's shown the way. And this "born again business" still goes on here in our Pelly Crossing village. When someone dies but doesn't want to go for good yet, his spirit roams around on this land. Pretty soon it finds a good strong stump. That's what old Indian say. But they mean some young woman. The fellow's spirit feels the stump around and finds a little hole. It's all warm inside. It gets in. And nine months later the fellow is born again. So we give him the same Indian names he had before passing away... And that's why some of our young women who've never been out with a man yet do give birth to a baby sometimes. Just like Virgin Mary. See, crow's done everything first. And he's done it for the Whiteman, for Jesus, and for the Indians. That's why the old timer said that this crow story is the true Bible story.

And now this trout girl's baby starts to grow real fast. Pretty soon he starts to crawl. Soon he starts to walk. He's already two feet high. And soon enough he starts to play. The more he grows the more they love him: everyone, his mother, his grandpa and his grandma. And one day this boy takes a fancy to his grandpa's sun. He cries for it.

"Bring down," he says. "Bring down, bring down, bring down..."

His grandpa doesn't want to let him play with it. But the kid gets louder and louder:

"Bring here, bring here, bring here..." he hollers.

He cries. He keeps crying. They try to make him change his mind. They give him all kind of different things to play with. But he throws them on the floor. He doesn't want them. He still stretches his little hands to the "light" up there. Finally, he tires them out. So his grandpa gives him the sun and lets him play with it indoors. It's not enough, though. The little kid wants to go outdoors with it. His grandpa says no. The kid: cry, cry, cry, cry. Boy, is he tiresome! His grandpa is getting mad but he gives in.

"My grandchild, what's wrong with you? O.K., I'll let you go out, but you're going to have to wait -- just for a little while."

He calls out for his people:

"Well," he says, "knock down all the trees around here. And use them to make a high fence all around my door. It's going to be a yard for this kid here to play in. I don't want him to let the sun roll too far away. I could lose it."

They go out... The muskrat slave walks with them. She is to chew the trees all right around and bring them down. They cut the branches, bring them in, and build the fence the old trout told them to make. Then the old man lets his grandchild out in this yard rounded up by a high fence.

The little kid is happy. He gives a push to the sun. It rolls around. Oh, it's funny. The boy laughs. He pushes it again, and he makes it roll back the other way... You can see he's having a real good time. His grandpa, grandma and mother are sitting down. They watch him rolling this sun around. Its shining rays go there, and here, and there again. It looks like the boy's playing with a flashlight. And you know, all little kids still love to fool around with this kind of light. It must be that it all comes from crow's story too... Otherwise, how do you explain it?

Anyway, crow's behind the fence, right where the kid might send the sun over if he pushes it too hard. He's waiting. And the rat woman knows that her boyfriend must be ready by now. So she starts to cook. She looks real busy. She does this, and that, and this. The kid is still playing with the sun. Now she's packing a birch-bark pan full of water. She pretends she trips on a root and she dumps the water on the fire.

"*T'roooohhhhh...*" it sounds.

Lots of steam comes out. The trout man, his wife and daughter all run inside their hole, to the bedroom. And this kid keeps on rolling the sun around. Crow's still behind the fence and he starts to medicine-think. He's thinking through to that boy. He says:

> "I wish you give this sun a bigger push, that you push it real hard, that it flies right over the fence. I wish that you get the strength to do this, that it can come to me, that I can take it."

The boy gives that sun a real hard kick. It hits the ground and from there it jumps right clean over the fence. Crow catches it with his two hands -- just like some kind of ball. Right at the same time, the rat woman climbs over the fence and runs to him. He grabs her too and throws her on his shoulders. He takes off packing the sun and his wife with him. He runs away over the trail he took to come down. He goes as fast as he can. Half of the time he's flying.

The trout people come out of their hole. The sun is gone. They all holler. All the fish in the lake start to run after that crow -- all everybody, and all the trouts, all the three big shot trouts too. Some of them fish are going to be catching up with him. So this crow grabs the top balsam tree he brought in and throws it behind him on the trail. The fish tumble up behind it. It makes like a little fish dam. Next, he throws the top of the spruce tree. And they all tumble up there too. Next, he dumps the birch branches. They all have a hard time getting through the fence. Next, he throws down the last one he got from the frog: the willow branches. It slows them down again. Crow's now getting pretty close to where he left the rope. But these fish are back right behind him again. So he takes the ice he's got with him and throws it in. It makes an ice-wall all the way right clean across the trail.

"Bang!"

The fish all get stuck behind the ice wall. They all get mad at crow.

> "*Ts'ehk'i sye de'ninyie',*" they holler, "*händye suna denintthye, ts'ehk'i ne'ye.*"

They mean:

"Gosh, that damned crow is getting away with everything. With the sun and with this slave muskrat woman. He's stolen everything."

And it's true. Crow gets to the rope and pulls on it. He pulls on it. And the water gets raised up again. The old frog woman is lifting it up for him. He comes out. He throws his muskrat wife down. He sits down and wipes his face with his own gopher blanket. He had left it there.

"Oh, jeez," he says, "I sure work hard for this land. This sun here gave me the hardest time I ever had."

Then, he gets busy with the sun. He calls everybody in -- all the birds and a lot of other things. He tells them:

"Try to put this sun way up in the sky. Try to make it stick there. It's going to be for the Indians, for the whole world. Until the next world!"

One fellow has a try at it. But the sun falls down. Everybody wants to try too. Everybody wants the chance to make the world better. So they all have a try at it. But it keeps falling down, again and again. Pretty soon crow says:

"Let me see..."

He goes out in the bush and brings back some pitch from a tree. He puts this pitch-glue all around on the back of the sun. He's holding it by the front side, flat on his hand. He looks at the sky, and, with all his strength, he throws the sun up, way up there. This time, it sticks. It stays up in the sky. It's glued there for good.

"Sun," says crow, "now you're going to come real big, and you're going to stay up there year round. And this world here can turn. But you, you're going to stay in this one place. You'll watch everybody; you'll watch the world and this land turning around. *Udjuu niints'in dekhaadye ddhaw 'otye,*" he says.

Kitty Smith, that old Indian woman from Tagish Lake, heard the same story from her old people. They told her, after that,

"that sun is going to stay for good. This ground turns, but that sun stays in one place – moon same, too. That sun does not move, he just stays there. That's what he said, that crow."

The man who writes the story for me just told me that. He read it in Kitty Smith's story, in Julie Cruikshank's book. See, old Indians knew lots of stuff. In our language, "sun" means *se*, and "moon," *edzeze*.

Anyhow, this world turns around, and daylight breaks. And noontime comes, and the sun is way high. And evening time, it gets dark again. Just like today. Crow looks at the sun and says:

"After I'm finished with this land here, I'm going to go back to you. And I'll stay there with you until the next earth comes in."

And this came true. The old timers said that after his last story, his mind went to the sun. That's God's power this one. It's also where people's minds go to after they die. It's why old Indians called this crow story the Bible story. And it must be true. My old man told it to the old Anglican bishop and he too said that it was a Bible story all right along.

So this is the way crow made the land and put the sun up in the sky.

Yeah, it's what crow did. And this story, old Indian people heard it. And these old Indians passed it down to their grandchildren, and next these fellows to their own grandchildren. On and on, down to this day. And me I got the story from my old grandpa Copper Joe. That's why all Indians know about this earth's turning round and round. Same thing for the moon! The old timers said that it stays in one place too. The sunlight hits it and it shines back down our way. You know, old timers knew lots of stuff. And, nighttime, you see some kind of man sitting down on the moon. Well, they also knew about that. Some day I'll tell you the story. And these old timers also knew about the land being all round. But I told that before, didn't I. That was when crow jumped all over the land to make it bigger and bigger. He told it to fit all right around. To be round. So that's why Indians know that this world is round right around. And it just proves that Indians have been in this country ever since crow made the world. Otherwise, how would they know about all these stories?

And from there, crow takes care of his muskrat wife.

"There is going to be summer and winter now," he says, "and you got to sleep and eat somewhere. Come on, come with me... I'll fix a place for you."

He takes a long sharp stick, walks to the bank of the lake, and jumps into the water. He holds his breath and he stays under there. He starts to dig a long tunnel straight through the bank. It's what the sharp stick was for. Some place he starts to go up. He is still underground but pretty soon he's back above the water level underground. He makes a room there. Then he walks out and comes back into the lake, and then back on top of the water, and he tells his wife.

"Dive in, go see, look."

She goes in and comes back out. And crow says:

"Well, it's the kind of lake-bank where you're going to make a home for yourself. You make an underwater tunnel just like this one I dug in and you make your bed in there, in your inside room above the water. This kind of home is going to be good year round: winter and summer. And these white carrots I showed you before, the kind that's good to eat, you pack lots of them in it. Hard times come; you'll live on them. And this kind of fresh grass you see here, you can eat it too -- it's a good eat. And you pack lots of it in your cache too. So, wintertime, you're still going to have some of it to eat. And for the cold winter days, for sixty or seventy below, you can make another kind of house. You build it ahead of time, though, when the lake ice is not too thick yet. You go some way from the shore. There you cut a hole in the thin ice. You make it big enough. This way you can dive in it and come back on your ice-floor inside what's gonna be your other home. After that, you bring in all kinds of sticks. You use them to build something like a little teepee on top of the ice -- all right around over the hole. Right inside, you keep some room for your bed, right by the water hole. It's where you're going to sit inside in the winter. When you're finished with that, you dive in and you bring back lots of mud from the lake bottom. You plaster all your walls with it -- real good. Don't leave any air hole, not even a small one. Otherwise, the water in the ice hole is going to freeze real hard and you're going to have no way to get back un-der... back into the lake to get your food. If you let your hole freeze solid, your teepee is going to be like a jailhouse. You're going to starve and freeze to death. But if you fix it good, you

102

can come in and stay in there anytime, as long as you want. Somehow, it's always going to get a little fresh air through the mud. And you're hungry in there; you go down into the lake through the hole in the ice. You pick up your grub. You bring it back through the hole. You get inside your home and you sit down. Then you eat and at the same time you can drink water too, from the hole."

Handy, isn't it? And that's what crow tells the muskrat woman. It's what he shows her. And she does as he says. And after that crow goes out again through the world.

THE FIRST MATCHES

Soon, he walks by some kind of big river. It could be a big lake too, or maybe the ocean. Anyway, something is going on way out over the water. Every once in a while, a big spark flies up in the air. It goes up quite high and then it starts to fall down. It hits the water and gets blown out. It looks like that kind of firecrackers you send up in the sky. But they're just big sparks coming from the *tl'ya* rock, the same kind of stone that Indians used to have for matches before the White-man. Crow looks at these sparks for a while.

From there, he calls for everybody to give him a hand. And all the birds come back to him -- his nephew, the *Kushekok* little owl, too.

"You bring one of these sparks down here," he tells them. "This way, you're going to have matches to start a fire and cook on it. Then you can eat your food cooked. I could get one myself but you guys have got to do it this time. You should make a name for yourselves now."

And pretty soon everybody tries. But they can't make it. Each one gets to the spark, grabs it with his beak, hauls it halfway to the shore, and then lets it drop in the water. It burns their faces fast. It's too hot. Nobody can hold it long enough to bring it back.

"Well," says crow, "I really was hoping you guys could do it. But I'm not going to get it myself. What about you, my nephew? You haven't not gone yet!"

At that time the *Kushekok* had a two feet long beak.

"Try to fly around," crow tells him, "but not too close. When it starts to fall down, grab it and come right back to the shore. Don't worry if your beak or face burns up. It doesn't matter. I'll fix them back after. But when the fire gets into your eyes, throw that spark down to me and I'll grab it."

And now that's what the *Kushekok* does. He's flying out. One spark's going way high. It's starting to come down. *Kushekok*'s grabbing it. He's flying down to the shore. And his beak and face are all being burnt, half-burnt.

> "My beak is getting all burnt up now," he hollers. "I don't want to lose it."

> "Just the same," crow shouts to him, "hang on to that spark. That's all. I'll fix your beak back. If you do it there'll be lots of new stories. All the countries in the world are going to know about you. Just do it. That's all."

And crow is talking and keeping talking to him. The *Kushekok* is coming down closer and closer.

> "Keep on going," shouts crow, "you'll make it pretty soon. Pretty soon you'll be landing on this shore. Go on."

But the *Kushekok* is getting his whole face burnt up.

> "Now, it's going to my brains," he hollers, "my eyes are going to bust. I can't hold it no more."

He throws the spark out to crow the best he can. Crow looks, jumps out, and grabs it before it hits the water, and throws it on the shore. A big fire starts there. All the grass, the entire bush, all everything burns.

Crow walks all right around the place that's been burnt. Then he comes to the middle where everything is still burning and he says:

> "Forest fire, yeah, you can go ahead like that. It's all right. Mash it up; burn out everything so that new stuff can grow back; so that all animals can eat good. You go like that around the world once in a while. That way they'll live good."

And you know, in the old days, Indians used to do just like crow did that day. When the bush and the grass were getting pretty skinny, they would start a forest fire. The bigger it would get, the more happy they would be. And they were not worried for their food "caches" in the bush: in those days they always built them where no fire could go. After that, they would go hunt some place else. Later on, they would come back to their old place. Lots of different kind of game would be feeding on the young grass and leaves. And then people would have plenty to eat. My grandpa Copper Joe used to do that. I used t see him doing it when I was a little kid. And springtime, he would also burn all the grass around Grayling Lake where we used to stay. That way the fish would get fresh grub to eat in the summer. But today, if you make a fire like that, you're sure to go to jail if you get caught. The Whiteman knows pretty good about cattle on a farm, but he sure doesn't know lots about wild animals in the bush -- how to farm for them. That's why right now we're getting low on moose. Dumb, hey!

Anyway, after that the *Kushekok* lands some place. His beak is all burnt up.

"I'll fix it," his crow uncle says.

And crow looks around. He finds some stuff. He makes a beak with it and puts it on the *Kushekok*'s face. It's sharp and straight all right, but it's way shorter than before, only about an inch long.

"It's not good enough yet," complains the *Kushekok*, "anyway,
I'm getting tired of straight beaks."

So crow works on it again. He makes it flat this time.

"It's still not good," says *Kushekok*.

"Let me see," crow asks him.

He holds the little beak and bends it down, all the way down, right over the *Kushekok*'s mouth.

"How about this?" he asks.

"Yeah, it's O.K. now, leave it like that," *Kushekok* says.

And that's why that little owl still has a little tiny crooked beak. And that's also because his face got all burnt up that his feathers all around it are all black. It's too bad you've never seen one yet. He looks real funny. Anyway, the way the story goes, crow still has got something to do. He says:

"Well, *Kushekok* now you have made a name for yourself over this fire thing. You brought it back. I sure could have done it myself. I made everything so far. I made the world. But I wanted you guys to do something too. You brought back that fire. That's good for you. Now we're going to have it in this country, in the world."

CROW PAINTS THE BIRDS

And from there, crow calls back all the birds.

"You're all good people," he tells them. "Now, I'm going to give a name to each one of you, and I'm going to paint you all a different color."

So he makes all kinds of paints. Then he calls all the birds one after another. He gives them a name and paints them. He starts with his nephew. He says your name is *etthedzaat*, and he paints him. He calls the next one and he names him *tutsi*. He paints him black on top and all red on his chest and belly. The *tutsi*'s wife he paints her a little bit different. *Tutsi* that's the robin, Whiteman way. And the light red color, he uses it for some other birds. Then he takes the blue paint and calls some other birds. One of them gets *tet'o zoa* for his name. He gets painted half black and half blue. That's the jay. The next one gets to be named *chuạ denintl'run*. Crow covers him all with the bright blue color. That's the blue bird. And that's why there's a lot of blue paint in this Yukon country. Crow gets to some more birds. The *etsana,* the *ts'u̱k'ye*, the *mek'en'*, the *tadrua* are all named and painted. That's the woodpecker, the camp-robber, the seagull, and the small sandpiper. And crow keeps going with the rest of the birds. Pretty soon, he's all finished.

Oh gee, all of them are nice-looking now with their different kinds of paint. They're really beautiful and they all like their new look. Then crow tells each bird which way he's got to go, which way he's got to make a living. And on top he says:

"You all are going to be good people. You all are going to be my helpers."

The way he talks sounds like the Bible story, you know. You see, God made the angels and here crow makes all the birds. That's why I figure that. It's pretty close to the Bible story, isn't it? I figured all that out from the way the old timers used to tell that crow story.

Anyway, after painting up all the birds, this crow wants to be good-looking too. So he asks his helpers to find some colors for him.

"O.K.," they tell him.

They all go work on it. They come back with some paint and they cover him up with it. He looks at himself put he is not too crazy about it.

"Oh," he says, "I'm not very good yet. Paint me a different way." They wash him off, paint him with something different, and he looks at himself again.

"No, I don't look good yet."

Well, this time they all do the best job they can. They make the paints as pretty as can be. Well, crow looks at himself there.

"No," he says, "I don't look good yet. Gee, you guys here, I made you nice-looking, but me, I don't look good yet."

The birds get mad. They tell each other, let's do that and then this. All right. They make a big fire. After that they get *t'ro'* from it, you know, fire chalk, charcoal. They mash it up and make black paint. Crow hears them working.

"What are you guys doing?" he asks.

"Well, we ran out of paint, so we're making some more."

Maybe that's the way crow wanted it. I'm guessing but I don't know. Anyhow, they bring back some of the old colors and the new black one. They paint him with the old stuff. They pretend they just made some more of it for him. He looks at himself.

"No, I'm no good," he says.

"All right," they holler.

They grab the charcoal paint, pour it over his head, and they all rush off. The paint gets all over crow and he turns black, just all black.

Oh, gee, crow gets mad. He turns around and sees the loon not too far away. This bird is slow at taking off from the water, you know. Crow looks for something down on the ground. He picks up some poop. It's kind of white. Maybe it's the wolf's. He picks it up and throws it at the loon with all his strength. He hits him on the back of his head. That's why the loon has got a white mark there behind his skull. It's where crow hit him with the white shit. Funny, hey. But all the other birds are too far away now, too scattered. He can't do nothing to them. He feels pretty bad.

"After I made you fellows all look good," he says to himself,

"you fellows made me all black, more black. Look at me now."

That's all for this one story. Crow can't do nothing about it. So he just goes out again.

EYEBALL, WATCHMAN AND PLAYING BALL

The sun has been put up in the sky, and from there crow walks across the land. He comes to a big river. He doesn't know what to do yet. He talks to himself:

"Anyhow, I made this river. And I think this one here is the biggest one I made. I might just as well build something to travel it down by boat. Then I can look for dead fish or something. This way I can eat their eyes, the fat from their eyes... Yeah, I should make a raft -- you know a *khwan'*."

But a raft might not be too good. So he changes his mind. He's going to make a birch-bark canoe (that how White people call the *k'i ts'i*). He starts to work on it. He goes out in the bush. He looks for some birch trees. He finds some. He peels the birch bark out. He takes it down. And he works: peel it out, take it down; peel it off, take it down; peel it off, take it down.

"Well," he says, "it's about time. Now I got enough."
Next thing: fine long roots for sewing. He tears some roots out. He tears roots out... tears roots out. Next, he gets a whole bunch of pitch. He takes it out from a tree. After that he brings all this stuff to the shore and he starts to build his canoe. And the birch bark pannels, he stitches them together with the roots. And the cracks and holes in the bark, he plugs them with the pitch. And this way his canoe won't leak in the water. And then out of nowhere he comes to be the one to be saying:

"Crow, you should have somebody checking around for you -- kind of like a watchman. You can't keep busy like this with nobody watching out for danger."

It just crossed his mind that strangers might come down on the river. He had been forgetting about that. His boat was keeping him too busy. He's got nobody to help him, though. So he finds another way.

He takes one of his eyes out of its socket and puts it on top of a willow stick.

"My eye," he says, "you check for people coming down on the river. Me, I'm fixing this boat. I'm too busy. Somebody comes down: you holler to me, you let me know right away."

And crow gets back working on his boat. And he's working. After a while, his eye is shouting away down there.

"*Hata acha...*" it hollers. "*Hata acha... Hata acha...* Strangers coming down, strangers coming down..."

It sounds like it speaks in Coast Indian language or maybe in *Tzän Huch'än* Tutchone language from the White River. Maybe it says "*hata hachya*," you know. I think it says no more than three words. That's all. Crow runs down to the shore and looks around. There's only one big tree root floating down. It must have fallen in the water somewhere up the river.

"That's not *hata*, he tells his eye. "That's a dead root floating down river. Look here! You got to watch for people doing like that, paddling down this way. You see it moving like I show you, then you tell me. You watch for a boat, you know, or maybe a raft. That's the kind you got to look for. You see something like that, you call me. Me, I got work to do, you know..."

And crow gets back to the canoe. Pretty soon his eye hollers again. He speaks another language this time. It sounds like Tutchone from the Champagne Indian village.

"*Kat'a echol, kat'a echol*," he says.

Crow runs down to the beach. Some driftwood is coming down on the river. He gets mad at his eye.

"Why do you speak like that?" he says. "Do you want people thinking you understand all the countries, all the languages in the world? Only I know that much. I understand all the different languages --every one of them. You can't beat me. Anyway this thing here is not a stranger, it's a piece of driftwood. Don't do that again. Otherwise, next time I'll dump you out in the river."

And crow gets back to his canoe making. But soon enough his eye calls him out and in a different language again.

"Somebody's coming, somebody's coming," he hollers.

Crow runs down and checks around. He looks with the one eye he has left.

"That's a piece of log," he says, "not somebody. Now you can go. I'm going to throw you in the water. It's what you've been looking for all along. ".

He grabs his eye and throws it in the river.

"Float down this way," he says. "I'll find you back some other place."

After that, crow takes a little piece of birch bark. He cuts it out into an eye patch. He places this piece of bark over where he's missing his eye. He ties it up with a little string going all around his head. He goes back to his boat and finishes it. He puts it in the water, sits in it and paddles downriver. Now he's watching for his missing eye. He's looking everywhere -- on both sides, all the way down. No eye is there. Finally he says:

"How come? It must be it floated down pretty far. Maybe it went into the middle of the river. I don't think so, though. I'm pretty sure I threw it close to the shore. It should be some place, some-where close by."

From there, he comes to a place where a big bunch of people is staying. He lands among them. He comes out for them.

"*Ts'ehk'i tee'klinre*," they holler. "Oh, crow, crow, crow's com-ing, crow's coming."

All people, all everybody knows him ahead of time -- all over the place. It's what I mean when I say it's a Bible story. Jesus: people know him the whole world over. Crow: it's the same thing.

And crow is among these guys and he's holding his hand over his missing eye, hiding the patch. These people are some kind of animal: maybe gophers, or maybe weasels, or maybe some other kind. I really can't tell. There used to be lots of animals at that time, you know. But it must be a people who don't eat anybody else. Maybe it's the ground-hog... Something like that: a small animal.

Crow is covering up his empty eye socket. And these people ask him:

"How about eating? Do you want something?"

"Yeah, I want to eat, I feel hungry."

"And how about your eye?" they say. "What happened to you?"

"Well, you know, I was working on this boat here and a witch hit my eye pretty bad. That's why."

They bring him some good food and sit down around him. From there, some of these people start to play a ball game. Crow is still seating down, eating.

"Let me look," he says. "I want to watch this game..."

He leans sideways. Now he can see. He's watching with his one eye. They're throwing a ball to one another.

"Hey," crow thinks to himself, "that's not a ball there, it's my other eye! The one I threw away in the water."

The way the story goes, these people had found it floating down on the river. They knew it was crow's eye. But they wanted to play ball with it.

Crow gets up. He walks around through the people. Pretty soon he comes behind a man waiting for the "ball" to be sent his way -- about a hundred feet behind him. Crow stops there and waits. He's still covering up his eye patch with one hand. So he looks at his other eye down there with his one eye here. He starts to think with his mind, to medicine-think, you know...

"I wish this guy misses my eye," he says. "This way, it can come to me. I can grab it and get it back in here."

He takes his patch out. Now he's ready to put his eye back in its hole. He still stands behind the ball player, medicine-thinking.

"I wish that man misses my eye," he keeps saying. "I want my eye to go back to the same place again."

The "ball" comes into this fellow's way. It comes way high. The guy jumps up, hands wide open. But he misses. The ball flies through, between his thumb and finger. It flies to crow. And crow grabs it with both hands.

"*Whaaaiiii*..." he says, while putting his eye back in.

He covers his eye socket again with one of his hands. The ball player runs to him.

"Did you see the ball? I missed it. It went over to you... Some place around here anyway."

"Yeah, I've seen it. It jumped off right here, and then it rolled down this way. Look for it down there."

But crow's already put his eye back in. He's just hiding it with his hand. It looks like he is still covering up his eye patch like before. More people come down and look for the ball.

"It went somewhere... somewhere down there," he tells them.

They look all over the place. They can't find it.

"The ball is lost," they say. "We can't play no more. Let's quit. Everybody can go home."

Nighttime comes and crow camps with them. Next morning he jumps in his canoe and goes downriver again.

HO-HEI, HO-HEI, HO-HEI, HO-HEI

Crow paddles away. He lets his canoe roll down. He paddles a little bit more. And pretty soon he comes to another big camp. Lots of people stay in there. They talk the same way as human beings, but they're some kind of animal again. I don't know which kind, though.

Crow paddles down there. Everybody comes down to see him.

"*Ho-hei, ho-hei, ho-hei,*" they all call out.

"*Ho-hei,*" that's what old timer Indians used to holler when someone was coming down to see them on a raft or a canoe. My old grandpa Copper Joe used to say that. But I don't think it was a word that meant something. It was more like "hello, hello, hello..."

And crow stops his boat. Everybody there knows him already.

"*Ts'ehk'i* comes, *ts'ehk'i* is coming, crow's coming," they say.

Crow walks up to the bank. He sits down with them and they feed him. After that, he stays around there. He goes through these people. He looks how they're are doing. Which one is a good person -- stuff like that...

They are fishing right on the side of the river. They are making fish grease and storing it into fish's guts, the fish's air bags, you know.

"Gee," they tell crow, "these air bags are too short, they fill up fast."

"I know," he says, "us, we used to fill ten of them at the same time, and maybe more. We just glued them with some pitch, all one after one another. We would pour the grease at one end. The whole thing would fill up and stretch into a long, long, long, long kind of sausage... That's the way the old timers used to do."

Right here he is starting to fool people again.

"Well," he says, "now I'm going to walk some place in the bush. I'll sit down there and take a rest. I'm tired, you know. I come from a long way."

So crow walks away. And the people get busy gluing the air guts into a long sausage tube like he told them. They start to fill it up with grease. Crow's lying down somewhere in the bush. And, these guys' sausage gets too long, too much in the way. So they push out in the bush what's already filled up. And they keep pouring grease at the other end. Finally the sausage reaches to where crow's resting. He grabs it, makes a hole in it and starts to drink grease. Gee, a funny guy, hey! He's done nothing and good fish grease comes right into his mouth. He lies down and he drinks.

Pretty soon, though, he hears some fellow's coming up his way. He grabs a bear's skin he's got around here. He puts it on real quick and starts to walk up to the man. Gosh, the fellow sees some kind of bad animal... He takes off full speed. He runs around in the bush, then he comes back to the camp. Crow is already there too.

"Where've you been?" his people ask the guy. "You've been gone a long time, you know."

"Oh," he says, "I ran into some kind of big animal down in the bush. He scared the shit out of me. I ran away."

"What kind was it?" they ask him.

"Ah, that's a big black one. Real scary."

They all talk over it.

"That must be *sra*," crow says. "Yeah, from the way you speak, it's got to be a black bear. What did you do to him?"

"Nothing, I ran away, I was too scared."

"Well," he tells him, "old timers used to know about that kind. They said you got to hit him with a little stick, right on the end of the nose. Then, 'vrooom': he runs away."

"Well next time he shows up, I'll do that," the guy tells him.

Everybody goes back to work on the long sausage. And crow is gone again. He's back in the bush. He puts his bearskin on and he starts sucking grease again. Pretty soon another man comes up. Crow is down there drinking grease, drinking, drinking. The man sees a black bear. He remembers the story crow told at the camp. He picks up some kind of stick and he hits the bear right on his nose.

"Ouch!" hollers crow. He meant "*eh bye*," though. Indians say "*eh bye*" when they mean "ouch."

Then nothing! He's got knocked right out. Some more people come up. They all try to get a hold of this animal lying down there. They pull. The skin comes off.

"Oh," they say, "all that time it was crow... He lied."
So they all jump on top of him, grab his beak, and break it off. Crow's got no nose left. They break it off and they give it to an old woman -- and old one who's got no husband left. They give it to her and say:

"Now, you keep it."
Crow holds his hand in front of his mouth.

"*Abah, abah*" he cries. (In English he means "ouch.") "It hurts. Give me back my beak. Bring it back here!"

"No," the old woman says.
And everybody goes back to camp. Crow too. He is thinking.

Finally, these people are just sitting down, enjoying themselves. Soon enough, though, somebody hollers:

"He's gone!"

"What do you mean?" the other fellows ask him.

"I mean crow. His canoe is still here, but him, he's gone."
They look around. Nothing!

Well, he's about a mile or two upstream. He slipped away through the bush and headed for the river again. He landed one or two bends above these people's town. This way, they couldn't see what he was going to do. And now he's just finished making five rafts out of some pieces of driftwood. Yeah, five of them. He picks lots of thick moss from the ground and loads each raft with lots of it. Next thing, he sets the paddles the way they're supposed to go on rafts. Then he tells these bunches of moss:

"Now you can paddle. Look here. You do that and this."
He shows them moss bunches how to run a raft.

"You see this point way down? Right after this last river bend... All right! Well, make sure you stay clear from it so that people in the town below can all look at you when you come out of the bend, floating down in the middle of the river. They took my beak away from me and I want to get it back."

He shoves the rafts out into the current. He shoves all five of them out. And they go. They're so heavy it looks like they're going to sink. And him, crow, he runs back to the camp again through the bush.

"What were you doing?" the people ask him.

"Oh," he says, "I went to look for some good cold water. I stuck my nose inside it. It sure starts to feel better now."

And soon, pretty soon, everybody's hollering:

"Ho-hei, ho-hei, ho-hei, ho-hei."

Crow's rafts are coming out from behind the bend. It looks like some people are paddling them down. But that's just the packs of moss who're moving there on top of the rafts. Everybody is down at the riverbank.

"Somebody's coming, somebody's coming," they say.

That's what they holler. Everyone is looking at the river, turning his back to the camp. Crow is around there.

"Yeah," he says. "Some people are coming down now. That's for sure."

He goes back to the camp. Nobody's there. He looks around for his beak. He can't find it. He comes into the old woman. She's sitting down. He knows that it's her who's got it.

"Hey," he complains to her, "somebody's going to come: I'll be looking funny without my beak. Come on, give it back to me."

"No," she says, "I don't have it."

"Come on... I know you got my *dye* here." With *dye* he means beak.

"Maybe I got it," she tells him. "But I won't give it back to you unless you pay me."

"Which way am I supposed to pay you? I don't know."

"I show you which way."

She opens up her legs for him.

"Make love for me first," she says.

"Sure, sure, sure..."

He jumps in between there. He works at it. And he makes a good time inside there. And pretty soon he gets through with it.

"Oh, oh," the old woman says. "Here, after that you sure can have your beak back."

She hands it over to him and he puts it back on.

Everybody is still standing up on the bank.

Crow walks there to have a look. But pretty soon all the rafts break apart. There's just driftwood and moss floating around now. That's all. Nobody was coming downriver. The people all get mad at crow.

"He lied again," they holler.

So they start to chase him. But he flies off into the bush. He hides in there for the night. He gets up early, when everybody is still sleeping. He walks back to the camp. He sneaks in to get back to his canoe, jumps in it and drifts down the river again.

And he's thinking:

"Anyhow, why do these fellows holler *'ho-hei, ho-hei, ho-hei?'* It sounds like they mean 'somebody's coming.' But maybe I guess it wrong. Maybe they're meaning something different. I got to find out. It could be I don't hear it good."

Pretty soon, he sees another town way down. It looks like another bunch of people is staying in there. He turns around and paddles upstream for a little way. From there, nobody can spot him. He lands and builds a new bunch of rafts. He puts lots of moss on top and he says:

"Moss, I'm going to canoe down to that village below. You wait here and you figure out how long it's going to take me to land among these people. When you know I'm already there, you'll start to paddle these rafts down. This way, you'll arrive some time after me. And me, I'm going to tell these fellows down there that I just passed lots of people on rafts, lots of people that should show up any time."

"O.K.," the moss bunches say.

Crow jumps in his canoe and goes. The rafts wait on the shore, ready to float down.

And crow gets close to the town.

"Ho-hei, ho-hei, ho-hei," everybody hollers, up on the bank. These guys already know of him too:

"Ts'ehk'i's coming... crow's coming, crow's coming..." they say. Crow walks up to their camp and goes through them. They're all good nice people. Not bad ones. So he tells them:

"You're going to see lots of other good people coming downriver.
And you fellows are going be laughing, laughing, laughing away.
Yeah, you're going to see lots of good people coming down any
time now."

So everybody walks to the bank. They see people paddling down on
rafts.

"*Ho-hei, ho-hei, ho-hei,*" they all holler.

"*Ho-hei, ho-hei, ho-hei,*" they keep hollering.

Crow asks them a question.

"'*Ho-hei, ho-hei*': what do you fellows mean by that?"

They don't hear him... They're too busy hollering. The rafts are now
half way down to the village. So crow medicine-thinks and these new
rafts all break apart again. They turn back to moss and driftwood and
that's all that's floating down on the river now. These people look at
the water. Nobody's there no more. Crow walks away.

"Crow lied to us," they start to holler.

"I wanted to know about that '*ho-hei,*'" he shouts from his place.

"That why I did that. And now I know what '*ho-hei*' means."

They start to run after him.

"Crow lied to us... He lied..." they keep hollering.

I think they meant:

"He lied to us, just because he wanted to be sure of what '*ho-hei*'
meant. He tricked us, just to make fun of us because we say
words like '*ho-hei*' which have no meaning on their own."

But crow races to his canoe, jumps in it, pulls twice on his paddle with all his muscles and gets away as fast as a fish. He leaves all
these guys way behind.

A JEALOUS GOPHER

And after that, a long way down the river, crow comes to another big town with lots of brush-camps all lined up by the river. There stays another big bunch of fellows. They're the *tsaw* people. Whiteman way, "gopher" means *tsaw*.

"Well," crow thinks, "I come to help. I should look for which one are bad guys around here, which one to get."

This new story here, is where he catches a man -- but one man only.

So crow walks up from the beach to the village on the bank and meets with these fellows. They talk the same way as human beings. I guess gophers were like people at that time. And they already know he's crow. They all call him *ts'ehk'i*. It's his name in Indian language. Anyway, they're real nice people: they feed him and he stays with them.

Later on, some of them talk story with him.

"You know," they say, "down there stays a pretty bad man, the number one jealous man ever. It's *goen tsaw,* the 'jealous gopher.'"

"Where?" asks crow.

They show him down below:

"Ah... about two river bends from us."

And they talk story about that man: how he is, what he does, and everything.

"He's got a real fancy woman, you know: a real good looking one... And gosh, is he jealous. You can't talk to her. You can't look at her. You can't make love to her. You can't do nothing with her. Nothing. He doesn't let anybody come around."

Crow tells them:

"Me, I'm going to talk to her, and it could be I make love to her too."

"Hey, hey, hey," they laugh. "You black one, how do you think a good looking woman is going to talk to you and love you? No way... You're much too black!"

"Wait," says crow getting a little bit mad at the way people talked about him. "Who made the world? Who made everything on this land? I did. I'm the one who did. And I came all the way from across the world to see how things are making it out among you guys. And right now I'm still working on something for you. Why do you talk to me like that?"

They all can see he's going to get real mad. So they don't say one work back. They all stop bothering him.

"Right on," crow tells them." So tomorrow I'm going to go down-river. I'll meet that jealous man and I'll do business with his wife just the same."

"O.K.," they reply. "You go ahead."

From there, next morning, he drifts down with his canoe. Pretty soon he spots the "jealous gopher's place" As soon as it happens, he lies down inside his boat and covers himself with his blanket. He pre-tends he's sick. He's going to fool the gopher man.

"Eh bye... eh bye... eh bye... eh bye..." he starts to moan.

"Eh bye, eh bye..." that also "ouch, ouch..." Whiteman way!

His boat drift into a quiet eddy close by the jaelous guy's camp

"Eh bye... eh bye... eh bye..." crow keeps sobbing.

The gopher man is a little way down in a dugout canoe, pulling out fish-trap sacks with a long stick with a hook at the end. Pretty soon, this gopher hears somebody's moaning. He looks out and sees crow's boat up there. He drops his work and paddles up full speed. He comes to crow's canoe, hooks it up with the stick and tows it to shore. He sees crow in there.

"Ts'ehk'i," he says, "what's wrong with you? What're you doing in this boat?"

See again! Anybody who comes to crow knows him. Everybody knows him ahead of time.

Crow says:

"Oh, my brother in-law, I'm pretty sick... I need some help. Just take me out of here and pack me up to your place. I'll lie down out-of-doors by your campfire. I want to take a rest. I'll feel better."

"O.K.!"

The gopher man packs him up. His campfire is right by the entrance of his brush-camp. He puts crow on its outdoor side, across and away from his wife who's sitting down at home. But crow's blanket has been left in the boat. Crow asks for it. The gopher man goes back to the beach. When he's gone, crow raises his head a little bit. Smoke is coming up from the fire. But just the same, he picks up what the gopher's woman in the brush-camp looks like: a nice big woman with good fat legs. Oh, gee, crow doesn't know if he's going to be able to hold it...

He hears the gopher man coming back. There is nothing he can do right now. He drops his head down and pretends he's sleeping. The gopher man sets the blanket over him. Then, he watches around for while. He checks if everything looks O.K. Yeah, all sounds fine. So he can go back to his fishing. He's got to make his living, you know. But half way to the shore, this gopher man can't help it: he stops. Run, run, run: he's back to the camp. He goes inside his home. He looks in there for his *tsi det'ow* powder bag. It's a kind of red paint, Indian paint. It's made out of the ochre red rock. He finds it. His woman is sitting Indian way: knees on the ground and feet under her rear end. He throws some of that red powder on her lap, in the fold of her dress, between her thighs. And he tells her:

"Don't move, just keep sitting down in that one place."

Now, this gopher man is back fishing with some kind of hand-net. He checks on crow and his wife from down there. Crow moans once in a while:

"Eh bye... eh bye... eh bye..."

The gopher man figures out that he's still sick. Then crow pretends to be sleeping. He keeps quiet. That "jealous gopher" does not hear nothing no more. He gets real worried. Every minute... nearly every minute he runs back to his camp. The wind has blown some ashes over crow's blanket. They're still there. O.K.! The jealous gopher looks at his wife's lap. The red rock powder is still on her dress. O.K.! He goes back fishing. Crow there, on the other side of the fire, is just pretending. That's all. As soon as the man is gone he laughs:

"Ah, ah, ah, ah."

Then he raises his head again and snoops at the gopher's wife across the fire. This gopher woman there shows him her tits away and makes him more horny. And every second her husband is coming back up to the camp. He looks at that red paint on her dress. It's in that one place there yet.

"All right."

He goes back down. So, after a while, crow starts to think to himself. He sings over that "jealous gopher." He talks to himself and he's talking to the fish at the same time:

"I wish that this gopher man catches you, that your teeth get all tangled up in the mesh of his net and that you drag him all the way downriver. That's for giving me a chance. I want to fool around with this woman here."

So crow's way comes out true. The fish get caught in the gopher man's net. They drag him down and he goes way out. He tries to fight back, to pull the fish out. No, he can't do it! Them fish keep dragging him around.

Up there, crow tells the woman across the fire:

"Put your hands under your dress. Go easy. Then from under there fold the dress over the red rock powder and hold it in there. I want to go on top of you. Don't let it move. You hold it tight. I'll do the work."

The woman says:

"Sure, O.K."

She grabs the red paint from under her dress, holds it between her hands, lifts her dress up and lays down on her back for crow, legs wide open. He gets on top and gives her a ball. Old timers said that he made a real good time in between there.

After they're finished, the crow gets off and goes lay down outdoors where he was before. He pulls his blanket up and tells the gopher's wife:

"Blow ashes back over me, on my blanket and my face."

And "*pfffff... pfffff... pfffff...*" she blows ashes over him from across the fire. It looks like he never moved.

"Now," he says, "sit down and put back your dress the same way it was."

She does it and sets her dress as he tells her. It's just like the red rock powder as never been moved.

Pretty soon, the gopher man comes back up to the camp. He looks at the red paint mark. Everything is O.K. He never thinks his wife just got a piece of tail. All right, he runs down fishing again.

After that, the second time he comes up again, crow pretends he's waking up.

"*Ih lye*, my brother-in-law," he says, "you might as well pack me down and help me get into my canoe. I feel a little better now. I'm pretty sure I can go and move on again. I'll just have to drift down with the boat. But I can make it."

So the gopher man carries crow on his back. He puts him in the birch bark canoe, helps him to lie down in there, and covers him with the blanket and some old bags. When he's finished, he shoves the boat out, away from the shore, right into where the river is flowing fast. He goes back to look for fish.

Crow's canoe is now floating away. From inside there, crow figures out he must be some distance from the gopher. Hiding under a bag, he raises his head a little bit and peeks overboard to check how far. The gopher sees two eyes starring at him from under there.

"Why is crow doing that?" he thinks to himself, looking at the boat drifting further down.

A while passes. Crow's still watching him.

"Hey crow!" hollers the gopher man. "What is it you're doing now?"

Crow pulls the bag off and sticks his head out. Then he gets up in the canoe.

"Gopher," he yells, "you're the man I heard a story about. I heard you were the number one jealous man and this story came out true: you're the number one jealous all right. But this crow here, he fooled you. He fooled you good. That time fish got tangled up in your net, well, that time, I fed your wife right. I had good love making with her. I slept with her. I stole her from you. And you know, she's a good love woman, just right for me. And me here, I thought you were smart."

And that gopher gets mad... He runs to his dugout, jumps in it, and tries to catch up with the crow's, paddling with all his strength.

Crow is already drifting down by a long and narrow sandbar. He sees the river flows through another big channel on the other side. He lands, lifts his birch bark canoe out, and packs it across to the other passage. He puts his boat back into the water and takes off full speed. The gopher gets what's going on. He's been outfoxed. His dugout boat is a log chopped off inside. It's too heavy to be packed across all alone. He's never going to catch up with the crow now. He gives up. He's more mad.

He turns around and paddles upriver. He gets back to where his camp is, jumps on the beach, runs up to the top of the banks, grabs a big club and:

"Paw, paw, paw, paw..."

He pounds his wife down and kills her. After that, he walks back to the shore and starts fishing again.

All the while, down in the other channel, crow beaches his canoe and walks back, up to the village above the jealous gopher's camp. He gets there and tells these people:

"Listen to this one story. I went to see this man's wife all right. I talked to her and made her love, good love making. And I didn't hide away from that jealous man. He knew I was there all right along."

They don't believe him.

"You black thing, nobody can make love with you. What are you talking about?"

"You don't believe it!" says crow. "Well, go down and see for yourself. I heard him. He clubbed her to death after he found out. He killed a good looking woman over me."

Some of these people go down to the jealous gopher's place. He's still fishing. They walk up to his brush-camp.

"Ah, that gopher killed his wife all right!"

They come back to the village.

"Crow was right," they tell everybody. "That jealous man killed his wife."

"Yeah," says crow, "and I didn't hide."

So they tell him:

"You're the best. If you had hidden away, it would be no good. But he was with you, see. So..."

And from there, crow goes out again.

WHO'S THE OLDEST ONE IN THE WORLD?

Crow drifts downriver, down to look for more animals or people, down to check who's bad and who's good. He wants to go through them all.

Well, pretty soon he comes to the osprey, to *tuundye*, the one he stole water and fish from when he made the world, earlier on. I guess *tuundye* must have kept walking around the world. Just the same as crow. He is a kind of eagle, but at that time he was like a man... like an Indian. Crow comes to that man and they talk together.

"Who's the oldest?" *tuundye* asks him

"I'm the oldest one," says crow.

"I'm older than you," argues *tuundye*.

"No, I'm much older than you," disagrees crow.

"No, no," says *tuundye*.

"O.K.," answers crow, "then, we're going to check it. Let's shoot arrows. We race with that. Let's try it. Then we know for sure who's the oldest one. Go ahead. Go first. You shoot first."

Tuundye aims at the other side of the river. He shoots and his arrow nearly gets across. It falls into the water but just close to the shore.

"You see that now? How I shoot?" he asks crow,

"Well," crow tells him, "I'm going to try now. You'll see I'm older. Me, I know it. There's no way you can beat me. You're only a kid."

He takes an arrow out. It's got magpie feathers at the end. I guess it's what he uses to make his arrows fly straight. He gets it out and starts to medicine. Something like a medicine anyway. He talks into the feathers with his mind.

"This arrow goes down," he tells them feathers, "you make it go up again; it falls down, you bring it back up; don't let it hit the ground."

He takes his bow and shoots. The arrow goes a little way and starts to fall down.

"Up again," he says in his mind.

That arrow flies right back up. It hustles a little way and then down again.

"Up, up, up," he orders the feathers.

The arrow goes higher up.

Crow keeps it going like that for a while. His arrow goes over one whole high mountain, never touching ground. And did you see magpies fly? They still go around just like that, you know: always down and up, up and down, never in a straight line. That's why. It's all because of crow. What he did and everything.

Anyway, *tuundye* gets beat. He tells crow:

"You're right, you're the oldest one all right. Me, I was just kid. Now I know."

Crow asks him:

"What kind of thing do you live on?"

"I live on fish," replied *tuundye*.

"That's good..."

And from there, crow gets into his canoe and goes out again.

A CANNIBAL HORSEFLY-MAN

Crow drifts down. Pretty soon, he sees a big camp. It's on a point of land in between two rivers that run into each other... Crow is coming down on one river and there is another one that flows into his river. The camp is in between the two, just before the two rivers meet. Crow lands on shore. There are lots of people in the camp. Crow walks through them and asks how they're doing. Everybody talks nice to him. They're sure happy to see him. They ask on what river he came on. He says:

"Right on this one; why you want to know that?"
They show him the other river and tell him that people go up on this other one all the time but never come back.

"They go only one way, they get killed, something eats them, they never come back, we cannot get the guy that eats us."
Crow asks them:

"What makes that?"
They tell him:

"We don't know, we can't find out what kind of guy it is."
Crow says:

"I'm going to go look for him. I'm going to find out. I'm going to get him. Maybe there is something bad, some bad man on that river..."
He walks to the beach where he has landed to make himself a new boat, a fancy canoe. But this time he is not going to use wood and birch bark. He takes sand. He builds and carves his boat out of fine sand and gravel -- you know, like kids do all kinds of things with sand on a beach. Pretty soon he is finished. He looks at it. But he finds it a little too rough. So he stands up and pees inside. He puts his hand in his pee and, round and round, smooth out the inside. When he is done with that, he uses the rest of his pee to smooth out the outside too. He gets a good canoe right there. He has got one long paddle too. He puts

his canoe in the water, jumps inside, and paddles upstream, toward where he came from. The canoe slides real easy, real fast. Crow has got only a paddle -- he doesn't use poles or anything else. His mind does all the work... His mind makes everything move like nothing.

Crow still paddles upstream. Pretty soon, he turns around and drifts down. Then he makes a sharp turn and starts to go upstream on the bad guy's river. He is going for that man. His boat goes just as fast as a speedboat... You know, just like a motor boat. Now you see: that's the way the Whiteman got the speedboat too. He got it from crow. Crow made it first...

Crow keeps on paddling upstream. He passes many river bends. And then, some place, he sees a man sitting on a rock on top of some kind of cliff. As the river turns behind this high bluff, he cannot see beyond. The man who sits on the rock at the top is like a watchman. His name is *tr'o*. Whiteman way you call it horsefly. But at that time *tr'o* was a man and a horsefly, back and forth. Not like nowadays, just a horsefly.

And *tr'o* watches and sees a boat coming upriver. He has got his own canoe hidden upstream, right behind the bend, where nobody can spot it from downriver. As soon as he sees crow's boat coming, he gets up and runs downs to his own boat. He thinks he is going to get a good lunch. Crow sees the horsefly disappearing behind the bluff. His mind tells him that something is going to happen -- that *tr'o* is going to come out somewhere on the river. So he paddles to go hide himself behind *tr'o's* bluff, on its downriver side. He knows the horsefly will show up upstream but not exactly where. He goes slow. He wants to get this man who eats people. When he reaches the eddy behind the bluff, he stops his boat. He knows *tr'o* has to come out from above. And soon enough he sees the bad fellow paddling down in the middle of the river. The man has real big eyes, just like a horsefly. He is looking for crow's boat all over the place. He does not understand why it's not where it should now be. He looks round and round. And then he spots it at last. He swings his canoe and paddles toward it full speed. The bad man's got a real big knife. About a foot and a half long. When he gets close to crow, he swings it above his head like a sword. He is going to kill him and eat him if he can.

Crow hollers to him: "*ih lye, ih lye, ih lye, ih lye, ih lye,* my brother in-law, my brother in-law..."

You remember: this is the nice way to talk to a friend. But that horsefly man wants to eat, not to make a friend. He shouts back:

"You are not my brother-in-law. What's the matter with you? Are you crazy or what?"

And he keeps swinging his knife at crow. He looks real mean. He is going to eat him for sure... Crow puts his hand up and hollers again:

"*Ih lye, ih lye, ih lye*... Let's not fight... Let's not fight... I am brother in-law to you. And you, you are only a little kid to me. I am much older than you are. I am the oldest one in the world. That's why my father told me all kinds of stories. And from that, I know everything, E-VE-RY-THING... My dad explained real good. I come from across the world. And my father told me: 'You are going to see your brother in-law this way.' He said right where we are now. And he told me: 'You got to be friends with your brother-in-law.' My father told me all that... That's why I know. So it was you who were my brother-in-law during all that time."

Crow steps out of his boat. He wants to make the horsefly his friend. He talks some more:

"Where you come from?" he asks.

The horsefly man answers:

"Me, I'm just looking around. I hunt for people. I want to eat them."

Crow replies:

"Me and you are friends. You see, your father and mine were friends with each other. Mine told me that. How about you? I don't think your father told you anything. What did your father tell you about all this? Tell me."

Crow beats the horsefly right there. The bad man doesn't know what to answer. He shouts back:

"My father told me nothing... NOTHING... ABOUT... THAT... AT... ALL..."

Crow answers back:

"This just proves that I am the oldest one. If you don't believe me, let's try to race across the river with our boats: the oldest one is going to land first; the youngest one is going to come behind. You see my boat here: with it you can go right clean across the river with one paddle push only."

The bad guy looks at it and says angrily:

"Where did you get this kind of boat? One paddle push and you get across? Are you crazy or what?"

Crows says:

"It goes like a speed boat."

The horsefly man answers back:

"We'll try it then."

He pulls out and paddles away like hell. Crow is left behind but he pushes his sand boat twice, flies on top of the water, and reaches the other shore like nothing. He sure beats the horsefly right clean through. But it's crow's mind-power -- his medicine -- that does the work. Now he is going to kill the horsefly man. He steps out of his boat and hollers to the bad fellow:

"You see now! I'm the oldest one. You, you are young."

The horsefly man comes up from way behind. He gets close to the shore, breathes and says:

"You are right. You are the oldest one. You are the old one all right. You know everything. You beat me."

Crow says:

"You know this boat here? It's a good boat. With it I catch up with moose pretty fast. With my boat and paddle, a moose can never swim away from me. I catch up with it right away."

The horsefly man smiles a little bit and looks at crow's boat with his big eyes. Then, crow says:

"How about if we trade our boats? I'll give you my boat. It's just right for you. You can chase and get moose with it. You see? You want to try it? Go ahead! Jump in! Uh-huh, uh-huh?"

The horsefly man agrees, steps outside of his boat, and jumps into crow's sand boat. Crow takes the horsefly's wooden boat. The horsefly's big knife is still in there. And they both paddle across. But crow is left way behind. He pulls like hell and he goes slow. The horsefly reaches the middle of the river like nothing. Now, as soon as he is there, crow starts to medicine-talk to his sand boat:

"My boat just sink right down... Turn back to sand and gravel. Go down into the water. My boat go down all the way."

And right there the boat turns back to sand. The horsefly man falls into the river and starts to drown. For sure he fights back like hell. Sometimes his head comes out from under the water but guy sinks down again. And then his head sticks out again. Crow keeps on going with the wooden boat. He paddles toward the horsefly man. Soon he comes close to him.

"*Ih lye, ih lye*," he says. "My brother-in-law, I'll pull you out. I'll bring you in. I'm going to pull you back into your boat right here. But I'll handle you very easy -- other ways, you start to pull too and the boat will be upset. Don't tip the boat over with me or both of us are going to drown."

The horsefly man says: "O.K! O.K!" Then he disappears down another time. Pretty soon he swims up out again. Crow grabs him by the hair, reaches for the head and turns the body so that its back is against the side wall of the canoe. He raises out the horsefly's head slowly. When the bad guy's back neck is on the edge of the canoe, crow bends it backward in one quick swing, takes the guy's big knife at the bottom of the canoe and, right there, cuts the man's throat open and chops off his head.

That's why nowadays the horsefly's head can turn pretty near right around all the way. Did you ever look at one of those horseflies? They can do lots of tricks with their head. They can go nearly right around and then wind up right back again the other way. They don't do this all the time, but once in a while they really go like that.

Anyway, crow lets the horsefly man's body sink back into the water and throws the head in the boat. He killed the horsefly for good.

After that crow turns around and paddles downstream towards the people's camp. Pretty soon he gets close to their town. They look at him paddling down. They say:

"How come crow has got a different kind of boat now?"

They all run down from the bank to the shore to meet him. They holler to him. Crow lands among them and tells them to all line up on the beach and look. Then he asks them a question:

"You fellows know what kind of man ate you?"

Nobody answers. Crow bends over to look at the bottom of his canoe. He grabs the horsefly man's head and throws it on the shore -- the big knife too. And the people look at that dead fly.

"That's *tr'o*, the horsefly. It's the kind of people that eats you -- the kind that ate your friends. He is not going to eat you any more, he said. I stopped him."

The people are all surprised. They ask questions: "How did you kill him? What did you do with your boat?" Crow tells them what he did:

"I gave him my speed boat. He went in the middle of the river and my boat turned back to sand. That's the way it happened. My boat sank. It's how I got him."

That's the only man that crow killed for good, though. He only killed one man throughout his whole story. You see, he made the world and after that the horsefly man ate people. Crow found out and fooled him. But the old timers say that no bad luck and no law comes out of that one story. The horsefly you can handle it any which way you want to. There is no *duhuli'* about it... No *duhuli'* that means no taboo about it, Whiteman way. But something else happened with the story anyway. Take any kind of boat: steam boat, anything, big boat, anything, any kind of little boat, gas boat, whatever. It hits something and it sinks right down to the bottom. That's because of crow... Because of his sand boat. It's crow that's done that. That's why boats sink. Crow's mind has made it to happen first.

After that, crow stays around there in the camp. He walks through the people. They tell him that lots of men live on the main river yet -- down below. Crow says that he is going to go through them too. And from here he goes out again...

CROW MAKES THE FIRST WOMEN

Soon enough, crow comes to a new camp on a small bank, just above the shore of the river. The people see him and everybody hollers:

"*Ts'ehk'i, ts'ehk'i*, crow, crow... Crow is coming over with a boat," they say.

Crow lands on the beach, climbs up to the top of the bank and walks through them. He looks around and listens to them talking. They already know about the crow and wolf clans. But in those days the crow people are called *handyaat* people. *Handyaat*, that must come from the word ants, from the *dedya'*. Maybe it's the old Indian word for ants. Ants were people in these old days. That's why crow clan people you can call them *dedya'* or *handyaat* or *tse'shk'i*, or crow people. Either way, back and forth!

So when crow comes into the camp there are ants and wolf people. And some place crow finds out something funny going on among them people. There have no women yet. They don't know about that kind and they make love with each other. They fool around with each other assholes: but ant men with wolf men because they already know that ant or crow people have got to go out with wolf people and wolf people with crow people only. It's the Indian law. And the wolf clan people you can call them *egay* just like you call a real wolf or else *hagundye* (this means wolf too but it's just for people) or else you can call them *mehk'en'* which means seagull.

Crow finds out because he sees two men who are going to make love to one another. They are hard and big and they need to get a ball real bad. But, poor things, they are all swollen up where they poop. They talk to crow:

"That's the way we do it. How about helping us, making something for us? You see that bluff over there, further up the river. Well, on this side, there is a tunnel going in there from the river.

It is like a flooded cave. It's quite big and deep enough for paddling inside with a canoe. There is something in there. It sounds just as if something is sucking on something under water, you know. It sounds like something is boiling. But all the men who try to get in and see what it is get drowned. At the door of the cave, there is some kind of a log looking thing moving up and down and barring the way to the inside. It's got the same look as a drift-log, but it's made of stone. It's big and scary: about two feet and half across and twenty five feet long. It sits on a rock to the right of the tunnel door. The other end goes all the way to the other side, but there is nothing to stop it there. So that end goes up in the air and down in the water, and back and forth. When it splashes it makes a big noise: *whaoooooooo*. It sounds like big waves crashing on a lake beach. Many people try to go through, but nobody can make it. The drift-log moves too fast. As soon as a man tries to paddle in, the stone log comes down from above, flaps the canoe and sinks it right there. Sometimes the stone log comes back from under the water. But it upsets the boat just the same. Then, the canoe drifts down to a sand bar below, right in the middle of the river. And the man is gone for good. All the men who try to get into the cave drown like that. They never come back. They are just a few bodies we find once in while. How about you, crow? You think you can get these things out of the tunnel and make something for us? Then we can grow more people, we can build up."

By this time lots of people have joined the two men talking to crow. Crow looks at them and says:

"Me, if I am going to go there, I am going to get through. But if I do this, are you fellows going to hold up my words? Right up? Otherwise, I don't want to do it."

All the men swears to it:

"You do it, you do it, you do it," they tell him.

Crow agrees and everybody watches him and waits to figure out how he is going to do that. He doesn't tell them anything, though. He starts by building a canoe. Then he makes himself a small bow out of a willow stick. He uses sinews for the string. He also makes a batch of short arrow shafts out of willow branches. Then, he cuts out some arrow points too. He sharpens them at the tip and carves into them a corner shape at the other end. They look like some kind of hooks. He ties the blades to his arrow shafts. When it's finished, each whole arrow is no longer than about a foot and four inches. That's all. Crow has got a boatload of them now. He ties them into a bundle and loads them up. He takes his bow, steps in his canoe, and paddles upstream toward the tunnel. He reaches it. The opening of the cave is a pretty big hole in the bluff. In the middle, its roof is about nine feet high above the water. Right under the surface, it's as deep as the eyes can see. The drift-log moves just like the people told crow. When it goes down it makes a big noise: "*WOOOOOOOO...*" When it comes out from under the water and starts to go up, it is only a little bit quieter: "*woooooooofff,*" it says. And it goes *WOOOOOOOOO* and *woooooooofff, WOOOOOOOO* and *woooooooofff. C*row can see that it's pretty dangerous. He thinks about the whole thing. Then he medicine-sings to the drift-log.

"Drift-wood, stay down for a little while; I want to go over you."

"*Gawndye...*" he shouts.

He talks Coast Indian Tlingit language to that log. Old timer Indians say that crow knows Tlingit and all kinds of different languages from around the Yukon and the Northwest Territories. Any language... Crow understands anything. Even animal's talk! They all speak with different kinds of words but he understands them too.

Crow's song has got lots of power. The drift-log stays under water for a while. Crow paddles through the entrance and into the tunnel. The log comes out and closes the door again, going up and down. Somewhere inside the cave, crow finds an eddy. Long grasses are floating up through its muddy water. A lot of foam covers it too. It's too thick for crow to see through the water. But something funny is happening right here. From under the water some kind of things are sucking the foam. You can't see them but you can hear them from all over the eddy:

"*To..., to..., to..., to..., to..., to..., to...*"

It looks like it's a bunch of suckerfish feeding on the foam from under water. Same way like with the suckerfish. Bubbles come out from all over. It's like water boiling. Crow looks at one place close by where one of those things is sucking from below. He takes his bow, one arrow and shoots at it through the water. It must be he hits it for the arrow starts to move by itself. Crow quickly grabs the shaft, plays around with it and, with the blade pointed corner, hooks it into the meat of the thing under there. He pulls out and throws it inside his boat, arrow stuck in. And then he knows. It's about as big as a big man's fist with the thumb sticking out between the two big fingers. But it's soft and nice. That's the woman's own he caught. The arrowhead went through in the middle right under the thumb-like little thing. So all that time it was the women's *druu* that was in there.

Whiteman way, *druu* means cunt. But *druu* doesn't sound bad in Indian language. I don't know why cunt looks dirty in English. It's a surprise to me! Maybe the Whiteman has no respect for the woman's own. This may be why! But there are lots of other words like that too. They sound cute and funny in Indian; and, Whiteman way, they all have mud on their face. So I don't know...

Crow keeps on going at the woman's own with his arrows. He keeps the shooting going. And pretty soon he has got a boat load of them in his canoe. The water reaches to the edge of the boat. *Druu* are heavy, you know... That's why women are heavy too. Old timers all knew that.

Crow paddles out of the tunnel now. When he come to the gate he sings to the log:

"*kaaan dyeeeeeee...* Log stay up for a while."

The gate stays and crow paddles under it and gets out. After that the log goes down and under water again.

And, crow now sings again:

"*K'at k'ala kiiin...*

Gol.. gol...

Gol... gol...

I got the woman's own.

I went through...

I got it.

I bring it back now...

Gol... Gol..."

He sings Coast Indians way. But "*gol... gol...*" I don't know what it means.

Crow paddles downstream to the people's camp, singing all the way. He lands. Everybody hollers:

"*Ts'ehk'i uga nin kl'in, aaaaaaahhhhhh.* Crow sure is back here. He is the oldest one in the world."

Crow tells them again about their promise:

"Are you going to hold up by my words? By the Indian law? Are you going to go the right way?"

People all just look at him. They are all scared. Nobody talks or acts smart. Crow waits for a while. Then he says:

"How many wolf? Raise your hand. How many crow people now? Just the same much. O.K., now line up along the riverbank. And hold one another by the hands -- each crow man holds a wolf man by his hands."

Then, he walks up to one man:

"What kind are you?"

The man:

"Wolf."

Crow says:

"How about this one fellow with you?"

The man:

"Crow."

Now, crow asks him:

"Which way you're going to be? You want to be a woman?"

The man speaks up:

"Yes, I want to be a woman. I want to stay with this crow man. I want to get married to him."

Crow talks to each crow and wolf couple in the same way, all right down by the riverside:

"Which one of you two men wants to be a woman? You? O.K.!"

Then he speaks for everyone one who wants to be woman:

"Take down your pants and open your legs. I'm going to put the woman's own in between them, in your crotch. You'll close your legs for a minute and you'll be a woman. You already got tits, so you don't worry for that. Go ahead! Open your legs."

Crow takes a woman's *druu* from his boat and walks to one of
the man woman-to-be. He flops the *druu* over the man's dick. It slides
right on, right clean through. Crow pushes the *druu* down between his
crotch. The man closes his legs. His dick sticks out. Dick that means
lelro' Crow makes it disappear and the man gets a hole inside, between his legs. It must have happened just like that. I mean I never
heard anything on how that hole came about. Now the man has got a
woman's own. Crow makes the first woman right there. That's the first
free-male. I mean the first female English way. I always get mixed up.
I don't know why. I always say free-male, not fe... fe... female as you
guys say.

And all the men who want to become women, crow makes them
free-males, you know... with the women's owns from the tunnel.

After that, he speaks out to the people. He tells them about the
law -- Indian law:

"You women, you keep the thing between your legs away from
your own relations. You too men: your own, you can stick it
out... but you keep it away from your own relations. Don't poke
them. You don't listen, you go the other way, you keep doing it;
well, your friends are going to kill you both and burn you up.
And if more go crazy with their relations, I'm going to come back
and mash them down on you people."

Crow explained them real good:

"Crow women have got to get wolf husbands only. And a wolf
woman has to take a crow man. It's the law and you have to hold
it up. And a crow woman's kids are going to be crow, just like
their mom -- their dad belongs to the other side. A wolf woman
makes children: they will all be wolf kind. Same law like with
crow women. And next generation crow will marry wolf again.
And their children are going to belong to their mothers' side
again, not to their dad's. And next generation: same thing again,
same thing again..."

Crow keeps on talking:

"See, you, you are a wolf; and you, you are a crow. Well, you're
going to be *duhuli'* if you talk to you own relations. You turn into
real bad luck if you do that. That what I mean by *duhuli'*. It's the

Indian law. A wolf man can't talk at all to a wolf woman his own age -- any wolf woman his own age, even if he has never seen her before. He can speak only with crow women. But he can talk to any woman, crow or wolf, who is not his own generation -- except to his mother-in-law. The same backward for the crow man: he can't speak to the crow woman his own age. You understand? You better do it. You, same side men and women are all relations with each other. You are brothers and sisters to one another. Same story for you women. It's just as good against the law for the wolf woman to speak to the wolf man and for the crow woman to talk to the crow man. All you same age wolf women and men are all brothers and sisters to each other. All you same generation crow women and men too. Follow my law! Don't get mixed up! It's *duhuli'* to do it; it's taboo to talk with your own relations. If you get mixed up, people are going to have to chop you to death with their axes. Keep the law! And later on your kids too! If they fool around with their own relations they got to be killed. No choice. Their own relations, people on the bad kids' mother's side do it. Maybe their own mothers' brothers... It's best that way. After that, nobody can argue, nobody can fight back. Anyway, whatever happens, you get them chopped just the same and you burn them up. That's what you got to do to keep the world the right way. You are a man and you want your sister to know something? Any kind of sister? Don't speak to her. It's real *duhuli'*. You tell it to her husband. How about you? You are a woman now. You need to say anything to your brother? Real brother or same clan brother? Any which way, don't talk to him. Speak out with his wife. You fellows do like I say and you'll keep the world clean. You got to remember my Words and pass them along, generation after generation. Otherwise you're going to spoil the world... spoil the people. You do that, and your world will start to go this way... You'll all start to go crazy..."

Everybody agrees to go by crow's words. They all agree to it. And today we keep on doing it too. Me, that's how I know crow story is a true story. That's why I believe it.

After that these people get up and start a big party. Everybody makes love all over the place. Every man is poking his partner. All of them men and women have lots of fun. The whole town is doing business. Well, you know, it's the first time they taste it that way. They all like it so much. Everybody is happy.

All the while, five dogs walk through the camp and one of them makes fun of people making a good time.

"Ha, ha, ha, ha, ha," one dog laughs at one of them guys. "*Dedjoso*... down here... *Deak'iaraaaaa*," he hollers to everybody.

"Everybody's cock is working... Everyone is working like hell." One man doesn't like the way the dog talks and pulls out of his partner. The dog walks through the town and laughs at more people and more people stop making love. Crow sees that. He sits down and he thinks about the whole thing:

"If it keeps on going this way, people are going to be ashamed by this dog. Maybe lots of them are going to argue and split apart. They are not going to go into one another good. They are going to make good times no more and they are not going to build up the number of people. That dog is going to spoil everything."

So crow walks around. He looks for some poop. He finds some. He takes a little stick. He holds it by one end. He dips the other end in the poop and butters it all over -- thick, you know. Then he calls the dog:

"Come on, come see me here... I'll tell you something..."

The dog comes to crow waving his tail and crow talks to him:

"You are a good fellow... Now open your mouth for me real big and stick your tongue out as far as it can go, and keep it there until I'm finished."

The dog says "O.K." He sticks his tongue out all the way. And, crow paints it all over the top with the shit on his stick. (Other people say that he painted his lips only. Some others tell that he painted the sides of his tongue all around. Me, I don't know about that). When crow is finished, the dog pulls his tongue back in and shuts his mouth.

"Now," says crow, "go make fun of the people some more."

"Mmmmmmmmmmmmmmmmmmmmm," that's all the dog can answer.

Maybe that poop is too sticky.

"Now, talk!" crow asks him.

"Whaaaf, whaaaf, whaaaf," that's all that's coming out now.
No more talk. Then crow shows the poop to the dog:

"You know this kind?" he asks him. "That's shit. And you are
going to eat this kind all the time. You can live on the people.
What else? When wolves come to you they are going to eat you.
But to eat you guys can hunt small animals for yourself too."
Do you know that wolves eat dog still to this day but that dog will
never eat any wolf meat? I know a Whiteman who tried to feed wolf
meat to his dog. They never touched it. They let themselves starve
even though he cooked it for them.

And crow told them dogs:

"When people move camp, you'll go behind. You'll look for this
kind. From now on it's going to be your grub. And now try to go
through the people, try to laugh at them again... You do that, you
speak to them and you're going to be 'real bad luck' for them.
They all are going to die within a day or two. Don't talk no more
to people. It's *duhuli'* for your kind."

But this dog still wants to go up look through the people and
make fun of them making love. He walks around and he tries to speak
again. But all that comes out is:

"Whaaaf, Whaaaf, Whaaaf."
That's all that's coming out. No more talk at all. And that's why dogs
don't speak any more nowadays. Crow fixed them up that day and he
told them not to speak Indian language to people no more.

"I fixed you," he said.

That's why today's dogs only bark and that's it. But you still got
to be careful with them, though. If you suffer your dog real bad, he
can still talk back to you with real words and then you die right then
and there. That's what happened with a girl from Aishihik Lake about
forty years ago. And in my grandpa's times too. Some boys bothered
an old dog for days on end until he turned around and whined back,
speaking in Indian language. They all died.

I'll tell you what happened with the girl too. That was around Aishihik Lake or maybe Burwash Lake, sometimes in the 1940's or 50's.
Jack Allen, an Indian from there, told me that story. There were lots

of people together. They had been fishing on the lake and the men had also been hunting around. They already had some dried moose meat, sheep meat and everything... Now they were on the move to a new camp. Everybody was packing something -- heavy packs, you know. And this girl was way behind. She could not keep up because her dog would not walk fast enough. That was an old one and he was carrying a big load on its back. As the girl had a big pack herself, she could not help the poor thing. And she was getting mad and more mad. She wanted to catch up with them people ahead. Her mother was walking with them, you see. The dog would walk for a little stretch and then he would sit down to catch its breath. She would chase him out, make him move on. No matter how tired, the dog would get up and pack again... And a little way ahead he would sit down some place and rest again. She would chase him out again trying to make him catch up with the people. The dog was getting mad too. So the next time she pushed him out again, he looked at her and started to talk Indian. He told her:

"*Te ka sin ishi o dye laku, nat'ane etsien.* You suffer me too much. I'm tired, that's why I stop to rest."

The girl didn't answer anything. She passed the dog, left him behind and walked on. She got up to where the people were making camp, took her pack down, and sat by her mother. She told the story:

"The pack dog I had talked back to me, Indian way. He said: 'I'm tired.' Me, I never knew he was tired. He lay down all the time. So I just tried to keep him going. I chased him ahead. That's when he said: '*Te ka sin ishi o dye laku, nat'ane etsien...*' The dog talked to me like that..."

That's all the girl said. She fell down and she was gone: dead.

Tl'aku! it's the end of that little one story.

That's how crow fixed them dogs. You see now. And in the crow story, after crow does this, he stays among the people some more. Lots of women are having babies already. Crow shows them women what to do:

"For diapers, you use moss. I'll show you. See this kind of moss: that the kind you take. *K'eitsak'* you're gonna call it and you put it this way for the baby. Then you put it in that way. Then he shows them how to make baby clothes like this and that, on and on."

The mothers do it.

Then crow tells them about the birch bark baby cradle. He makes one for them. All the women look. All those who have got a baby make one. Crow puts moss in it and sits a baby on top. Then he covers the baby.

"That's the way you got to do it," he tells them. "You keep doing this all right along."

One more thing he says:

"You got to cover up this country I made. The world I made it for you fellows. You stay friends. Sometimes I see you people again."

There is a lot more people already. The country starts to build up.

MOOSE, CARIBOU, SHEEP AND GOAT

And crow goes downriver to another country, to another place again. He comes to a new camp. There are already lots of Indians there. The world builds up fast. But the people tell him that they are short: some men and women have disappeared. Crow counts them all. Two days latter he counts them again and finds out for himself: some more people have disappeared. Crow asks:

"What's doing that?"

"We don't know," they answer.

So crow starts looking around in the bush. Pretty soon he comes to where a new whole bunch of people are staying: moose, three kinds of caribou, sheep and mountain goats are all in there together. Crow walks through these people. They all look at him. And as he walks around, he finds out how the other people have become short: there's a woman's chest here on the ground; another place, a man's behind - the bum has been all chewed up and eaten up. Moose and some other animal people have been eating the Indian people. Crow doesn't show he has found out. He just thinks about it. He doesn't know which way he is going to stop them people eating Indians. He can't find out what to do. Finally, he just thinks these man-eating people through. He picks out which way to fix them. He thinks to himself:

"I do that... This way... Then they're going to turn to a different way. They're going to turn to animals -- for the ever and the ever, I can tell them that. I'm going to change their lives."

And crow medicine-thinks about them man-eaters.

"I hope they all get sore teeth," he says in his mind. "I want to make the right medicine for them."

And moose, the caribou, sheep and goats, all get toothaches right this same moment. Bull moose, that means *denyäk* and cow moose that's *dezra*; caribou, that's *hudzi*; sheep that's *mäk*. Everybody holds the front of his mouth with a hand. They hurt real bad. Crow made this sickness for them. But that's also why people have been getting toothache after that. Crow invented it... You see. It's better to laugh about it, though. That's the only way he could straighten out those man-eating people. Now crow goes to a moose.

"What's the matter with you fellow?" he asks.

"I'm sick. I got a bad toothache," says the man. "See all my teeth here are all covered up with something and..., and..., it hurts like hell. I don't know what to do."

Crow says:

"I know it. I know that kind of sickness. I know a good medicine for it. I'll get that kind for you. I'm going to fix you quick. You're going to feel better right away."

He goes out in the bush with a large birch-bark pot. He picks up cranberries. Lots of them. Pretty soon he has got enough in his pot. It's almost filled up. He walks back to the camp. He puts one big cooking stone in a fire. While the fire is going he pours water in the cranberry pot. When the stone is red hot he takes it out with some sticks. He throws it inside the bark pot:

"To, to, to, to, to, to," says the water.

It's all boiling in there. Now his medicine is just right -- hot and good. Crow makes a big birch-bark spoon. He calls the sick man:

"Come on... Come on... Come to me. I'm going to fix your toothache. Open up your jaws."

Crow shoves a big spoonful of his boiling medicine in the fellow's mouth and makes him close it.

"Hold it shut now," he says. "Don't spit nothing out. Hold it all in your mouth."

The man's tongue, teeth, and all everything are burning.

"Tiiiz... ho... hot..." he mumbles through his teeth.

He means, it's too hot.

"Just the same," says crow. "Keep it in there. Keep going. Hold it up. Otherwise you're going to get worse. It's a good medicine I give you."

The moose man keeps his mouth shut as best he can. Crow goes out in the bush. He picks up fresh leaves. He mixes them... Rolls them up into a bunch for the moose, and comes back.

154

"Now," he says, "throw that hot juice out."

The moose spits it right out.

"Now, open up your mouth again."

The moose shows his tongue and teeth. Crow shoves the leaves inside.

"Leave this one in your mouth," he says. "Hold it in there for a while. From now on you're going to live on this kind. And then you're going to be smart -- for the ever and the ever. Now you got to know what you're doing. You find a woman, you get married. But you get a woman like you: a moose woman. Don't eat man any more."

All the moose walk away. They go eat leaves.

And crow doctors all the other man-eating people all the same way: the woodland caribou, the timberline big bull caribou, the tundra travelling caribou, the sheep and the mountain goats. All of them get a spoonful of real hot juice and crow makes them hold it in their mouth until it cools down. Timberline caribou is the biggest one -- he's about the size of a two-year old moose calf; he's got a long head. The other woodland caribou is only a little bit bigger than a "travelling" bull caribou.

After that he calls back the sheep.

"Hey, you sheep, come here too," he asks.

He picks up the sheep's hay, rolls it up, and throws it in the animal's mouth. (Though I should not say animal yet: at that time sheep were people too.)

Caribou? He gives them *edju*: that white dry stuff that caribou eat -- it looks like little small caribou horns. Someday, when we go hunting, I'll show you where it grows. Crow bundles up some of that kind and shoves it in the caribou's mouth. Big timberline bull caribou? He gives him *ts'u̱ shye̱*. That kind of caribou grub grows off the trees at timberline.

"You eat this kind too," he tells him. "And all of you don't eat people no more."

And now crow turns around and calls the moose again:

"From now on, your head is going to be *duhuli'*," he says. "You know about little children? *Dän*'s (people's) kids? The kind that sucks milk at his mother's tits? Well, he can't touch your head and he can't eat any of your meat from it. It's going to be 'bad luck' for his family if he does. You won't give yourself up any more to his dad when he hunts. You'll look the other way. You won't look for him no more. He doesn't handle your meat the right way: you keep away from him. And all your four feet and your four big bones right above them, don't let people throw them in the fire with the skin and hair still on top. It's going to be *duhuli'* for you. People who do that are going to have real 'bad luck.' They want to eat the marrow from these bones? They want to feed some to their little kids too? It'll be O.K., but first, they skin your legs and clean up your bones before they can fire them to crack up. Otherwise your skin is all going to curl up. That's what's *duhuli'*. And when the people don't look after your body good, keep away from them too."

And then crow makes the same *duhuli'* for all the other man-eating people: sheep, caribou, goats... all of them. And they all say they're going to go by crow's way. They'll all watch good for their head, feet, and lower legs.

You see now: all our *duhuli'*, all our laws about the big animals that we hunt come from this one story. And we Indians got to respect all these *duhuli'*. That's why I can never sell a moose head to a Whiteman -- more worse, to a tourist who wants to put it up on a wall as a trophy. How is he going to handle it? The more he comes from far away, the less he knows about animal laws. He is not going to take care of it the right way and after that moose are going to keep away from me for the ever. Who's going to take care of my wife and kids then? Whiteman? Forget it! He is going to spoil my sons' luck too. The Whiteman does any kind of crazy things with the animals he hunts and he gets away with no "bad luck" because he's got no laws about it. But us, we have like a whole book of them laws. Write them up and it'll be as thick as the Bible book.

You forget this *duhuli'* or you forget that one, and you're in trouble. The animals don't look for you any more.

And it's no bullshit story. It's five year ago now: I talked about the five-finger and the four-finger kinds in the same story. (That's the porcupine and the beaver). Nobody is supposed to do that. From then on I haven't got one single beaver. The porcupine too: I have not seen any for the last five years. Now I tell these two animals' true names together again. That's because I already got "bad luck" for them anyway. It can't hurt no more.

So you see now, the minute the Whiteman would handle my moose head the wrong way, I would get "bad luck" for moose too. That one moose's spirit would pass my picture along to all the other moose and then they would all know about me not taking care of their heads good. Yes, the animals know the face of who's done something *duhuli'*.

It's about the same way as the police get a man's picture. I saw that one time at the R.C.M.P. station here in Pelly Crossing. I was saying hello to Glen, Sergeant Glen. Someone had killed somebody in Whitehorse and straight away, right here in Pelly, Glen got the guy's picture on his machine -- through the phone wire. Then he posted it for everybody to know and everyone saw the bad guy's face. And that guy's good luck ran out.

Moose's spirit, caribou's, sheep's, all of them animals' spirits pass the news around and get them about the same way. It's more like TV, though -- through the air. You don't believe me. But that's because you don't know about animals' spirits. And, anyhow, it maybe just as well. There is lots of *duhuli'* in there. When you don't know, maybe "bad luck" keeps away from you. So let's forget about Indian laws for now. Give me a minute. I want some tea. I'm getting dry...

What about crow's story now? Let me see. Ah yeah... After he talks about the *duhuli'*, he calls them sheep in:

"You see that high mountain up there," he says. "You see that high rocky bluff on top. This is going to be your country. You go there. And you goats, you're going to be the sheep's partner," he says. "You got to go up on that mountain too. That's going to be it for you fellows. Don't go nowhere else. Don't come down in the hills or on the flat lands. That belongs to the moose and to the caribou. You'll make your living high up on the land. But your grub is going to be there for you year-round. You'll live on that."

Crow also tells the moose where to go:

"You'll live in the hills. Your grub is going to stay there for you for ever."

Caribou don't know yet what to do. So crow tells them too:

"You, small woodland caribou, you go live on the flat lands and you stay in the same country year-round. It's where you going to find your grub. You're going to be called 'year-round caribou' or 'this country caribou.' You, big bull year-round caribou, you walk up to timberline. It's going to be your land, your country. You stay there. You eat that *ts'u shye* that grows on the trees. Don't travel nowhere else. And, last, you, the smallest of you caribou fellows, you're going to be the 'travelling caribou.' You'll live on the flat lands with no trees. And you're going to move across two countries once a year: winter country down south; and summer one up north. And if you clean up your grub in one place, all of it, you'll go look for another country. While you're gone it's going to grow again. When you're finished with the new country you come back this way again and you eat that. Maybe it takes thirty, forty or fifty years but it's going to be here for you to feed on. This way, you'll be walking through the whole world, back and forth."

And you know, the "travelling caribou" keeps on going like crow told him. He's been walking around pretty near all over the whole world by now. These last thirty years, there were lots of them on the Peel River and Fortymiles River. There used to be lots of them around here in the Yukon and Pelly River country when I was a young man. Thousands of them. Then, in 1939, they all went up some place North and never came back our way for the next winter... and for the next winter... and for the next one... It's only in 1990 that they started to come back to us, right here, in their old Pelly winter country. That's why I know that this crow story is no bullshit. It always comes true. That's why I believe in it. It's the Bible story. And I better tell my sons and grandsons to watch about the *duhuli'*. They don't know much about this kind of caribou yet. Maybe they make a mistake and burn their legs with the skin on top. Then this "travelling caribou" is not going to come back here for good. It's going to scratch its legs and walk somewhere else for next winter.

Tl'aku! That pretty much does it. That's all for the story of crow with moose, caribou, sheep and goat. After that, crow leaves them animals and walks overland. He does not paddle down any river anymore.

CROW'S MOTHER-IN-LAW

And some place in the bush, there is this woman and her daughter living by themselves, alone. They're people. Indians have built up you see. The girl is grown up all right. Her mom is thinking of having a husband given to her pretty soon. He will stay with them and help around a lot. The two women live in a small brush camp. Like all Indians then.

In this country, here in the Pelly, Indians didn't know about tents and cabins before the Whiteman came in the Yukon. Around the Pelly River, we just had the brush-camps. We called them *man ku̲*. It's easy, and quick to build up -- and cheap too, not like houses today. The women and children made it. The men too -- sometimes.

First, you send the kids to break lots of spruce branches -- you know, the bottom ones with lots of green needles. You pick up branches all around and pile them up on top of one another to make three walls: one back wall about nine or ten feet long and four feet high; and two side walls about six feet long and the same high. The other long side stays open. For the roof, you sit some rafters on the walls. This gets covered up with brush. Then you put one or two moose skins flat on the top of the roof so no water drips in. Your kids bring back several loads of green spruce branches. It's for the floor. You set them branches flat all over inside. And you put more... and more. The floor's got to be about one foot thick. Otherwise, you're going to feel the cold from the ground. You watch for the needles too. You look at each branch. You see the way the needles are. They go up. You flap the branch over. Them needle points are going to be looking down. This way, your bed doesn't scratch you all the time. The brush-house is all finished in three or four hours. The whole family can go to sleep: heads against the long back wall and feet in the open, where there is no wall. This way everybody can jump out of bed real quick if something happens.

Wintertime, people keep some logs burning outside, just two feet away from the opened door. Days and nights. So it's always hot in there. Seventy below zero, eighty below, it's still warm. You have to sleep between two moose or caribou skins with the hair inside, though. And you got to get up all the time to keep the fire going. But you get a lot of fresh air from the opened door. You breathe good all the time, not like in my new Indian Affairs house.

I slept in this kind of brush-camp when my grandpa Copper Joe was raising me in the bush around Grayling Lake. That's a long time ago, hey. I never got cold. I never died. What's wrong with them kids now? You take one out in the bush. He cries for his house. He's scare to poop outdoors. Maybe he thinks his bums 're going to freeze right the minute he takes his pants down. And he misses his home, and his bathroom, and his TV. As soon as he is in the bush, he wants to go back to the village. I don't know how these guys are going to make a living later on. I bet you a hundred bucks they're going to eat cow meat all the time.

Anyway, what I am talking about is the kind of brush-house these two ladies stay in, when crow walks into their camp. Maybe it's already late summer or early fall. They keep a small fire going at the front.

"*Ts'ehk'i yaadah*, crow's coming," they say.

Any place he walks in, people tell him that. Everybody knows about him before he comes in. He's famous in any which land he goes to. He made the world, you see.

Crow sits down outside, in front of the campfire. He smiles. He has seen that girl in the brush-camp:

"Gee! I wish to get married to you," he tells her. "What kind of people are you?"

"I'm wolf side," she answers. "You see my mother is a wolf."

"Me, I'm crow side," he says.

Then he pretends he just figured something out.

"MY GOSH," he hollers, "this is just right. We're just RIGHT for one another. Me I'm crow. You, you're a wolf. We get married and we make some more people."

All right, they get married. Crow moves into the brush-camp with his wife and wife's mother. Nighttime comes and everybody goes to bed. The girl lies down in the middle, between crow and her mother on the other side. The fire is going on strong. The girl's mother is already lying on her back. But she's getting too warm. She lifts her bottom and legs up and pushes her pants out. Crow hears somebody moving. He raises his head a little bit over his wife's head -- just a tiny bit. He looks sideways and sees what his mother-in-law is doing. That fire throws too much light around, you see. He watches. And when she pushes her pants up, he sees her legs -- her bare naked legs.

"Oh, my gosh," he thinks. "What nice good looking legs I see there. All white and just the right shape. My, my, my... I don't know what to do."

Now, crow's mind is getting real crooked. Let me tell you. Indian ways, old timers' ways, you're not supposed to look at your mother-in-law at all. You got to look the other way. And you're not allowed to speak to her. Same law for her: she can tell you nothing. And you never listen to what she says when she talks around in the camp. She never listens to you either. It's like she doesn't hear you at all. It starts from the day you were promised to her daughter. Mother-in-law and son-in-law are supposed to be "shamed" of one another all the time. If you talk big story, your wife, or your sisters-in-laws, or your father-in-law will tell her later on. Or maybe your wife just repeats it as you go along:

"My husband says that..." she tells her. "And now he says that. And on and on."

This sounds crazy, I know, but that's the way it's supposed to be. See, me, right here, I lived with my wife's folks all my life. I helped them right until they passed away. Well, I never said one word to my mother-in-law. It's the law. Wait though. One time I talked. I had hurt myself bad with an axe and nobody else was in camp to help me. So I turned around and asked my mother-in-law. But my god, did I feel ashamed that time. Her too. Her face turned all red. She could not speak. She looked another way. She couldn't do nothing. So I stopped the bleeding myself the best I could. And I waited for the others to come back. She was not mean, though. She was a real good woman.

But that was the Indian law then. So, after that, I never told her one more word. My wife talked to her every day, but me, nothing at all -- even when we camped in the same tent. And something more, too. Our way, you can't call your mother-in-law "mom" like White folks do. That would sound crazy. My mother-in-law can't be a "mom." See, I'm a crow. That's because my mom is a crow. And anyone I call "mom" has to be a crow like me. She has to be in the same clan as me and my mother and be like a sister to my mom.It's our law. That comes from when crow made the first women. Now any wife I take has to be a wolf.It's our law again. So my wife's mother has to be a wolf too. She can't be crow. If she was, my wife would be crow and that would be real bad luck, real *duhuli'*. They would chop her and me to death. For a wolf man, it's the other way around. His wife and wife's mother have to be crow. And that's why we can never say "mom" to mean mother-in-law. In my language, we can say *ih mbi'* -- same thing like dad's sister. That's because the mother-in-law is always in the same clan as the dad's and, so, as the dad's sister's side. But we don't use *"ih mbi'"* too much. Most of the time the word we say for the mother-in law is *"ih tsu̲"*. That means, my "grandma." And people have got to guess who you're talking about: your real grandma or your mother-in-law? It's a nicer way to talk about her. It's more polite.

So that's why I mean that crow's mind gets crooked after he sees his mother-in-law's good looking legs. He's not "shamed" at all. He does not care about any mother-in-law business. He is lying down and thinking about those legs:

"My gosh, they're so white."

Do you know about Indian people? Only their faces and hands see the sun and turn dark. But under their clothes they have a light-colored looking skin. Never had any Indian girl friend? So you know! But these legs crow sees are almost white. And this crow keeps thinking about them in his sleep. He dreams and he finds out what to do.

Next morning, he gets up. He looks real sick.

"Gee," he says, "my head aches bad. My head is so sick. For sure, I'm going to die: help... Help."

His wife and mother-in-law sit up. Crow looks at his wife:

"Your mom right here, tell her to go find some medicine for me, real quick. Otherwise, I'm going to die. I got that kind of headache before. There's just one kind of medicine for it. Tell her to go in those hills behind, where there is a lot of thick moss. It's the kind of place where it grows. Tell you mother that this plant is real easy to find out. This kind calls for you when you look for it. When you hear it, you just walk straight up to it. When you are right close to it, you turn around, you take your pants down, and you sit on top of it. And, first thing, you make sure to let it poke you inside. When you stand up again, you pick it up and you bring it back home. Old timers, they all say that it's the best medicine for this kind of headache. Ah, I was going to forget something. Tell her that when the plant calls you, it says: '*dänaazak... dänaazak...*' That's the one, that's the one. It's the good kind. That's the one she's got to pick up."

Crow's wife repeats to her mother what crow just said; how he is going to die; how she is going to find the medicine; all everything. Crow's mother-in-law gets all worried as she listens. She is going to save her son-in-law. Sure. So she goes and starts to walk up to the hills.

As she is walking away, crow tells his wife:

"My headache is getting more worse. I'm going to look for some cold water. I want to shove my whole head inside. Maybe it'll help a little bit. I don't want to die. What about that little creek I saw down on the trail? It must be real cool, isn't it?"

Crow starts to walk. He's staggering all over. He looks worse than a drunk. So he picks up a dry stick and helps himself with that. His wife gets real worried for him. But him, as soon as she can't see him no more, he throws his stick down and runs to the hills where his mother-in-law is going. He runs fast. Pretty soon he catches up with her. He takes another way. She never sees him. And he comes up way ahead. The plant his mother-in-law is looking for is called *shra tsok*, Indian way. It grows on the ground. It's yellow or brown. It sticks out straight up between two or three bottom green leaves. Same look as some spruce tree corn -- you know, the thin long one with a sharp end; about six, seven or eight inches long. Same shape and same big like a man's own -- hard one, though. But it's only a bunch of hard tiny things all closed together on one stem. It looks like the *detr'uu* plant too. Crow picks one of them *shra tsok*. He lifts the thick moss and goes lie under it with the medicine. Nobody can see him no more. He makes a hole in his moss blanket. Just the right size and the right place. He pushes his medicine plant through. Now it sticks back up outside. Just like if it had grown there.

Crow hears his mother-in-law coming up. He hollers:

"*Dänaazak... dänaazaak... dänaazaaak...*"

She hears the call. She looks around.

"*Dänaazak... dänaazaak... dänaazaaak...*" crow hollers again.

She listens to figure out where it's coming from. Then, she walks up to it. She sees the medicine.

"Ah," she thinks to herself, "that was right: look there is one here."

She gets to it. She turns around, pulls her pants down and sits on top of it.

But as soon as she's turned around, crow pulls *shra tsok* back under the moss and sticks his own thing out through the hole. She sees nothing: she's turned around, she is looking the other way. Crow's mother-in-law grabs the "medicine" with one hand, she feels for where thing are, she moves a little bit, and she shoves it inside her own. Then she sits down real good...

It makes me laugh, I tell you. It's crazy. I know. But my God, I swear it's the true story. It's what happened. That's all in the real crow's story.

And crow under there, he can't move. Women are heavy, you know. He passes his hands and arms through the moss and he grabs his "grandma" by her hips. He holds her tight with his three fingers. Then he works her out from under. Pretty soon he works like hell from the bottom up. The moss is moving all around.

"Boum... boum... boum..." it says.

Gee whiz: he makes me laugh. He is a real funny guy this crow fellow...

Now his "grandma" is getting up. Quick, he pulls his thing out, back under the moss. And, quick, he shoves the *shra tsok* medicine back in the same hole, same place again.

His "grandma" pulls her pants up. She turns around and she sees the *shra tsok*...

"Golly..." she says to herself. "That one must be a real strong medicine. I'm pretty sure, though: I've seen two hands on my hips. Nothing here now! What's going on?"

She bends down to pick up the plant. Crow is still under the moss. He holds *shra tsok* by the roots. She pulls a little bit. Nothing. She figures out it's got strong roots. She pulls more. Crow lets it go slow. She gets it out. It comes out just like the real thing, you see -- roots and all. Crow doesn't want her to know he's done it. Now she can't figure out what happened no more.

She walks home with the *shra tsok* medicine. She is thinking about the whole thing all the way back to the camp:

"There must be something wrong with that medicine story... I'm pretty sure."

And it's another *duhuli'* crow has broken here. It's "bad luck" for a man if a woman steps over him. Real "bad luck." Everybody knows that. When I worked on the steamboats on the Yukon River, one American tourist wanted to make it out with me. She was pretty good looking and I was not married then. So we went some place. But then she was trying to step over me to sit on top. I told her about the *duhuli'*. She didn't understand nothing about it. She just looked at me with her big round eyes. Me, then, I didn't know the Whiteman didn't know about any "bad luck" laws. And she still wanted to go on top. She wouldn't change her mind. So I said:

"Never mind about the *duhuli'*, I just found out how to get around it anyway. You stand up here with your legs opened. Me, I am going to lay down on the ground and move and push my legs all the way through yours' until I'm right under your bunny. Then, you'll sit down on top of me."

So that's the way we did it. She never stepped over me. It's me that moved under her. No *duhuli'* this way, I guess.

What you think of that? I'm just as crooked as crow, hey? Ah, I guess it's all right.

Anyway, crow waits for his mother-in-law to be out of sight. As soon as she is gone, he comes out from under the moss. He cleans himself up and he runs back home. When he is going to pass his "grandma", he runs through some bush. She doesn't see him. Pretty soon he gets to the creek where he was supposed to get cold water. He soaks his head in it and walks up the trail to the brush camp. He sees his stick along the way. He picks it up and walks with it. He looks sick again. His wife is waiting for him. She is worried.

"Where have you been?" she asks. "You were gone for so long."

"Ah... my wife..." crow answers. "Cold water... All that time I soaked my head inside. I feel a little better now. Your mother came back? I see nobody yet."

Crow sits down outside. He rests. After a little while his mother-in-law walks into the camp. She gives the *shra tsok* medicine to crow's wife. Crow looks at it. He tells his wife:

"That's the one. It's the kind the old timers talked about. Yeah, that's the right kind. I'm going to use it later on, though, in case I get real sick again. Right now my head feels good enough."

He keeps it. Nighttime comes. They all go to bed. And early morning crow gets up. He goes to hunt. He walks around in the bush. He walks around... He keeps on walking. But he gets nothing. He doesn't see no moose tracks at all either.

Now you believe me about the stepping over bad luck business? It sounds like even crow can't do nothing about it. So it's late when he gets back to the camp. His wife and her mother are in bed. They wait for him. Crow sees something different. What's going on? His wife used to sleep in the middle. Now that's his bedding that's there. His wife lies on one side. His mother-in-law is on the other side, lying down just as if nothing was going on. They made room for him in between them. They set the beds just like for a man with two wives. Gosh, it looks like them women have decided to be married to him both at the same time. And that means he is going to have to marry with his own "grandma" too. Gee whiz.

Now, I'll tell what happened with these women. While crow was out hunting all day long, his "mother-in-law" spoke with her daughter. She asked:

"Was your husband home, after I left from here to look for his medicine?"

Her daughter says:

"No... Right after you left he went for cold water. He said he wanted to wash his head. It ached so bad, you know. He stayed there for quite a while, soaking it up. But he said it helped."

Right this minute, crow's mother-in-law figured out what had gone on.

"What the matter with your husband? He never went to cold water. He went in the hills and fooled me up. I see the medicine. I sit down. It gets inside. But then, someone grabs my hips with his hands and holds me down. And some thing works me up inside all over from under in the ground. Now I know that's him. I saw the hands. They had three fingers. Just like his own. That's the one who's done it."

The mother told the whole story to her daughter. They talked about it for a while. And then they made up their mind on what to do about it.

But crow doesn't know anything about it yet. So he looks at his bed in the middle. His wife is on one side. It's O.K. And, from one corner of his eyes he looks at the other side. Remember that he has to look sideways for he is not supposed to even look at his mother-in-law. But never mind, anyhow he sees her on the other side of the bed. She is going to be right next to him too if he sleeps in the middle.

"What's going on?" he thinks to himself. "How come my 'grandma' is there? It's not supposed to be that way. Where am I going to sleep now?"

So he stands up outside the brush-camp door way. And he waits without saying a word. After a while, his wife sits up in her bed and calls him:

"Why don't you come in? Don't wait there. Come in."

Crow looks at her:

"How come my mother-in-law sits down beside where it is my place?" he says. "I mean, how come I'm in the middle now? That's why I am standing up outside."

His wife:

"That's not your mother-in-law no more. Now she's your wife too. You must know... You crooked thing, what did happen in the hills with the *shra tsok* medecine...? Or was it with your own? So, as for now, both of us are married to you. How come you never said you loved my mother too?"

Crow:

"You really mean what you say?"

Crow's wife:

"Yeah, I mean that. After what you've done, my mother is already your wife anyway. What's the matter with you?"

Crow smiles. He's real happy now. He's going to have two wives. He tells the young one:

"O.K., I get married to your mother too..."

And he can't wait. He jumps on his bedding in the middle, between the two women. Then, he sits down and talks:

"My wives," he says, "tomorrow, early morning, I'm going to hunt. It's going to be real hunting now."

He doesn't promise he's going to get a moose. That would give him "bad luck." But the women know what he means. They are Indians. Then everybody goes to bed. Crow talks to himself about what he's going to do:

"The new one... I got to try the new one now, isn't it?"

So he goes on top of his "mother-in-law" again. He gets a real good look at her legs this time. They're good fine legs. And he said:

"My two wives are all the same good... I'm going to keep them all right along."

His young wife's seen everything. But she didn't mind. Tomorrow night, she'll be the one who gets a ball. You know, two relations with one husband, get along just fine. I've seen that when I was a young man. The husband slept in the middle too, and nobody was jealous.

After that, next morning, crow gets up early.

"I got two wives now," he thinks to himself. "So I'm going to hunt with all my strength."

And he goes out hunting. He looks all over the place. But he doesn't see nothing all day -- no tracks. When nighttime comes, he has got nothing to bring back. He sits down and thinks. He wishes he had a moose. He would skin it, gut it out, and cut the meat parts: head, hind and front quarters, ribs, backbone, on and on. He would roast some of the moose fat and eat it. He would cover the meat with the skin. The guts: he would clean them and pack them home for his wives. Tonight, they all would have fat innards to eat -- it's the best part, it's what everybody likes best after a moose just got shot. Tomorrow, him and his wives would come back for the meat. Or, maybe his wives alone would go there. They would follow his tracks. Him, he would go out hunting again. That's what Indians are supposed to do when they get a moose.

And crow keeps thinking about it. Pretty soon he figures out what to do. He stands up and he looks at his asshole between his legs.

"That'll do it," he says. "I'm going to bring back some moose guts."

He pulls his knife out and starts to cut his meat all around his asshole.

"*Eh b-i-aaa-eaah*," he hollers.

Whiteman way, that means: "ouch, ouch." He keeps going. He gets his shit hole loose and he pulls on his own guts. He takes about two feet of them out. Now he's got his whole bum-gut outside. He cuts it out. He is bleeding from his asshole. So he goes to pick up some moss and he plugs it with that. He takes the same kind of moss like for baby diapers or for women's blood -- every month blood. That's a good moss that one. It keeps you real dry. He cleans his bum gut a little bit. He uses some water to rinse it. His job is not too good. But maybe he doesn't know about cleaning guts. So he shoves his own gut in his packsack just like it is. And he walks back to the camp. Every little way he feels like going to the bathroom. So he takes a shit. But all he shits is blood -- lots of it. He doesn't notice. And he keeps on going with his packsack on his back. After a while he gets home. He sits down between his two wives. He tells them:

"Finally, I got a moose now. I bring in the bum gut, the best part. Just a pretty short piece, though. A whole moose gut is too heavy for me. The new wife can eat it. It's for her." (I guess he's still "shy" with his old mother-in-law turned into a new wife -- he still doesn't talk straight to her.)

So his new wife cooks the bum gut he has offered her and starts to eat it. But after a few bites she says:

"How come it smells like shit?"

"Well," answers crow, not looking at her, "that's because this moose must have fed in a muddy place on a lake. I bet he swallowed lots of mud with the moose carrots he found there. That's why it smells a bit like shit."

His wife finishes the guts. Everybody goes to bed.

But all night long, crow wakes up. The moss gets filled up with blood and it slides out. His stomach is bleeding inside, you see. It hurts inside. So he walks out and takes a shit to get rid of the blood. He sticks a new moss pad to suck out what coming next. It does not work too good, though. He keeps going in and out of the brush camp. Finally, the noise wakes up his new wife.

"What's the matter?" she asks. "How come you go outdoors all the time?"

"Gee," he says, "my stomach ache. It must be I ate too much of that moose fat, down in the bush. My stomach is sick. I'm shitting like hell now."

After that crow tries to keep quiet. He lies down in the middle between his two wives. Finally, he falls asleep. All the while, the blood keeps on running off from his asshole. So he bleeds to death, he dies.

Next morning, his young wife tells him to get up, to make a fire.

"It's daybreak already," she says.

Nothing moves in crow's bedding. (He is already stiff.)

She sits up and lifts crow's blanket.

"My God," she cries, "my husband is dead. Crow is dead now." Her mother gets up and looks. She sees nothing but blood under crow's bums. She turns her husband around and both women look at his asshole. There is no asshole there, just a big hole.

"Gosh, mom, that's the one bum gut... that's the bum gut you ate. That's why it got a shit smell..."

Gee whiz! Both women get mad. They grab crow's body and throw it in the bush, way down. Crow disappears for a minute. After that, he comes back alive and he flies away again: kwack, kwack, he says. And there he goes out again.

INDIANS GET TO BE TOO MANY FOR CROW

The next story comes up quite a while after. After crow has been around all over the country and seen lots and lots of Indians.

Crow is talking to himself:

"People are getting to be too many now... There are too many of them in the world and they kill too many animals. Maybe some of them should die off. So I'm going to make them starve."

And crow goes to sit down on trees around people's camps. When a fellow goes out hunting, he figures out the way that the man is going to go. Then he flies ahead of him. He sees the animals, the game, things like that, before the man. He bothers this game and it runs away. People can't shoot nothing. They don't get nothing to eat at all.

Crow keeps doing that. People starve to death. That's what crow wants. He keeps chasing the game away. Pretty soon, people decide to fight back. Crow can't be everywhere at the same time, they think. So they all split up. But crow runs all the game away just the same -- he just has more work to do, a lot more flying. And from the air he looks for the dead peoples' bodies. They are covered up with green brush. Their friends put that on their bodies after they passed away. As soon as crow sees a green patch like that, he flies down and lands on the green patch of fresh branches. He watches if people are not here to grab him. No! He pushes the branches sideways. He takes the dead guy's eyes out and eats them.

"*Ihtsok'ye*," he says, "That's my eye fat. The fat around the eyes is the one I love so much."

That's why today all these crows around here still do that. You get a moose and leave the head out there in the bush. Some crows come around and first thing, they go for the eyes. Soon enough there is nothing left of them.

And some other place, there's this man and his wife. They live where there is lots of snow. Many moose are around. The man hunts every day. But every time he goes out, crow flies ahead of him and scares everything away. All the moose take off before the man can get to them. The other game too. These two people are starving. A few more days, and they'll be dying off. Yeah, it's what the old timer Indians said when they talked story. It's what happened.

So this man and his wife get into their last camp to talk about what to do. They just whisper into one another's ears. Crow waits for them on a branch nearby. They don't want him to hear what they are saying:

"Psss... ps... psss-psss, ps..." that's all that's coming out.
The man tells his wife that they'll make a new camp. He'll try to go hunt in another place. To go there, he will make a tunnel under the snow and go out that way. So crow won't see him leave. He asks his wife to stay home, in the new camp.

"You'll sleep," he told her. "If I get anything, I'll come back. And after I come back I'll lie down, pretend I'm dead, and you'll put green brush on top of me. We'll try to get a hold of the one who is bothering us."

From the top of his tree, crow hears somebody whispering in the camp.

"What kind of things are you whistling about, down there?" he asks.

"Ah," the man says, "we just talk... you know, it's just talk. That's all."

Then the man and the woman walk out to find their new campground. They look for a big tree all covered with a lot of snow and with big branches low down at the bottom. It's the kind of place where you can make a camp real quick. You just have to crawl under the bottom branches. Right under the branches there is no snow. It's all dry. With all the snow on the ground around and on top of the branches, there are no cold drafts to bother you. It's like a ready-made home. The two fellows, the husband and his wife, find that kind of tree and they make room for themselves under it.

Nighttime comes. Crow is still around. He has followed them. He sits on a branch on an other tree nearby.

"Well," he tells these people, "it's getting dark now. I am going to sleep. I am going to bed some other place now."

And he goes away to sleep. And down there, the man starts to shovel out his snow tunnel. He starts from the dry ground right under the branches so crow won't see any tracks when daybreak comes. The man digs out. He crawls up one hill under the snow and then down. He keeps on digging. He goes up another hill and then down on its other side. Now his tunnel is finished. It's still nighttime. He lies down some place and goes to sleep.

Morning time comes. The woman is still under the big tree. She wakes up. The man at the end of the tunnel gets up too. He crawls out from under the snow and looks around. When daylight is getting real good, he puts his snowshoes on and goes out hunting. He sees moose. He shoots with his arrows and gets two cow moose. He cooks them right where he got them.

Crow comes back to these two guys' camp. He flies right around. He just sees the woman. He goes to sit on a tree close by.

"Where's your husband?" he asks.

"My husband?" she said, "he is asleep right under this tree."

Crow wants to know:

"How long he's going to sleep anyway?" he asks. "He didn't die yet?"

"No," she says. "When he dies, I'll let you know."

"O.K.," says crow. "Then, for now, I'm going to go look at some other people's camps."

He flies away.

Way out in the bush, the man keeps roasting the meat and everything. When he's cooked everything, he ties it together and packs it on his back. He gets into his tunnel and crawls in it all the way home. He comes out right under his tree-camp. He sits down by his wife. They pull their blanket over their heads. They hide themselves under it and they start to eat before it gets dark.

Crow comes back. He lands on a tree branch. That's where he is going to sleep. Under there, the two fellows eat like hell. Crow wants to know what going on.

"What kind of thing are you chewing on?" he asks.

"Oh," they say, "we're just chewing on a rat here."

"It doesn't sound like it..." crow says.

But he goes to sleep anyway. The man and his wife eat all they can. They get real full.

Next morning they get up. The man goes lie down just like if he was dead; he puts his hands flat above each other on his chest, right above his stomach. His wife covers him up with green branches. She piles lots on his face, shoulders, body and legs. But she puts just a few above his hands.

The woman cries:

"My husband's gone now... He passed away... He starved to death."

She cries some more and then she walks off. Crow flies behind her.

"You woman, sure go quick... Where are you going? Which way are you going to go? Are you going to take this old trail?"

And this woman slows down. Pretty soon, crow asks her about it:

"What's the matter? You can't walk?"

"I'm pretty weak," she says. "I have a hard time walking now."

Crow keeps on flying up behind the woman. Then he thinks about something:

"What's the matter with me? What am I doing here? I am walking behind this woman and I am leaving that dead man behind. His eye fat is going to freeze. I got to get back to eat that quick."

So he flies back. The woman turns around too. She is walking back to her camp. After a little while, she hears her husband hollering. It's what the old timers said. She runs and comes to him. Her husband is holding crow by his two feet.

"Yeah my wife. He landed on my chest. He was going to go for my eyes. So I pushed my hands through those little branches and I got him."

And pretty soon, these two fellows pull a rope around crow's neck and they start to choke him. Crow manages to moan through his throat:

"What... are... you... going... to... do... to... me?"

(Crow sure is a funny guy. He always makes me laugh!)

They tell him:

"We're just going to choke you to death, right here. That'll smarten you up. After that, we're going to chop off your neck and legs and we're going to burn you up."

And crow gets choked to death and his neck cut off... Then, the man and the woman pile up lots of dry wood and get a big fire going. They throw crow's body in it and burn it up -- feathers and all. The woodpile goes full blast all day and all evening. The man sits around. He keeps on watching all night long too. Next morning, the fire is down. There is just a little bit of smoke coming out. The man gets up and looks through the ashes. Crow's body is all gone but there is one little piece of his liver left in there -- just one little piece, about two inches long. The man is really surprised:

"How come?" he says. "Crow's body is all burnt up and this little piece of meat is not even cooked."

So he builds a new fire and throws that little piece in again. After a while, he looks for it: it's still not cooked.

"What's wrong with this thing here?" he asks himself. "It's still here yet. It never burns up... It'll never turn to ashes. And it smells too much too."

So he takes a sharp stick, pokes it in the meat and throws that little piece of liver way down in the snow. And right from there he hears:

"Gawk, gawk, gawk, gawk..."

Crow is back alive again and he flies out.

"That's me," he says. "I'm me. I'm crow. I fly again. I'll come back to you Indian people. I'll come back on my land to see you in two days."

And, "zooooomm" crow disappears. And this man and his wife just look -- that's all. From there this crow story splits out. *Tl'aku*, I mean it ends here.

His last words were: "I'll come back in two days." But he has not come back yet. Maybe he meant two thousands years... Maybe more. He went some place way out east -- it could be Calgary, but I don't know for sure; it could be even more to the east. Anyhow, there he was born again but through the Virgin Mary. He turned into a White-man... Into Jesus. He went to work for the Whiteman.

See, crow already knew about being born again. He had done it before; when he had got that kid to steal the sun. You remember. He put his spirit into the lake trout's daughter's cup. That was like a little piece of dirt. She drank it. This way, crow's spirit went inside the girl and she got a big stomach. Then she made that little baby even though she never met any man yet. Just like Virgin Mary. And that's the way the little Jesus was born too -- from crow's spirit who was born again. That's why the old timers say that crow's story is the Bible story. And when some Indian or some Whiteman is born again through some woman, that's also because crow has done that before them, through the trout's daughter and through Virgin Mary.

From there this story split out. That's the way this story ends. After crow made this land he went outside and was born again through Virgin Mary as Jesus. And Jesus preached pretty near all over the world but not here, not in this Indian country. After he left it, way after, that's the little beaver man that came up here. And this beaver man cleaned this land from all kinds of bad animals. I'll tell this story at another time. It's a different one.

It must be that crow, after the Whiteman suffered him on the cross as Jesus, went to the sun for good. That's where all the dead people go when they don't want to be born again into some other new life on this land here.

Tl'aku!

FROM THE ORAL TO THE WRITTEN AND BACK TO THE ORAL: A POSTSCRIPT

Tradition [...]cannot be inherited, and if you want it you must obtain it by great labour.
Thomas Stearns Eliot

Mayo, Pelly Crossing, and Carmacks: three place-names, three tiny settlements lying about 100 km apart from each other, in the Western Far North, north of Whitehorse, the capital city of the Yukon Territory, Canada. These are today's hometowns of the Northern Tutchone Athapaskan Indians. Tommy McGinty, who narrated us *The Story of Crow*, belonged to the Fort Selkirk First Nation, which now resides in Pelly Crossing.

Obviously, it is now time to narrate much more about the historical and cultural context of the telling of this story. Mr. McGinty who intended its publication to contribute to an eventual Northern Tutchone renaissance would have wanted readers to know more about the Tutchone themselves. Who are they? What sort of life do they lead today? Where do they come from? What culture did they develop before entering into contact with the Euro-American world? What happened after this contact? How did Mr. McGinty handle and become interested in collaborating with an anthropologist? How did the contemporary field research context make the anthropologist change priorities? What difficulties were involved in transforming the oral transmission of a tradition into a written one? What are the dangers of having done so? Is there a way back to the oral when knowledge of a story comes from the written? Finally, who was this Mr. Tommy McGinty who "talked" stories. Let us enter into the present and the past of this Tutchone people only to return to the contemporary context and to the constraints of the production of the written version of *The Story of Crow* on the sole basis of oral "texts."

1. THE NORTHERN TUTCHONE CONTEMPORARY WORLD

The latitude of the Tutchone villages is that of the southern part of Greenland; their environment, one of the harshest in the world. First snow may fall as early as late August and after a brief autumn, winter settles and lasts until May when ice breaks up on the major rivers and lakes. In early January, temperatures may go down as low as minus 65° C -- or worse in some bad years. The brief summers are pleasant with temperatures ranging in the 18° - 24° C. The country is a plateau lying between the Rocky Mountains to the East and the Pacific Cordillera to the Southwest. Deep river valleys cut it. Lakes are very numerous. Up on the plateau is the realm of the tundra. Down in the valleys and around the lakes grows a thick taiga.

The village of Mayo is the home of the former lower and middle Stewart River people; Pelly Crossing that of the Fort Selkirk people and a few other former sub-groups such as the McMillan River people, Carmacks the hometown of the former Tatchun, the Little Salmon and of some of the Big Salmon River people. These villages count from 200 to 400 native inhabitants each. They are all interconnected by double lane year-round gravel roads, and, thanks to the Alaska Highway, are also directly accessible in any season by automobiles from anywhere in North America.

As soon as summer begins, flocks of middle-class tourists driving comfortable campers or motor homes come to visit the country. They are in search of the Wild, which, it is rarely suspected, can only be found beyond the road on which they drive, far away in the huge areas left undisturbed by the road network and accessible only on foot, horseback, or, for wealthier tourists or big-game trophy hunters, by water-planes or helicopters.

In Carmacks and Mayo, the native communities share space with a significant number of Euro-Canadians but native and Euro-Canadian living quarters are clearly divided. In Pelly Crossing, realities are slightly different: the Euro-Canadian population is limited to two policemen, a nurse or two, a few school-teachers, one social worker, a mechanic and a few road maintenance workers. Everywhere, the overwhelming majority of local Euro-Canadians is not native to the Yukon and considers itself in a frontier area -- the last frontier of North America. After some years in the Yukon Territory many of these "immigrants" return to live in Southern Canada. New outsiders replace them. Very few of these new newcomers ever intend either to migrate to the Yukon for life.

During the 1980's and early 1990's, when Mr. McGinty offered to tape *The Story of Crow*, almost all Tutchone dwellings were already of the standard Euro-Canadian type with bathroom, kitchen, and several bedrooms, electricity, phone, and running water. Very few people still lived in the single-room log cabins, which were the dominant form of housing up to the 1970's.

The nineteenth century traditional double lean-to dwelling referred to in *The Story of Crow* had disappeared altogether -- it was abandoned a little after 1900 when most Tutchone families adopted Euro-Canadian canvas tent to shelter themselves while hunting or fishing in the bush.

In each village, most homes had a color television set. Reception of signals was through a community satellite dish. The most popular shows were early afternoon American soap operas. And, tragic it was! Or was it tragedy in comic disguise? At any rate, every afternoon, groups of Tutchone women dropped their commercial beadwork to gather around TV. sets, watching the love adventures of Marcy and Kenny -- as American TV intended the story to be. Yet these Tutchone women did not focus on Kenny's and Marcy's relationship as the American producers of the story would have expected them to do. What riveted them to the TV set were the odd and unintended implications the said relationship had in the Tutchone matrilineal system for

181

Marcy's brothers and sisters (barely named faces which were there by chance in the plot and which American T.V never meant to be actual parts in the story -- but which, for women in a matrilineal and matrilocal culture, were the substance of the "exotic" soap opera they were watching ! Julie Cruikshank has noticed the same phenomenon in the 1970's among the Southern Tutchone. In one instance, a TV show portrayed a young (Caucasian) middle class girl getting pregnant with a hand-wringing mother anxious to marry her off. The Tutchone women watching the scene were all equally distressed, but *their* concern was that the teenager might actually be married *off* to the father of her child and have to leave her matrilineal-matrilocal nest (personal communication). In parenthesis, by spreading the world over their cultural productions, Americans expose themselves to world criticism when some aspects of their civilization are discovered by others as totally lacking in humanity. Such are some of the unexpected results of globalization.

Each village had at least a primary school as well as ready access to nursing facilities. Tutchone people dressed like any Euro-Canadian in the North. However, on ceremonial occasions (such as for funerary potlatch), some persons wore more traditional moose-skin clothing ornamented with beadwork. Their cultural distinctiveness, which otherwise was not truly perceivable by an outside observer, was thus made materially visible. All children from six to sixteen were schooled in English and Euro-Canadian culture. Young adults and older ones survived through some involvement in hunting and fishing, some seasonal jobs and thanks to supplements provided by welfare and old age pension cheques. The wealthier families owned cars or pick-up trucks, and, in Pelly Crossing and Carmacks, used these means of transportation to pay regular visits to Whitehorse where shopping was less costly than at the local trading post. In Mayo, which was further away from the Yukon capital city, most purchases were made at local stores.

Seeking refuge in alcohol affected to one degree or another close to half of the population. The other half who had found a haven in Christianity kept away from drinking altogether and did what it could to help those whose despair was too obvious. For many local Euro-Canadians normal life was also seriously jeopardized by alcoholism --

but as among the Tutchone, this affliction did not concern all and everyone.

Only a few Tutchone individuals under the age of forty fully understood the native language well but they, as well as all others in this age group, spoke English, even when addressed in their native tongue by elders. The teaching of Tutchone language had been recently introduced in the school curriculum but its effect was not yet tangible. Many people above the age of forty or fifty understood Tutchone but rarely used it, except, possibly, when conversing with much older persons. Many aspects of Tutchone culture and heritage were enduring and thriving in spoken and written English, but the Tutchone language itself and those traditions that were bound to the language seemed to be on the wane.

2. NORTHERN TUTCHONE BEFORE CANADA COLONIZED THEM

The incorporation of the Tutchone into a European-type of state organization is quite recent if compared to that of other North American First Nations. It roughly dates back to the Klondike gold rush of 1897-98, which, after it subsided, left their country settled with its first Euro-Canadian pioneers.

Prior to that era, no Tutchone knew English and naturally *The Story of Crow* was then narrated exclusively in Tutchone, a language which belongs to the Northern Athapaskan linguistic stock -- a group of (over 20) historically related languages spoken by the Indians of nearly the entire Yukon and Mackenzie River basins, but which were no longer mutually intelligible.

The Athapaskan linguistic stock is a reality comparable to the Indo-European linguistic phylum to which the majority of present-day European languages belong. Although English, Russian, French, German, Greek and even Iranian, Hindi, can all be traced back to a common ancestor language, it is nonetheless true that these languages are no longer mutually intelligible. Similarly, the Northern Tutchone language is only one Athapaskan language among many others, which are historically related, but no longer mutually intelligible, just as English is one Indo-European language among many others.

The Northern Tutchone language was further subdivided into regional dialects which were all *mutually intelligible*. Thus, middle Stewart River native people in Mayo pronounced some Tutchone words (but not all) in a manner slightly different from that of the Pelly River Tutchone or from the Little Salmon group living in Carmacks. For instance, the sentence "hand me an axe" is "*khwät de*" in Mayo, "*khwät je*" in Pelly and "*Shakhe je*" in Carmacks whereas the sentence "hand me a knife" is more uniform -- "*mbra de*" in Mayo, "*mbra je*" in Pelly and "*mra je*" in Carmacks. Within the group of the Pelly River drainage area where Mr. McGinty comes from, further differentiation existed between the Lower Pelly and the McMillan River. In the early seventies, I have seen speakers from these two sub-dialect communities of the Tutchone language make fun of each other's way of speaking just as English-speakers in Toronto may make fun of the English spoken by the inhabitants of Newfoundland and vice-versa. Yet, in both cases, speakers of the two sub-communities as well as from the three larger areas mentioned understand or understood each other without any serious difficulty.

Researchers working on the basis of linguistic distribution and glottochronological evidence have concluded that the ancestors of the Athapaskan came from Asia and first occupied Western Alaska around 8,000 years ago. Between 8,000 and 6,000 year ago, they settled into the interior of Alaska and the Western Canadian Subarctic. Quite a few archaeological sites located in the heart of the Tutchone country are as much as 4,000 years old; some may go back to 8,000 years ago (Clark and Morlan, 1982, Gotthardt, 1987). By approximately 3,500 years ago, the Athapaskan languages of Western Alaska (Tanaina, Ingalik and Athna) and of Canada (Kutchin, Tutchone, etc.) had evolved along separate lines to the point that they were no longer mutually intelligible (Krauss and Golla, 1981: 67-68). Tutchone became a separate language sometime after 3,500 years ago but it has not yet been determined at what precise time and in what precise location. However, strong evidence suggests that Tutchone Indians first settled into their present country in the very distant past. In the central Yukon where they live, all geographical native place-names are either in one of the dialects of modern Tutchone or in older forms of that language which are not understood anymore, just like Middle-Age English is no longer understood by modern English speakers. None of these very old words or expressions seem to correspond to possible previous other Athapaskan or non-Athapaskan languages.

While the early culture of the Tutchone will probably never be known in precise details that of the nineteenth century has been fairy well reconstructed on the basis of ethnohistorical evidence (Legros, 1981, 1982, 1984, 1985, 1987, 1988; and for the Southern Tutchone, McClellan, 1975). In these remote days, the Tutchone were the sole inhabitants of the largest part of the upper drainage system of the Yukon River which is located in the southern half of the Yukon Territory. They were then free from any actual foreign domination. Their population counted about 1,100 individuals (women, children and men included).[1] It was divided into a dozen or so small independent regional societies. Each regional group was further subdivided spatially into local camps. In each region, the biggest of these camps counted up to ten or so nuclear families (around fifty individuals) whereas the smallest ones could count as little as one or two such nuclear units (five or ten individuals). Every camp was subjected to a year-round form of cyclical nomadism. The Tutchone territory was as large as England in the restricted sense of the term and the population density was one of the lowest in the world. The Tutchone economy was based almost entirely on hunting and fishing – the gathering of berries and of some edible roots never contributed more than 5% to 10% of the aboriginal diet.

---

[1] *This figure included some of the people counted as Southern Tutchone by McClellan (1975) but excludes about 300 Southern Tutchone who were immediate neighbors of the Tlingit to the South, and who, by the 1850's, had been culturally "Tlingitized." All Tutchone Elders consulted in 1972-74 reported that "real early on" (probably meaning the end of the 18th century), the Northern population was as "thick as the trees in the bush." While these phrases were definitely hyperbolic, it is nevertheless fairly obvious that by the 1850's, the population had already been heavily decimated by European disease transmitted indirectly through inter-ethnic contacts (Legros, 1981).*

There existed a form of social stratification: families named *dän nozhi'* were richer than others and at the head of the largest local camps; some families who were described as poor or destitute (*chaekadyae*) usually formed small local camps; finally some individuals of both sexes were domestic servants for life (*händye*) to the rich families. *The Story of Crow* refers to such bonded status when crow's muskrat wife is taken away by the lake trout.[2]

Based on linguistic evidence, the original kinship system of all Athapaskan peoples was matrilineal at the time they first settled into interior Alaska, some 6,000 to 8,000 years ago (Dyen and Aberle, 1974). In the 1980's, the Tutchone were still recognizing who were their blood relatives on the basis of this system. Among them, as among many of their neighbors in the Yukon drainage basin, descent was still counted through female links exclusively (matriliny). In addition, the members of each local group were divided into two social groups: the crows and the wolves. This cultural feature may have been of less antiquity, however. Be that as it may, one belonged to one's mother's social group only (either the crows or the wolves), never to one's father's, and one's father had to belong to the group opposed to that of one's mother (if the father was a wolf the mother had to be a crow and vice versa). There were no other kinds of descent groups (phratries, sibs, clans or lineages, etc.). Such a division of the population into two unilineal groups only is known in anthropology as a *moiety* system and in this case as an *exogamous* moiety system (from the Greek *exo-* (outside) and *gamy* (marriage); *moiety* from the French

---

[2] *Tutchone Elders translate the Athapaskan term* händye *by "slave." That slavery existed worries younger Tutchone. The fact could be used by Euro-Americans and Euro-Canadians to further diminish the value of the culture of their ancestors. However, they could always remind Europeans and their North American cousins that, at the same time, in the 18th and 19th centuries, they had slaves on a grand scale and that the average lifetime of a slave on an American plantation was roughly seven years. Much earlier, during the Roman era, Europeans also took each other as slaves and in many countries a third of the population had such a status (cf. Braudel, 1991: 92-93). Tutchone slavery never reached these proportions and a corresponding degree of exploitation.*

moitié meaning *half*). In the 1970's and earlier, Tutchone used to speak of "two kinds of people" or "two sides" but nowadays they talk of a "*two*-clan system." In such a structure a man has less authority over his own children who are not members of his social group or moiety and much more rights and power on his sister's children who do automatically belong to his own half of the society or moiety. For example, if a man is a crow, his sister who is born from the same mother is also necessarily a crow; the man marries a wolf woman and his children are wolf; his sister marries a wolf man but her children are crow because descent is matrilineal, in other words it is counted exclusively through female links. Because of this peculiarity, an individual man knew that for help he should first count on his sisters' children and in turn his sisters' children felt that they had to oblige him first and act as his "helpers." This is why the crow called the *Kushekok* (the little owl he made himself at the beginning of the story) his "sister's son."

The fact that one had to marry outside of one's matri-moiety was strictly enforced. Any sexual relations between individuals of the same moiety were punished by death. What would be for Euro-Canadians an absence of genealogical or biological connections between the culprits never was an excuse. In fact, consanguineal kinship terms (blood relatives) were always applied to anyone in the same moiety (even if from a far away regional group and totally unknown) and affinal kinship terms (relatives by marriage) to anyone in the moiety opposed to one's own. Thus, for a crow man or woman visiting an unfamiliar camp, any crow man in this camp of one's maternal uncle's generation was *ipso facto* addressed as a maternal uncle (what anthropologists call a *classificatory* mother's brother) and was regarded as having such a status in relation to one's self. Any woman of the same moiety and same generation as one's mother was addressed by a term meaning "little mother." Any man of the moiety opposed to one's own and of one's father's generation was called by a special term that translated as "little father." Any woman opposed to one's moiety and in one's father's generation was designated by a term that has no equivalent in European languages for it must be translated as meaning both and at once father's sister and mother-in-law. Alternatively, one's actual mother-in-law could be designated by the more polite term of grandmother, which, in this sense, was most likely used to denote that one's mother-in-law was one's own children's grandmother.

Furthermore, there was total speech avoidance between individuals of opposite sex belonging to the same generation and the same moiety except that an older sister could address herself to a younger brother. Kinship terminology was of the Iroquois type and preferred marriage was between actual first degree bilateral cross-cousins.[3] In other words, a young man was encouraged to marry either his father's sister's daughter (this is why the Tutchone term for father's sister also translated as mother-in-law) or his mother's brother's daughter, if any such cross-cousins were available. Alternatively, second or third degree bilateral cross-cousins could do. One's parallel cousins such as a mother's sister's or a father's brother's daughter could under no circumstance be married for they necessarily belonged to the same moiety as one belonged to. If one is crow, one's father is wolf, one's father's brother is wolf too. Thus, one's father's brother's wife has to be crow and one's father's brother's children are therefore crow.

Residence of a married couple was strictly matrilocal and in many cases the husband lived with his wife's parents, until the latter died (or avunculocal when a man married his actual mother's brother's daughter). Polygyny and polyandry were prized forms of marriage. Some leading men are known to have had more than ten wives at the same time, but this was exceptional. Most polyandrous women never had more than two husbands at the same time. It was also a duty for

---

[3] *Today, members of the Fort Selkirk First Nation disapprove of marriage between first degree cross-cousins and assert that it was always so in the past. A special story explains and justifies this ban. Yet, one generation ago some such marriages have been arranged between members of the Fort Selkirk Nation and were not then considered incestuous by the parents or the community at large. Even today, those who condemn them do not do find them as abhorrent as sexual relationship between members of the same moiety. In this respect it should be noted that the Fort Selkirk First Nation has been the earliest one among the Tutchone population to be constantly exposed to missionaries, starting in the early 1890's. In Carmacks, in the early seventies, several male and female friends which were about my age (then 26) or younger told me about the pressure their mother, or maternal uncle and father, were putting on them to marry their first degree cross-cousins.*

a man, even if already married, to take his deceased brother's wife as a spouse (levirate) and symmetrically for a woman to take over her deceased sister's spouse as a husband (sororate). Without exception, there was total speech avoidance between actual mother-in-law and son-in-law, although the rule of matrilocality made them live in the same camp for most of their lives. We have seen how the crow dealt with this and what ensued. For further details on 19th century culture, see Legros (1981, 1982, 1984, and 1985).

To state that Tutchone were left alone and continued to be an independent people until the 1890's does not mean that they were isolated, however. By the early 1800's Russians were trading with and settling among the Tlingit of the Pacific coast. The Tlingit traded with the Southern Tutchone and these with the Northern Tutchone. By the late 1830's, Northern Tutchone entered into direct trade contact with the Tlingit. Accounts of the Whiteman's ways and Christian beliefs were then indirectly circulated. Campbell, a European explorer working for the Hudson Bay Company briefly set foot among the Tutchone in the early 1840's and in 1848-52 opened a trading post, at the junction of the Pelly and Yukon Rivers (the original Fort Selkirk). However, because it competed with Tlingit Indian traders, the venture failed. In 1852 the post was closed and abandoned. A close analysis of the relevant documents reveals that for all practical purpose the presence of this trading-post had no economic or cultural effects on Tutchone society (cf. Legros, 1981).

By the late 1840's, Northern Tutchone's native neighbors to the East and the North had all entered into direct and permanent contact with Euro-Canadian fur-traders and missionaries. During the next three or four decades, they spread further information on the Whiteman's world among the Northern Tutchone with whom they were in contact through inter-ethnic exchanges.

3. THE END OF TUTCHONE INDEPENDENCE AND THE AFTERMATH OF DEPENDENCE.

However, during the 1890's several truly significant changes occurred among the Tutchone. A trading post was re-established on the site of the old Fort Selkirk. An Anglican mission was opened on the same location. Both remained opened until the early 1950's. During the 1897-98 gold rush some thirty thousand Euro-Canadians and Americans en route to the Klondike gold fields crossed the Tutchone territory. They brought with them recipes for making home-made alcoholic beverages known as "homebrew." Some settled in Northern Tutchone territory -- all in all, a few dozen individuals (trappers, storekeepers, missionaries). The Klondike gold rush also brought the first detachment of the Northwest Mounted Police to be dispatched to this far off corner of Canada. While this police force was first sent to keep order between gold-miners, it also made it illegal for natives to use force between themselves and thus deprived them of their traditional means of enforcing Tutchone laws. Consequently, the hierarchical division between rich families, poor ones and domestic slaves weakened and some breaking of the infra-moiety incest taboo went unpunished, snapping the old culture's spinal column.

Starting in 1900 steamers sailed not only the Yukon River but also its main tributaries such as the Pelly. New stores and missions were built at various locations. From 1910 onward, most Tutchone groups stopped spending the whole year in the bush and gathered for a few months around the mission and store closest to them. Deliberate attempts to uproot Tutchone traditional religious beliefs were initiated by the Anglican missions.

The Second World War and its aftermath led to the replacement of summer river transportation by year-round road traffic. New permanent villages were established near the new roads. Fort Selkirk was abandoned for Pelly Crossing; Little Salmon village for Carmacks. Children were forcibly taken away from their parents and sent to spend years in religious boarding school where the use of any native language was strictly prohibited and severely punished. The intent was to "de-culturize" and re-educate the children into Western ways and, so it was hoped, to give them a 'future' within the population of European stock in Canada. Tutchone couples like Tommy and Annie McGinty were deprived of their children for most of the year, year after year. Many were disheartened. Time spent in trapping hunting or fishing camps was drastically reduced. Irresponsible drinking behaviors developed. "Why should we have worked?" a middle-age man and a shaman from Carmacks asked me in 1972...

Anyway all your children were raised far away by the mission school and as for your wife the Indian Affair agent was like a second husband to her -- when she needed some stuff like a tent, she just had to ask him and he would give her the stuff or some money.

When children, robbed from their family at an early age, were sent back to their villages, they had often developed a total dislike, if not disrespect, for their parents' culture. In any case, they were totally unprepared for making a living in the bush and had lost all but a few words of the Tutchone language they had spoken in their early childhood. And it was dramatic for although some wished to recover their language, they had been made psychologically unable to re-learn it after the trauma of the boarding school. Investigators of cultural genocides will perhaps one day explain how such mental blocks are set in the mind of the victims.

Starting in the 1960's, the welfare state, the legalization of alcohol consumption for native people, and the development of village schools did the rest, bringing Tutchone into the too-well-known contemporary "reservation"[4] scene of unbearable idleness. However, in the 1970's and the 1980's, no doubt out of despair, some Tutchone elders moved to revitalize their society. Land claims were launched and cultural renewal was attempted. Band councils put pressure on school boards to hire bilingual native elders to teach the Tutchone language to their grandchildren in the school rooms. The Yukon Native Language Centre headed by the linguist John Ritter made a huge effort to provide these teaching elders with a writing system which, up until then, did not exist for the phonemics of their language.

---

[4] *There were no treaties and no actual reservations in the Yukon. Thus the quotation marks on the word reservation.*

4. THE MEETING BETWEEN Mr. McGINTY AND THE ANTHROPOLOGIST

This version of *The Story of Crow* was recorded in this new cultural and socio-political context. Even though Tommy McGinty had nothing against either European fairy tales such as *Snow White*, which were then the only lore taught by the Euro-Canadian teachers assigned to the local Tutchone primary schools, or against parts of the *Old* and *New Testaments* being read by missionaries to Tutchone pupils, he was very much stymied if not deeply angered by the fact that no sacred or secular Tutchone traditions were ever being passed down alongside.

How, when and why Tommy McGinty opened up to me so I could tell his stories ought to be sketched out for it illustrates how long-term fieldwork gradually makes one part of the community one studies and ineluctably changes one's research priorities.

My first fieldwork among the Tutchone goes back to 1972. I then was 26 years old, straight out of Paris, and quite embarrassed at trying to interview people whom I quickly felt had more pressing matters to attend to than speaking about their culture, past or present, especially to someone whose English was then even more rudimentary than theirs. However, the truth is that I was too much of an armchair researcher, did not know how to formulate my questions and asked about topics such as clans or cross-cousins when nobody knew these terms. No wonder people rapidly found out that they had something else to do every time I showed up at their houses! Before I realized the degree of my inexperience in field interviewing, I was working in the Carmacks village (mainly inhabited by members of the Little Salmon regional group) with "drinking" Tutchone whom I found more welcoming, loquacious, open and available. I befriended one of them and on several occasions when he was penniless and thirsty, I "lent" him some money to buy beer. I shall not give his name but we may call him "Black Label" from the brand name of his preferred beer, which as he said was Indian beer because it was black. He was a member of the crow moiety, married to a wolf moiety woman and had had five children. Some years before, four of them had been forcibly taken away from him and his wife by "Welfare" and given up in adoption to Euro-Canadian families "down South." His morale was low. Under the circumstances, I considered the dollars I gave him as a form of payment for the help he had given me and never expected a return. A month or two later, however, he came to visit me in my log cabin and handed me fifty dollars. "That's the money you lent me!" he said. I refused to accept it -- this was part of his Welfare check and he needed the cash for himself. However, he insisted vehemently: "What's wrong with you Whiteman? My money is not good enough for you!" In the end, remembering Mauss' *Essay on the Gift* and the necessity of accepting a return, I acquiesced, telling him that it was so nice of him that I would now regard him as a true brother. As soon as news of what I had said spread I became regarded by all as an actual member of the crow moiety and when later on my female companion and her son joined me in the field, quite logically, they were immediately counted as members of the wolf moiety.

During the summer of 1972, I made a brief visit to Pelly Crossing and attempted to interview Mr. Tommy McGinty. He was then in his early fifties. Although I spent a fine day with him and his family at their fish-camp, the interview went nowhere in terms of serious ethnographic work. I did not know then that Tutchone etiquette dictated that a man or a woman in this age bracket still had to keep quiet about one's knowledge and had to defer to elders on any elaboration on any important matter being discussed -- the rule being even more strict with strangers. When I returned to Carmacks I met Mr. Johnny Mack, a wolf moiety elder and widower who was born in the Fort Selkirk regional group around 1890 and who had been sent to Little Salmon around 1910 to be wedded (matrilocally) to a woman from this regional group. This man answered my queries patiently and thoroughly and I got through him my first break-through on Tutchone culture. As I did not know that it was his advanced age that allowed him to speak his mind, I wrongly assumed that he was simply less shy, more outgoing and knowledgeable than Tommy McGinty. While I worked with Mr. Mack in Carmacks, I often drove him around to various locations and in particular to Pelly Crossing which he wished to visit. In this village, he "fell in love" with Ellen Silverfox, a sixty year old crow moiety widow. When I went back to Carmacks, he and she came along with me. They settled in his cabin. A few weeks latter she insisted the "marriage" had to be more "normal" (that is, matrilocal) and made him move back with her to Pelly Crossing (the new hometown of the Fort Selkirk regional group of his childhood).

Being settled in Carmacks and unable to find an empty cabin to borrow in Pelly Crossing, I was thus deprived of my best collaborator so far. To solve my problem, I regularly visited Pelly Crossing during the winter of 1972-73, helping the new, albeit old, couple in wood-cutting, house cleaning, grocery shopping, in exchange for lodging and long conversations with them. During these visits I met several times with the then younger Mr. McGinty but nothing special occurred between us except that we discovered that we both enjoyed telling each other our best jokes, especially about sex. However, Mr. McGinty asked why I referred to Mrs. Silverfox by the Indian kinship term meaning "my mother's sister." I explained that in Carmacks they had made me a crow, that she was a crow like me and of the same generation as my mother. I added that my "boss" -- David F. Aberle, my research director -- had insisted that I use kinship terms when addressing older people, instead of Mr. or Mrs. so and so, or worse, first names. Based on his experience with Navaho Indians in the Southwest of the U.S.A. this was the truly polite and nice way to address each other in Athapaskan cultures.

At some other point, the old Johnny Mack confirmed to Tommy McGinty that in Carmacks I was regarded as a crow moiety individual and that my companion and her son must be wolf for at one funerary potlatch the three of us behaved and acted in the way proper to each moiety (J. Mack had forgotten that I had asked him what should the crows do on the one hand and the wolves on the other).

I left Carmacks and the field in late 1973, and came back to Pelly Crossing only some eight or nine years later for a short visit, at the invitation of the band council which wanted me to explain to younger Tutchone band officials what elders had told me earlier about Tutchone culture, kinship and marriage, as well as proper rules of behavior toward animals. Mr. McGinty was also a speaker. He was then in his early sixties and much more open to talking "old stories." He dared for instance to tell in front of a large native audience (and even more surprising in my presence with an open microphone) how he became an Indian doctor or shaman and in particular the illuminations and trances he went through around the age of sixteen before gaining "medicine power."

Among the spirits that came into his dreams to give and teach him the songs that help save the sick, there was already then (it must have been around 1935) the mind-power of Jesus. All his life he kept in contact with both his animal spirit protectors (such as the wolf) and the main spirit helper of the New Testament. His understanding of religion was truly inclusive. Baptized an Anglican early in his life, he followed the footsteps of Copper Joe, his famed shaman grandfather. Sometimes in the mid forties' he added the catholic beliefs to his Anglican connection with Christ while maintaining his faith in the Tutchone native religion. To this end, he requested an Oblate missionary (Father Bobillet) who was visiting his fishing camp to baptized him. Mary, as a virgin mother, had become an important figure in his mind for it allowed him to better integrate the Christian stories into his Tutchone religious belief in crow. Later, in the sixties, seventies, eighties and early nineties he kept his faith as ecumenical, attending and serving in catholic mass, Anglican services or Pentecostal revivalist meetings (depending on which services were offered in a given month in Pelly Crossing). And he kept on being visited in his dreams or in the bush by his animal helpers. As late as 1991, I saw and heard him ask better hunting luck from a wolf which had hollered from behind a hill. He explained to the animal that they used to be friends and that his wife "had been hungry for moose meat for over a month and bugging him about it, all that time." (To my surprise "one young bull gave itself up to Mr. McGinty and I for his meat for us to eat" two days later and we shot it). And yet, ten years earlier it was the good Jesus who had showed himself into one of his dreams to give him the power to quit drinking altogether.

Ironically, Mr. McGinty's intense religiosity did not go with an introverted personality as it could have, or still less made of him some kind of sour grape about the earthy and mundane urges in actual human life. Nor was he a fundamentalist in any way. He remained facetious all his life. In the summer of 1990, during a band council meeting which was deliberating on how to attract tourists to Pelly Crossing, he proposed to the much younger band officers, seemingly most earnestly, "that the band built a nice-looking motel with a bar on the side of the highway," adding that "it would even be a better idea if...," he paused, "the band would hire three or four 'sport-women' to run it" (in other word he was proposing the opening of a brothel). Just before going to the meeting, he had told me that he would keep his best poker face and make that joke. He made me laugh about it, adding in a whisper, tongue-in-cheek: "it sure would make a lots of truckers and tourists stop over"). I did not expect him to really go through but when he did it became funny. The bar-motel proposal was met with intense disbelief. Heads went down and eyes looked at papers on the table or went to muse about the ceiling. How could an elder not realize that it would increase opportunities to drink in the village? Then, the "sport-women" idea was thrown in to everyone relief and a burst of laughter filled the room, dissipating the thickness which had quickly accumulated in the air. Would Mr. McGinty's idea have led to an economic take-off? In a village of 300 inhabitants it surely would have brought in some extra activity. So much for his practical sense of what some men need but should not. But for a crow's witness (as we say a Jehovah's witness) was it truly a paradox to be religious and mischievous? To tell the truth, one of his old Indian names meant "the mischievous or the facetious one."

Yet, one should perhaps be, like the ancient Tutchone, wary of the meaning of naming. For McGinty could also be at once playful, quixotic and romantic. For example, in the summer of 1991 he pitched his tent just behind his very comfortable modern house and, whenever he had a chance, went there to rest each time it rained. Why? Simply to listen to the music raindrops make on a thick cotton canvas, to hear the changes of rhythm accompanying the variations in the intensity of the rainfall outside, and to bask in the warmth of that very special kind of home that makes you hear, feel and comprehend that it protects you from outside circumstances as it shelters you.

In 1982 (but it may have been in 1983), his niece, that is his sister's daughter who necessarily was a crow and thus, in this case, an older sister to me, invited me to stay at her house. I frequently visited Tommy in his log cabin nearby and always addressed him as "my maternal uncle." He returned the compliment by calling me nephew or more precisely *mbra'* or sister's son, speaking as a male[5] (not brother's son for a brother's son would have to be from the wolf moiety for the simple reason that Tommy's brother would have had to be a crow like him and would therefore have married a wolf woman whose children would be wolf). While we chatted, he informed me that Ellen Silver-fox and Johnny Mack had passed away in a car accident. He then told me that Ellen was his older sister and that he remembered what I had done years earlier for her and Johnny Mack. Because I had previously discovered in Carmacks the strength of the taboo on talking to or about one's adult siblings of opposite sex I was not too surprised that neither Ellen nor he had ever told me about their blood relationship. When I left two weeks later, I promised to come back.

I did so in 1984 to spend the summer with him, his wife, daughters and some grandchildren, at his salmon fish-camp on the Pelly River. As I was a crow moiety member and like his older sister's son because of my former relationship to his late sister Ellen, I was to him like the little owl *Kushekok* was to the crow in the *Tutchone Genesis*: i.e. his helper. It was just as well for there was no other man to help him -- his sons who were wolf moiety members, like his wife, were, as should be expected, far away either in other camps helping wolf men whose daughters were crows or on contract jobs for some government agencies. Being the only "man of the house" present, (beside Mr. McGinty), I accompanied him twice a day on his motor boat, two miles downriver to his salmon net. There, twice a day, late morning and late afternoon, I worked for him, clubbing to death and entangling

---

[5] *The kinship term* mbra' *is used by males only. It means sister's son or sister's daughter, as well as son-in-law or daughter-in-law. Females use two different terms for the equivalent relationship: (1)* yaa'ara, *for brother's daughter as well as daughter-in-law; (2)* yædiye' *for brother's son as well as son-in law. It is to be noted that a maternal uncle belongs to the same moiety as his sister's children whereas a paternal aunt belongs to the moiety opposed to that of her brother's children -- thus, perhaps, different terms for a male versus a female speaking about their respective cross-nephews and cross-nieces.*

some twenty huge king salmon, which had been or were still fighting his net. Each time, upon our return to camp, we unloaded the fish. And his wife and daughters would gut and process them in the traditional way so that they could be hung on horizontal poles and let to dry for many days without putrefying at all. Once dehydrated these salmon were stored for winter use. One or two fresh fish were boiled in a common pot for all to eat whenever hungry. Much of the rest of the time we spent "talking old timer Indian stories." I taped most of these moments without him objecting. On the contrary, he encouraged it.

At last, circumstances were propitious for a real exchange. Most of the elders he had deferred to in the past had passed away. He was then old enough to be regarded as an elder himself and was thus free to speak up without passing for a show off. I was no more entirely an outlander but some kind of "estranged stranger" who had internalized many Tutchone mores such as giving a hand without being asked to, or helping himself when hungry to cooked food from the common family cauldron without asking anyone's permission (bad manners among the French or the Euro-Canadians but "really class" among Tutchone) --someone who thanks to the moiety system was a maternal nephew to Mr. McGinty.

As a matter of prudence, Tutchone had stopped a long time ago offering their food to non-Indians for fear of seeing uncontrollable expressions of disgust on their faces because of the latter's unwarranted but nonetheless real feeling of superiority over anything native. Thus, helping yourself without asking and clearly relishing the distinctive mix of, say, the well-known seven different tastes and consistencies in the boiled muscles and cartilage of the cheeks and nose of a salmon head turned you *ipso facto,* in contrast to other Euro-Canadians, into some sort of Indian, or put in other words, into a weird Whiteman.

In this family context, taken together with the atmosphere surrounding the launching of native land-claims, we did not discuss any more in terms of Tutchone *culture* but of what he more pointedly termed the Tutchone *law*-- a set of rules of behavior and beliefs which should be re-instituted and enforced if Indian *culture* (or *law* as he rightly preferred to call it) was to truly survive. As I witnessed his eagerness to speak his mind and vent his age-old resentments, as he listened to and answered my questions of clarification on the relationship between culture and the politics of today, an affection developed between us which went much deeper than the friendship that had come years before from our common sense of humor and our shared liking for salacious plays on words. During the summer of 1984 he truly treated me as a sister's son and I always listened to him with the greatest attention and respect, as one should with any Tutchone maternal uncle, and especially with a particularly learned one as he was. He knew that elders had already taught me the broad outline of Tutchone laws over the years 1972 and 1973. He went over what I knew and elaborated. I taped all these sessions.

When he discovered that I had been told only some episodes of *The Story of Crow,* he was surprised and offered to tell all the rest at once for it embodied the fundamental Indian laws. As a matter of method, we taped the story first in Tutchone. He was supposed to listen to his Athapaskan version with headphones and translate it verbally into English, dictating word for word into a second tape-recorder. However, the task proved impossible to him. Years before, he had already adjusted the story to a narration in English and he chose to tape this ready-made version. Had he had Lévi-Strauss read to him, he may have agreed with this French scholar according to whom the value of such stories persists even if very roughly translated, for the simple reason that their substance lies not in their style or, as in poetry, in their language of original composition, but entirely in the story that is told in them (Lévi-Strauss, 1958; 232). Which is not to say, as we have seen, that Mr. McGinty had no style in his telling the story.

Later on, we moved to various other subjects. To my surprise, I soon discovered that his knowledge of Tutchone culture was truly encyclopedic. As the summer was drawing to an end it became clear that he could not, in the time left, teach all he knew. Again, I had to promise to come back.

As the date of my departure was only a few days away we relaxed and it is at this time that an incident, which could have turned into a tragedy, drew us even closer culturally. Mr. McGinty had just bought a new and powerful gun for big game (a 30.06). He was very impressed by the ease with which its trigger could be pulled and showed it to me. I asked to be allowed to try. He rearmed the gun making sure that no cartridge from the magazine was loaded into the barrel. I aimed at a tree nearby, pulled the trigger -- it was indeed an easy trigger. Mr. McGinty was facing me, standing to my right, at the height of the mouth of the barrel. His wife was beside him, to his left. Impressed by the trigger mechanism, I wanted to try again. I rearmed the gun, aimed at the same tree and pull the trigger another time:

"Paoww!"

A bullet came out of the barrel mouth, two feet away from Mr. McGinty's ear, perforating the tree trunk all the way through. I had inadvertently let the magazine mechanism load a cartridge into the barrel.

Mr. McGinty who by then was totally deafened by the shot fumed at my stupidity. His wife was totally panicked. The shot and the shouts made everyone in the fish-camp run toward us. Soon, we were surrounded. Nasty observations fused. "How could you be so stupid? You could have killed him! His hearing is already not too good! What will happen to him after that, etc?" I felt worse than confused and as I was apologizing, memories of what I had learned during my first fieldwork came back in a flash. Johnny Mack had been a witness to a similar but more tragic incident in 1916 around Little Salmon. Playing with a .22 gun, a crow boy had accidentally killed another one from the wolf moiety. A four-day-long peace ceremony involving three or four regional groups had to be enacted. At the meeting ground, all the wolf went on one side and all the crow aligned themselves on the other side, facing the wolf. Every single nuclear family was thus divided for the time being -- whereas a woman and her children were on one side, a man was on the other side facing his wife and children. Ceremonial hostages were exchanged between moieties. Freeing the hostages involved considerable payments and counter-payments between all the crows and all the wolves from these groups. The ceremony was successfully concluded. Then the leaders instructed the crowd that the homicide was never to be mentioned again for ever.

What I had to do became clear. In the case at hand, Mr. McGinty and I were members of the same moiety. For this reason, in the old days no peace ceremony would have been called for. Johnny Mack and another elder (George Billy) had been specific about that. Nevertheless, some form of a minimal compensation would have been essential to settle the matter. Saying that I would be back right away, I rushed to my camper, opened the cupboard where my money was and came back with a pile of bills worth perhaps $100. "Here my maternal uncle," I told Mr. McGinty,

> This is to pay for your ear. Old Johnny Mack told me that it was the old Indian way to settle a problem like this one. I have been completely stupid. It must hurt a lot.

Mr. McGinty looked around at the small crowd, smiled and addressing himself to everyone said that it was indeed the right thing to do, old Indian way, to settle a matter like this one. Although the money was unimportant to him, (he had often refused to be paid for his work with me), this time he willingly accepted the bills and pocketed them. We all had supper together, and the incident was closed. And closed it remained, for neither himself nor any members of his immediate family or of the fish-camp ever evoked it again.

The next and last extended visit I paid to Tommy McGinty was from July 1990 to August 1991. It is during this period that I came to the realization that anthropologists had to stop the old and time-honored practice of raising and answering questions linked to the observer's curiosity arising from the differences between her or his culture and that of the observed. From the beginning, the first priority should have been to empower the people they are studying with the material and data they (the people "under study") really need from the anthropologist and are really interested in, all this with as little interpretation from without as feasible. Questions arising from cultural differences between observer and observed people are certainly fully legitimate for they are queries about a universally recognized paradox: all human beings are the same and yet they all express their sameness through specific cultures which are all different from one another, just as all people speak a language and yet each one uses a specific one different from the next one. However questions related to this paradox need to be treated separately from the more urgent questions raised by the people interested in having their anthropologists act as go-betweens between their small indigenous communities and the outside world which is more and more infringing into their world. In a way, this line or reflection represented the climax of a very slow process of appropriation of a stranger, me, into the Tutchone world by the Tutchone themselves.

Mr. McGinty never thought of our relationship in terms of observed and observer and, if he ever did so in terms of Indian and non-Indian, he did so no more. In as much as I had behaved as an older sister's son over so many years, no matter my origins and physical appearance, I was first an older sister's son (a *mbra'*) and only second someone from the "Old Countries," by which he meant Europe.

As a sister's son I was both someone he should give in marriage to one of his daughters and one of his blood relatives (i.e. members of his moiety -- in the Tutchone matrilineal kinship system, a man's sons-in-law or daughters-in-law are always his blood relatives whereas the reverse is true for a female). Exception made for the "consanguineal linkage" between him and me that was established by the moiety system (we were both crows and therefore consanguineal kin), his way of integrating me into his family was somehow analogous to what prevails in European and Euro-Canadian cultures. Don't we too make members *of our family,* individuals who are married to our relatives, irrespective of where these *in-laws* were born and the language they first spoke? The obvious drawback to all this was, as Mr. McGinty facetiously pointed out to me one day, that I should stop "smiling" at crow women no matter how nice-looking. Even the crow himself had to bend to this moiety law when he met the foggy woman. I was not anymore just any Whiteman with no laws to respect in matter of sex (we, Euro-Canadians, were often compared to dogs by older Tutchone because of our too narrow definition of what constitutes an incestuous relationship). Then, Mr. McGinty had the kindness to let me know that I was out of luck in Pelly Crossing. There were, by far, a lot more crow females than wolf women like, say, his daughters or wife.

As Mr. McGinty's *mbra',* the Tutchone kinship system made me his helper and not the other way around. Crow and the *Kushekok* had set the way at the beginning of time. As such, I was also inevitably connected to everyone in the community, either through marriage or blood ties -- either through bonds of affection seasoned by family disputes or through oaths of hostility tempered by alliance between opposed moiety members. No more was I like in earlier days some privileged stranger who could choose to be or not to be implicated. In brief, to be a total stranger had become an impossibility.

The political climate of the days also contributed to a stronger assertion of native political will to self-determination. In July 1990, Indian land claim negotiations were picking up steam in the Yukon Territory. July 1990 was also the time the Mohawks of Oka in Québec were revolting against judicial decisions which were to transform one of their old burial grounds into nothing less than a municipal golf course. Or was it into nothingness? Mr. McGinty's Fort Selkirk First Nation band council had a large advertising board set on the side of the highway asking in vain passers-by, mainly summer American tourists driving mobile homes, to support Mohawks in Oka.

In this context, the conditions of my work as a field anthropologist were rapidly transformed. To begin with, I had to formally request the Fort Selkirk First Nation band council permission to conduct research with Mr. McGinty and more generally with any native person in Pelly Crossing. Consent would depend on my initial intents and willingness to modify them in accordance to the band council's objectives. In a way, these were the conditions that any native researcher paid by a band council would have had to meet. So I accepted. Thus, Mr. McGinty and I met with band officials and discussed with them what we intended to do. Mr. McGinty's position was that it would be very useful for future generations to tape and then write up all the Tutchone sacred stories. Another concern of his was to record how one should behave in respect to each animal species and what were the taboos to be upheld in each case. To him, Whitemen could, without consequences to themselves, "disrespect" animals by killing and butchering them "any which way," but not Indians who were subjected since the beginning of times to "bad hunting luck *laws*" (not just simply taboos) for breaking rules of proper behavior towards animals. On its side, the band council was interested in additional subjects such as traditional game management, mapping of Tutchone place-names on topographical maps. An agreement was reached and permission was granted to go ahead.

Mr. McGinty had then just moved into a new and large modern house with running water, an inside bathroom, and a basement. It had been built for him, ten yards away from his former four-room log cabin, which was now empty. Both were nicely located on a high bank overlooking the Pelly River. He arranged with the band council so that I could settle with my companion Véronique Raison into his old home. I bought second-hand furniture from here and there and the place was soon ready with one of the bedrooms turned into an office reserved for his work with me. It was now my turn not to have running water, but especially inside toilet facilities, a convenience which would have been highly appreciated when outside temperature in our backhouse went in the - 60°C range. I had become Mr. McGinty's poor relative and him, some kind of rich Whiteman who could watch color TV, all day long if he pleased. We had a good laugh over it.

But this did not change his diagnosis on the difficulties facing his nation and his eagerness to proceed with a project which was to supply a written Tutchone heritage to be used, ultimately, for the perpetuation of Tutchone society and culture. Most every day, he would walk the ten yards separating our dwellings, come to my door, knock, and asked if I was ready to "talk story." He already had cardiac problems, and depending on his health, he would lock himself with me into our office and spend from one to three hours, and sometimes more, taping stories or discussing freely as two friends who enjoyed each other's company. This lasted for eleven months. In July and August 91 we moved to his salmon fishing-camp, some ten miles downstream on the Pelly, and resumed our work there, in the bush. The overall result was astounding to me for in thirteen months he managed to recount enough stories and ethnographic descriptions to fill over five thousand pages of printed text. This material included four different types of data: (1) sacred stories from times immemorial; (2) more recent historical tales; (3) ethnographic description of various cultural practices; (4) animal behaviors and religious powers of animals.

The first category consists of stories such as that of crow, of beaver-man, of the man on the moon, and of the giant man. Historical tales include many narratives of bushmen, cannibal men, of stolen girls made slaves by other groups, chief Lane's story, a war a Tatlaman Lake with the Tlingit, and an encounter with mountain dwarfs. Some of the cultural practices discussed at length were the traditional funerary potlatch, shamanism and its related worldview, the traditional marriage ceremony, the rites of passage for boys, traditional games such as wrestling, witchcraft versus medicine, and traditional game management.

The cultural ethology of Yukon animals, the fourth category, was perhaps the most rewarding in the sense that it led him to narrate stories he would most likely have forgotten to tell if it had not been for this part of our work. We covered almost all beings living in the Yukon with the exception of non-food and non-medicinal plants and most insects. For each animal, the discussion started with the recording of its name or names in Tutchone language. This was followed by a description of its annual cycle: time of mating, procreation; time to be hunted or captured, where and why; techniques of capture or acquisition; food and non-food usage; spiritual help the species could provide to people; taboos and proper behaviors to be respected. In the course of these interviews many a time a long-forgotten story about this or that animal would come back to Mr. McGinty's memory, and every time he seized the opportunity to tell it. He thus enriched his accounts of Tutchone traditional narratives considerably.

Mammals which were discussed included beavers, muskrats, porcupines, squirrels, groundhogs, gophers, lynx, wolverines, wolf and dogs, foxes, otters, martens, hares, mice, bears, moose, and caribou. Among birds, he reviewed the cranes, the swans, the ducks, geese, loons, eagles, ospreys, hawks, owls, grouses, ptarmigans, ravens, magpies, swallows. All the fish species were covered one by one. In order not to neglect uncommon species in any category of beings, we used illustrated guides to the mammals, fish, and birds of the Western Subarctic, which we reviewed, page by page.

From this account, it may sound as if Tutchone culture was still well alive and that community life in Pelly Crossing went on smoothly. However, it would be quite misleading to leave the impression that such a state of affairs concerned everyone and everybody. Only a few elders shared Mr. McGinty's extensive knowledge (or was it life experience?). Many adults and younger persons did not even know how to tell the beginning of even one of his stories. The debilitating effect of cultural deprivation was everywhere to be witnessed. Drinking parties were used by some to free themselves from the Tutchone ethos. As least, this is what one younger Tutchone in his late thirties asserted:

> We have too many laws about animals, and this and that, while the Whiteman has none -- when I am drunk I am like a Whiteman because I don't feel I have to respect any damned Indian laws anymore.

Sometimes, drinking parties turned into real dramas. Two such tragedies occurred in thirteen months. A Tutchone half-breed from Mayo murdered one of Mr. McGinty's crow nieces, Linda Joe, hitting her with an axe. The victim was a sixteen-year old girl. She had chided her Mayo lover for his impotence during a drinking party. Her body was thrown away in the snow, fifty yards away from Mr. McGinty's house and the old one he had lent me. As she was missing from school, the principal went to look for her and discovered her corpse. Later on, in early 1991, a wolf moiety member, Robert Alfred was drunk enough to jump down the Pelly River bank to let himself freeze to death by fifty below on a very soft white snow-mattress, twenty yard away from my cabin -- at age twenty-four. This young man had returned to Pelly Crossing a few months earlier from an alcoholic treatment center in British Columbia. However, as soon as he was back, his former drinking partners in Pelly forced vodka in his mouth and he had been since then unable to resist drinking any longer.

The second dedication at the beginning of the book is to the memory of these two young Tutchone friends who left us for good in 1990-91. May Tutchone succeed in their attempt to repossess the instrument of their own destiny, their land and their culture! This will be one of the ways to end most of the internal violence and despair born out of having been colonized -- of having had one's own parents', grandparents' and great grandparents' lifestyle and worldview systematically made irrelevant. Victims like Linda Joe and Robert Alfred will never be forgotten, but it is hoped that one day they will be seen as belonging to a time which has long lapsed from consciousness. This, at least, was what Mr. McGinty was longing for.

Once again, not every Tutchone was affected by drinking, acculturation, or anomy, but problems of this nature were sufficiently commonplace to vindicate Mr. McGinty's worries as well as his attempt at revitalizing Tutchone culture, or more precisely, in his words, the Tutchone *"rules of law."* These, he felt, were the only means to re-institute a sense of dignity and pride among all his people. To go the Whiteman's way like some Tutchone had attempted to do to some degree or another in the last forty years was clearly for him and some other elders a total failure. He knew, for he had quit very heavy whisky drinking himself only some eight years earlier.

The Story of Crow was thus only a small part of our work during this particular year of 1990-91, but it is precisely in this social, cultural and political context that Mr. McGinty recorded it a second time for me and narrated it in public in its entirety for a younger Tutchone audience. He did this within the framework of a Yukon College outreach course on Tutchone laws and culture, taught on a weekly basis in Pelly Crossing by him and two or three other elders in the band meeting hall of the Fort Selkirk First Nation, from January to April 1991.

The idea of the creation of this course came from several Tutchone students from Pelly and Jane-Lee Goudreau, the person responsible for the local campus. Yukon College, with a main campus located in Whitehorse, has local campuses in most settled indigenous communities in the Yukon, even in very small one such as Pelly Crossing. As a university teacher, I was asked in the fall of 1990 to negotiate the creation and content of the course with the college administrators as well as its financing with Indians Affairs, in Whitehorse. With both administrations I argued that the course ought to be defined and taught not by me but by elders who should be paid the standard remuneration per lecture/hour for college teachers; that is at an hourly rate of $100 (it may look considerable but it is not so if one considers that hours for preparation are not paid). To me, what Tutchone students were after went beyond the regular course on Tutchone culture I could have offered. To them, I thought, it was as fundamental and probably more decisive that the college make room for their elders and recognize their knowledge and high social ranks, that is, give its teaching positions to insiders who not only could teach but also *celebrate* Tutchone culture and who, for this reason, were the only appropriate persons to cover the subject at hand.

Why the most suitable? An analogy may help to clarify the matter. A boiled salmon head is a Tutchone delicacy. I have learned with elders to appreciate the various tastes and textures of its meats and cartilage by simply connecting fish cartilaginous viscosity, for example, to similar consistencies in some French dishes -- the snout of a veal in *sauce grébiche or vinaigrette* for instance. Now, if I am to verbalize what I experience in eating "boiled salmon head" to a Tutchone class, I will inescapably refer to what it reminds me in French cuisine, since I was born and raised in France. Moreover, the dish or dishes it evokes in me may very well be disgusting to my audience. On the opposite side, a cultural insider will most likely never discuss "boiled salmon heads" as a special topic. He or she will assume that its tastes are known by everyone, that it is universally liked, that it is a pre-given in the culture. He may refer to these tastes. If he does so, however, it will not be *to explain them*, but to explain *with them*, metaphorically, another and different domain of reality which is less primary, such as a rarer dish for example. In the case of an outsider, the focus is on a reality which is taken for granted by Tutchone culture -- on a reality which does not truly call for any commentary except in the context of another culture where such a dish may be baffling. Then the fact which is exotic to the outsider is explained through a point of reference within his different foreign culture, a point which may or may not make sense to the Tutchone. In the case of an insider, Tutchone culture is not explained but reiterated to provide its students with primary points of reference with which to explain the world, including the one that has just invaded its world.

Given the context, what Tutchone college students needed was a frame of reference, not a reference to the cultural frame of an immigrant among them. Thus, at times, there is an obligation for non-native anthropologists like me and others to withdraw. At certain stages of research, there is the necessity for the "foreign insider" to abstain from analyzing from without a story like that of crow if people need it foremost to have it re-told as a primary frame of reference or charter narrative.

History is full of similar predicaments. Russia provides a good example. The writing of its history did not truly begin before the 1700's when a few German scholars devoted themselves to it entirely. However, the efforts of the German historians did not satisfy their Russian audience, and won them bitter reproaches rather than gratitude. History was expected to bolster pride in being Russian, while the pedantic scholars persisted in discussing, from without, what was absent or lacking from their standpoint in the achievements of Russian society compared to that of others -- while missing the uniqueness of what Russia had accomplished, or what pitfalls it had avoided, in contrast to other European societies (Greenfeld, 1992: 246-247).

Be that as it may, some people (but not everybody) at Yukon College and Indian Affairs worried a little and hid it behind contrived smiles. How could the elders I was referring to be college teachers? How could it be justified to pay them $100 an hour? Didn't I know that they could not read nor write? Who would grade the student's research papers? The remuneration problem was surprisingly rapidly resolved. All I knew about Tutchone culture came from Tutchone elders. How could it have been otherwise? How could they be paid less than I would have been? The problem of grading and of the conception of a course to be delivered in three hour chunks over thirteen weeks was different. Tutchone elders do not count their time and are not used to counting it. They could very well have discussed with the students for seven hours in the first week, and be gone hunting or visiting relatives for the next week and the next and the next, and be back a month later for a two-day storytelling bout. A compromise was called for. I agreed to be, so to speak, their agent and work with them to section off what they wanted to tell in a standard three-hour time-slot. To reassure the College, I offered to help the students formulate their research questions as well as to grade their essays. Face was saved even though everybody knew that what was at stake went beyond students' aptitude for anthropological research.

However, to get myself into coaching elders to conform to the structure of a thirteen-week college course was to say the least enlightening about Euro-Canadian pedagogical culture. What is an introduction? What is a conclusion? What do you mean by first or second part? Very quickly, I had to change my approach and plan for the short term only. What do you feel you should talk about this week? Decisions were then taken in light of what was going on in the community at that particular moment, in light of what was deemed most useful to the student audience then and now. The remaining task for me was simply to rehearse with the elders how the selected topic could be delivered in three-hour time-slots.

5. TRANSFIXING THE ORAL INTO THE WRITTEN

Time came for Mr. McGinty to tell *The Story of Crow*. During rehearsal, we identified three possible difficulties. How the various episodes of the story should follow each other? How many hours will the narration actually take? Given the stress of telling the story in the unusual context of a course with two video-camera running, was there not a risk of skipping some episodes inadvertently? The first question was solved through a long discussion leaving only two or three segments for which a precise chronological order in the story was not completely certain and never became so, but about which Mr. McGinty decided. For the second and third concerns, Mr. McGinty chose to tell and explain the story to me again in its entirety, leaving me with the task to give a title to each segment and compile in writing the ordering of the episodes. I was to bring my notes to his public performance. Should he feel the need, he would just ask me what came next. In fact, except for one brief hesitation about one episode where he consulted by glancing at me (I simply had to stage-whisper a brief title), his worries were unjustified. Our discussion about the flow of the episodes, as well as the rehearsal of the narration of the story itself, were recorded on audio-tapes. His public performance was video-taped by two students. With the 1984 account of the story, this gave me two research versions on audio-tapes during which I often interrupted him for explanations, clarification or elaboration. As the course narration was a performance in story-telling excluding any sort of interruption, the video version provided both a more normal telling of the story and a visual recording of the non-verbal additional information communicated by Mr. McGinty through his body language. These three versions constituted the bases on which I have elaborated the written version offered in the present book -- the video-tapes being used exclusively for additional information given by the kinetics of the narrator.

The next pages offer in succession three versions of the same segment of the story: the beginning of the foggy woman episode. The 1984 version is a transcript of the audio-tapes recorded at Mr. McGinty's fishing-camp in 1984. The 1991 version is a transcript of McGinty's rehearsal with me of the story for his college course. In this 1991 transcript, words in square brackets have been added when there was a need to clarify what Mr. McGinty was referring to. Mr. McGinty stammers at irregular intervals and chews tobacco. Most of his stammering and all of his spiting are not included in the transcripts The written version is the version of the same segment of the episode as it appears in the present book.

1984 VERSION OF THE FOGGY WOMAN EPISODE (FRAGMENT)

McGINTY: And after that he walkin' down again. Pretty soon he found one woman there, really nice lookin' girl. Nice lookin' woman, nice tit; tit just sticking out, you know. And nice leg, nice fat leg. Crow see it, Oh gosh he said, Jeez...

LEGROS: That's foggy lady there?

McGINTY: Foggy woman. Gee, he said, you got nice leg and nice tit, he said. My god, where you come from, anyhow? Oh, he said, I live here all the time. That's what I do, I make my living. And he said there, you married? You got man? He said no, I got no man, nothin'. He said, how about I stay with you? He said, I don't know, I think so, you can stay with me. And he stay inside his camp there. By gosh, he say, I wish it get dark quick.

LEGROS: (laughs).

McGINTY: We make love quick, he said, and that woman there he said, I don't know that kind too myself, he told him. He said, I'll show you! I show you how to do it, he said. And after that, he throw his blanket in. We use my blanket for sleep, on top, and your blanket, we use it for mattress, he said. My blanket nice and warm. And he said, take all your clothes out, I take all my clothes out too. Bare naked, they go inside blanket. And crow started fooling around with her. And that foggy woman there said, What are you doing anyway, what do you do that for? And then he said, what for you pee on me? He said, that's the way, that's what you gotta do, he say. When man come to you, they gotta use you that way. Using woman for, he said, He sucking tit and every-thing there. Woman tit... and they make good love.

LEGROS: Ok, just wait. Who pee on him? Woman she pee on crow, or crow he pee on woman?

McGINTY: He pee on woman, he pee inside, I guess. He shoot up, that's what he mean. And he said, next time I do that to you, you're gonna go after me, you're gonna love me real hard.

1991 VERSION OF THE FOGGY WOMAN EPISODE (SAME FRAGMENT)

McGINTY: After he [crow] all he finished there, from there, he go out again [for his world journey]. He walk, he walk by, by river again... And he sees some woman stay there: nice lookin' woman. He come in there. He sit down from him [her]. Woman got lots of dried fish. Gee, he say, you make lots of fish. [S]he say, yeah I sure work hard, I work hard for my livin'. [crow] he said, ah, do you married? No [s]he said. Do you need man [crow asked her]? I need man but where I gonna get it from? [crow], he said I'm here, can I get marry [to] you? What kind are you? Wolf [she said]. Me crow, oh we just right, he said...

LEGROS: Uh-huh.

McGINTY: I stay with you. [S]he said O.K. go ahead and... bring, bring your stuff in [the camp]. And [s]he cook, [s]he feed him. And they fishin', they fishin', they fishin', they work. Pretty soon he wack [*sic*: "wipe"] his face again: I sweat he said. He said, ah, I tired now, turn over that fish. So his wife turn over the fish. [Crow] he see here under here.

LEGROS: (describing gesture and taping the description) Under her armpit, yeah.

McGINTY: Yeah, under her arm, yellow here [armpit hair].

WRITTEN VERSION OF THE FOGGY WOMAN EPISODE (SAME FRAGMENT)

So for now crow is just walking hungry. He is going along a river. He walks, he walks, and pretty soon he finds some woman living alone in a camp. There're lots of dried fish hanging on her racks. And this woman is really nice looking: you know, nice tits sticking out... And nice fat legs too. Crow sees all that.

"Oh gosh," he thinks. "Jeez..." He comes into the woman's camp. He sits down some way from her.

"Gee," he says. "You got such nice legs and nice tits. And you made lots of dried fish too. My God, where're you coming from, anyway?"

She tells him: "I've been living here all my life. Drying fish is what I do. That's how I make my living. Yeah, I sure work hard for it."

"Are you married? You got a man?" says crow.

"No, I got no man, nothing."

"Do you need one?"

"Yeah, I need a man but where am I going to get him from?"

"Well," he says, "I'm here. Can I get married to you? What kind are you?"

"Wolf side, wolf clan," she answers.

"Me, I'm crow clan," he tells her. "So we are just right for one another."

He raises his two hands and grabs one of her thighs.

"Please, you got such nice soft legs! How about me staying with you?"

"I don't know for sure," she says. "But I guess it's all right. You can come in and stay. Bring your stuff inside here."

He moves inside her brush-camp. She cooks some fish and she

feeds him. After that, crow lies down and starts to think all kinds of crooked ways:

"My gosh," he tells himself. "I wish it gets dark real quick. I can't wait."

Nighttime comes at last. He calls his new woman:

"What about making love right away?"

"Myself," she says, "I don't know what kind of thing you're talking about."

"I'll show you, I'll show you how to do it."

He throws his blanket on top of hers.

"We use my blanket on top. It's nice and warm. It's for sleeping under it. Your blanket, we use it as a mattress."

But that's just because he wants to keep his own one, nice and tidy. And he says:

"Take all your clothes off. I take off all my clothes too."

Pretty soon they're are bare naked and they go inside their blankets. Crow fools around with her. Then the woman complains:

"What for you do that? What's that you shoot up inside me? What for you pee in there?"

"That's the way," he says, "that's the way you do it. When men come to you, they got to use you this way. That's what men do with women. You'll see, next time I do it again to you, you're going to go after me for more. You're going to love me real hard then."

He sucks at her tits and everything and they make real good love.

Even a cursory reading of the two transcripts quickly reveals the sort of difficulties one encounters when writing down oral texts from a Tutchone elder for a broad audience. When the reader compares the two oral versions with the written one she or he can see that Mr. McGinty's English has been transformed into a more standard form of the language. The reason for this is simple. Other scholars have published *verbatim* transcripts in broken English, most often widely annotated to make the text comprehensible (as in my 1991 transcript). While this is more satisfying for some scholars in the field, it has also displeased younger First Nation students who speak English perfectly well -- they find that publishing their elders in broken English makes their old people sound pretty stupid. As a French speaker whose English is often at variance with the standard forms and who always needs an English-speaking editor, I fully appreciate their point. Nevertheless I do hope that my editing will be found minimal, unobtrusive, and leaving the text with most of the style of Mr. McGinty's oral performances.

In relation to the transcripts of the 1984 and 1991 audio versions, the first obstacle comes from Tutchone linguistic usage in English. The Tutchone language does not distinguish gender through pronouns (it does so by other means), and elders carry this over into English. Sometimes, they use "he" for "she," and vice-versa, and in other cases "he" and "she" are employed the way they are in English. In most instances, the context clarifies whether "he" is used to mean "he" or "she." Nevertheless, in other cases what is being told remains quite obscure. The 1984 version offers an example of this type of difficulty. Towards the end, when crow is already making love to the foggy woman who knows nothing about sex, the transcript reads:

And that foggy woman there said, What are you doing anyway, what do you do that for? And then *he said*, what for you pee on me? He said, that's the way, that's what you gotta do, he say.

When one reads "*he said*," and then goes through the last sentence, one assumes that "*crow* said what for *you woman* pee on me?" and that the woman answered "that's the way..." Yet one should never presume that what is being said with an English pronoun means what a Tutchone elder is actually referring to. This is why as soon as Mr. McGinty made a breathing pause I asked:

O.K., just wait, Who pee on him? Woman she pee on crow, or crow he pee on woman?

Then came the clarification:

he pee on woman, he pee inside, I guess, he shoot up, that's what he mean.

In the last instance, "he" clearly refers to the woman. In consequence, when working on the written version I rephrased this segment as follows:

Then the woman complains: "What for you do that? What's that you shoot up inside me? What for you pee in there? "

"That's the way," he says, "that's the way you do it."

In this case, I felt that the clarification brought about by my question could be integrated in the written text. To make the woman ask "What for you pee on me?" without elaborating was obviously a form of euphemism that Mr. McGinty felt obliged to use because he was speaking in English to a Caucasian. However, Tutchone culture is much less castigating about sex. One may remember, in *The Story of Crow*, Mr. McGinty pondered on why "cunt" is a dirty word in English whereas "*druu,*" the Tutchone equivalent, never is. Thus in his language he would most likely have said something like "What for you pee inside me? In the case at hand the verb *to pee* is the most likely choice for the narration is supposed to reflect that the foggy woman knows nothing about men, even less about being penetrated by a man, and still less about ejaculation.

A second type of difficulty comes from my own interventions during the narration. For instance, at the very beginning of the same segment of the 1984 version, I inquire about whether the episode Mr. McGinty just started is that of the foggy woman. My question is one of curiosity and I ask it only because I had previously heard this episode from somebody else and recognized its beginning. Perhaps it was also a form of bragging on my part: "see uncle this one I already know." But unfortunately this leads Mr. McGinty to refer to a "foggy woman" at the very beginning of his telling of the episode (see 1984 third entry for T.M.), destroying the dramatic effect achieved in the traditional narration when crow's wife runs away and changes herself into a totally unexpected silent form on which her insulting husband no longer has any sort of influence or power: a free-floating fog roaming over an expanse of water. This very singular outcome -- turning oneself into an unreachable reality in the face of an abusing husband -- is gripping for women, and even for little girls who hear the story. But for this effect to occur, crow's wife has to be presented as unexceptional at the beginning and as transforming herself into a fog only at the very end, after she has been too cruelly mocked. This is the reason why in the written version of this passage I entirely omit, in this case, the response I triggered by interrupting Mr. McGinty. Deliberately, in the subtitle of the episode as well as in the text I only indicate that crow meets with a woman and keep any reference to a "fog," until the very end, as it should have been had I not asked Mr. McGinty to identify the episode.

When comparing the 1984 and 1991 oral versions with the written one, it becomes clear that additional information is integrated into the latter. For instance, at the very beginning crow is described as "walking hungry." Such indications are in neither the 1984 nor the 1991 transcripts. However, this information does come from somewhere. In one case, at this particular instant in the telling of the story, Mr. McGinty impersonated crow as yawning. In Tutchone culture to yawn is not interpreted as indicating tiredness but as a sign of hunger: thus the portraying of crow walking "hungry," a description which is consistent with the end of the preceding episode where crow has stupidly lost his only meal to a root (see full story). Another example of precision based on visual information may be found in the passage where crow is trying to convince the woman to take him in as a husband. The written version describes him as raising his hands and grabbing one of the woman's thighs. Nowhere is this mentioned in the transcripts of the oral versions. However, this is what Mr. McGinty mimed in his public narration to the students, which was video-taped. He rose from his chair, walked to a huge wooden pillar in the band office hall, raised his hands and embraced the pillar high up with both arms and hands expressing how soft the thigh was by rubbing one of his cheeks against the pillar and making everybody burst out laughing. By raising his arms and hands he also ridiculed crow's pretensions by making him appear as a dwarf who can hardly reach the height of the thighs of the woman he is lusting after.

Some other phrases in the written version, which may appear as unwarranted by what is said in the 1984 or 1991 transcripts, are the results of different considerations. For example, in the 1991 version crow asks the woman "what *kind* are you?" Here, the answer given by the woman proves beyond any doubt to the ethnographer (but maybe not to an outsider) that *kind* refers to the moiety the woman belongs to. Twenty years ago, the use of the word *kind* for moiety was common among all older Tutchone. In fact, when they used it, they often seemed to think of the two moieties as two different kinds of humanity. At other times, when conflicts occurred between moieties, to convey the idea of a pivotal opposition, they also spoke, in English, of the wolf *tribe* and the crow *tribe*. As moieties are not territorial groups, as they cut across the division of people into geographical groups, in so doing, elders were changing the English meaning of the notion of tribe, which in ordinary circumstances refers to territorial groups irrespective of internal moiety or clan divisions. However, by the same token, these elders reveal that, to them, the complementary relationship between moieties could also be conceived of as antagonistic, just as an opposition between actual territorial tribes in the normal sense of the words.

So, how to clarify in the written version what *kind* is referring to? The word could not simply be replaced by *moiety* for the single reason that Mr. McGinty who ignored the very existence of this word would simply never have pronounced it. *Tribe* could have been employed if the context had been one of friction -- but this was not so in this episode. It left me with the word *kind* and with the task of clarifying its meaning for both younger Tutchone and Euro-Canadians. To do so, I chose to introduce the words "side" and "clan" in the written dialogue between crow and the woman. "Side" for moiety is readily understood by all potential Tutchone readers but most likely not by Euro-Canadians. "Clan" is the word employed by many younger Tutchone for moiety, and by Yukon Euro-Canadians. It is also a term which is familiar to eventual other Euro-Canadian readers and which better than any other, short of moiety, conveys the idea of two dispersed postulated descent groups which Tutchone moieties are (as opposed to two territorial groups).

This is why the written version departs from the actual phrasing in the 1991 oral version. Excluding the editing in square brackets, the original segment in question read:

- I need man but where I gonna get it from?
- He said, I am here, can I get marry you? What kind are you?
- Wolf!
- Me crow, oh we just right, he said.

The written version reads:

- Yeah, I need a man, but where am I going to get him from?
- Well, he says, I'm here. Can I get married to you? What *kind* are you?
- Wolf *side*, wolf *clan*, she answers.
- Me, I'm crow *clan*, he tells her. So we are just right for one another.

Clearly, the notions of *side* or *clan*, which are surreptitiously inserted into the dialogue, clarify the notion of *kind* for non-Tutchone without altering fundamentally either the style or the content of the exchange. In fact to solve the problem I asked myself how Mr. McGinty would have responded if I had asked during our taping session what he meant by "*what kind are you?*" While I know that he would never have talked of *moiety,* I am equally sure that he would have been, first, slightly irritated by the interruption, and would most certainly have snapped back something like:

You know... he means what side, what clan... crow or wolf.

In the transcripts of the audio tapes, many passages are similarly equivocal for an outside reader. After many interviews spread over nineteen years, I understood most of Mr. McGinty's obscure formulations and in such cases never requested him to make an effort to be more explicit for an outside audience. In the written version, for every such case, I clarify the text by appending the type of wording that Mr. McGinty would most likely have used to answer me had I questioned him.

Along the same line of thought, I have avoided altogether any footnotes. This would inevitably have made the story look like a subject of study and not, as I wanted, a narration in itself and for itself. When further details were visibly required, I solved the problem by integrating into the text of the story how Mr. McGinty answered my questions and, after his death, how I imagined he would have elaborated. The beginning of the first episode provides two examples of the kind of ornamentation he offered. All through our years of acquaintance, Mr. McGinty had always presented crow as being the God Christians believe in. However, in both his 1984 and 1991 narration he omitted to say so. A few days after the taping of the 1991 version

I was having lunch in his home and asked him about that. "Yes," he said, "you gotta write and tell that crow is God," and then he qualified his statement which I summarized as follows in my note-book:

Crow means *ts'ehk'i* in our language. But *ts'ehk'i* has got to have two names Whiteman way. Sometimes you have to call him God because that's God who made the world. And sometimes you have to call him crow too because that's him, the crow, who really made the world we live on. You call him God or crow, either way, back and forth.

So, instead of a distracting footnote on the Tutchone' interpretation of crow as being the Christian God, I integrated into the text Mr. McGinty's own statement which I found, because of its special phrasing ("Crow means *ts'ehk'i*" for example) much more complex in meaning than what I could have mustered on the issue in a footnote.

A second example of avoiding footnotes and replacing them by inserts in the text is provided a little further down, when the flood is coming and when crow catches and kills two birds to save himself: one *yaazok* and one *chät tadjia*. Mr. McGinty wrongly assumed that I knew what these birds were. I did not and said so. He answered that he did not know their English names either. Stranded, we stopped the tape recorder and spent two to three hours looking through bird guidebooks with pictures of northern birds. All along, he made comments about which I made "headnotes." In the end, I made the following summary of our discussion which I would not dare to put in a narration in front of an elder audience which will know what these birds are, but which has to be provided to an audience of younger Tutchone who speak English only and to Euro-Canadians who do not know Tutchone at all.

Yaazok, that's the gray bird with yellow legs and a real sharp beak like a pencil [his comment on finding the picture at last], about seven or eight inches long [shown with hands]. The Whiteman doesn't know this bird's true name. So he calls it the great yellow leg sandpiper [after I read him what the English name was]. That bird hangs around lakeshores and marshes in the evening. Its grub is way down in the mud. It's got to shove its whole beak down there to get it out. It eats, eats, and when it's got enough eat, it goes some place else. It flies way high in the sky, saying: "tigidigidigidigidi..." That's why they call him *yaazok*. And nighttime, you can hear it all the way through: "tu-gudugudguk..." it whistles.

Once he found a picture of one *chät tadjia,* he offered the following comments:

Chät, that means any kind of duck but all the big ducks have their own names on top. C*hät tadjia*, that's any kind of small duck and that the only name a small duck gets: it means "big duck's fart." If it's a really small little duck, you can say "*chät tadjia zra*" too: "big duck's little fart." When people want to be nice to a small duck, they can call it *chät tadjia zra*. Indian way, it sounds like "big duck's fart darling" and it sure looks better.

Would a simple footnote on *yaazok* being the great yellow leg sand piper and on *chät tadjia* being any sort of small sized waterfowl have achieved the same narrative effect? Surely not. Probably even less so with Latin names added.

After Mr. McGinty's death, when writing up the remainder of the story, I limited myself to inserts I was sure he would have made. To be certain, in all cases I relied on comments or anecdotes he had told me at various times over the years to explain this or that aspect of Tutchone culture. Such is the case, for instance, in passages I added concerning the relationships between brothers-in-law, between a mother-in-law and her son-in-law, on the danger of letting a woman step over a man, or on the physical appearance of a brush-camp.

So far, everyone might agree that the editing discussed is justified. However, the attentive reader of the three versions of the beginning of the foggy woman episode will not have failed to notice some more significant reworking between, on the one hand each transcript taken separately, and, on the other, the final written version of the same segment. This should come as no surprise for this section has been deliberately selected as illustrating a more important editing difficulty which was encountered here and there when comparing the transcripts of the 1984 version with that of 1991.

In the case at hand, the differences are obvious. In 1984, Mr. McGinty focused the opening of the episode entirely on crow's desire to have sex. The fact that the woman encountered was a hard-working person on whom crow was going to count being well fed is evoked, if at all, only in a very brief and oblique statement: "Oh, [s]he said, I live here all the time. That's what I do. I make my living." In the 1991 audio-taped version, the opening goes the other way. Mr. McGinty focuses entirely on crow's desire to eat and to be fed. The only passage revealing that crow may be sexually attracted is, to say the least, rather cursory. It occurs right after crow sees the woman for the first time when the narrator adds: "[a] *nice looking* woman." True enough, crow marries the woman and one assumes that he has sex with her, but nowhere in this segment or in the rest of the 1991 transcript is there any single evocation of crow's impatience to have sex, of him finally having sex when nighttime comes, or of how his wife reacts. The focus is on crow's hunger for food alone.

For the written version a dilemma had to be faced. Should it be based on only one of the two versions? But which one? Would it be legitimate to merge the content of the two versions? Mr. McGinty's practice in storytelling provided the answer. In his public performance with students, which was given a week or so after the taping of the 1991 audio version, he kept the theme of crow's hunger for food but reintroduced the motif of crow's urgent desire for sex. In these conditions, I felt quite safe in assuming that merging the two versions was sound. This feeling was further reinforced by the 1984 account. In it, when Mr. McGinty makes the woman to say, "I live here all the time. T*hat's what I do*, I make my living." This "*That's what I do*" seems to make her answer a compliment about her work as a fishing woman that crow would have given her earlier but which Mr. McGinty forgot on that particular day to include in his narration.

How was the merging of the two versions actually made? Let us illustrate it by quoting a brief passage from the written version in which what is coming from what version is identified.

So for now crow is just walking [1984, 1991] hungry [yawning kinetics in 1991]. He is going along a river [1991]. He walks, he walks [1991], and pretty soon he finds some woman living [1984, 1991] alone in a camp [inferred from the rest of the story in 1984 and 1991]. There're lots of dried fish [1991] hanging on her racks [inferred from field data on the technique of drying fish]. And this woman is really nice looking [1984, 1991]: you know, nice tits sticking out... And nice fat legs too. Crow sees all that [1984]. "Oh gosh," he thinks. "Jeez..." [1984]. He comes into the woman's camp. He sits down some way from her [1991]. "Gee," he says. "You got such nice legs and nice tits [1984]. And you made lots of dried fish too [1991]. My God, where're you coming from, anyway?" [1984]. She tells him: "I've been living here all my life [1984]. Drying fish is what I do [inferred from the remainder of 1991]. That's how I make my living [1984, 1991]. Yeah, I sure work hard for it" [1991].

The date or dates given are those of the transcripts used for each phrase or fragment of a phrase. When a sentence is not in any transcript and is inferred from the rest of the story or from other field data this is indicated by the mention "inferred..." in square brackets. In as much as Mr. McGinty's own practice in his public narration legitimates the weaving of the food and sex themes together, such merging of the two motifs seems fair. In fact, one discovers to one's surprise that the various segments from the two versions can be mixed and then fitted with one another as easily as pieces coming from one single jigsaw puzzle. One will also notice that, better than anything else, the synthesis makes crow both human and bird in the same moment, or "back and forth" like Mr. McGinty has it at the beginning of the story. What make the crow human are small details such as his cunning in having sex without dirtying his own blanket. What makes him a crow is his ravenous appetite for other people's food.

Comparison of the two transcriptions of the audio-tapes reveals other instances where some details are given in the first version but not in the second, and vice versa. These passages are much briefer than the example of the foggy woman we have just considered. In all such cases I have treated the differences as complementary rather than contradictory and have merged the information. In the same line of thought, I have treated the two versions as complementary when one episode is given in only one of the two accounts. I am aware that this strategy creates a difficulty for researchers interested in how the same storyteller may vary his narration of the same audible "text." Yet the problem is solvable for the entire transcripts of the audio-tapes have been deposited in the Concordia University Archives (Montréal) where they may be consulted.

Nevertheless, one truly trying editing problem was encountered with episode 14: *Ho-hei, ho-hei, ho-hei, ho-hei...* In this case, the 1984 and 1991 versions are quite different. A segment by segment comparison of the plot offered by each version reveals to what extent. In what follows, the plot of each version is directly summarized from the way Mr. McGinty's worded it in the transcript.

1984 VERSION OF THE HO-HEI EPISODE (SUMMARY)

1. Crow goes downriver in his canoe.

2. He comes to a town where people are making fish grease storing it in fish air guts. Crow tells them that the air guts are too short and shows them how to make them longer by gluing them together with pitch. Then crow hides in the bush. He has taken one end of the long grease sausage with him and he drinks the grease.

3. A fellow comes by and crow quickly hides inside a bearskin. The fellow runs away and reports in town what he has seen. Crow who is back in town says that it must have been a black bear. Crow pretends that he knows about black bear and instructs the people to hit it on the nose with a little stick -- this will make it run away.

4. Crow goes back in the bush, hides under the bearskin, and again sucks the fish grease from the end of the sausage. Another man comes by and sees a bear drinking the grease. He does as crow said and hits the bear on the nose with a little stick. Crow is knocked out. The people grab the bearskin, pull on it, and find out that crow is inside. They break his chin or beak off and give it to an old widow, asking her to keep it for herself.

5. Crow goes hiding in the bush on the river shore, upstream. There he makes rafts and mannequins of moss to paddle them downstream. The rafts come downriver and everybody runs to the shore to welcome the visitors: *ho-hei, ho-hei,* they holler.

6. Meanwhile crow finds the widow who has got his chin. He asks her to give it back. She agrees on the condition that he makes love to her. He complies, having a good time, and gets his chin back.

7. People look at the phoney rafts, which crumble apart. They get mad at crow for fooling them and chase him. He flies away. When nighttime comes he gets back to town, jumps in his canoe and runs away.

1991 VERSION OF THE HO-HEI EPISODE (SUMMARY)

FIRST SUB-STORY.

A. Crow goes downriver in a canoe. He meets people in a town; they salute him with *ho-hei, ho-hei*. Crow wonders what "*ho-hei...*" means.

B. Crow is well fed by the people. But then he hides away without warning them, leaving his canoe in town. He is making a plan to find out what the people mean by "*ho-hei, ho-hei.*"

C. Crow goes upriver where he builds five rafts and puts on them mannequins made of moss. The mannequins are told to paddle toward the town. Crow runs back to the town faster than the mannequins can go on their rafts.

D. The rafts with the moss mannequins arrive close to the town. Everybody hollers "*ho-hei, ho-hei.*" Crow asks the people what they mean by "*ho-hei, ho-hei.*"

E. Crow makes the mannequins and the rafts fall apart, and the people are mad at crow.

F. The people accused crow of lying because, to find out the meaning of "*ho-hei,*" he ridiculed them by making them hail nonexistent rafts and people.

G. The people run after crow. He escapes with his canoe.

SECOND SUB-STORY.

H. Crow keeps on going downriver and soon spots a new town.

I. He stops and hides away to make more phoney rafts and raftmen. He goes downriver and orders some of the rafts to follow him, after they will have figured he has arrived in town. Some other rafts are to be launched later.

J. Crow arrives in town where nice people salute him. He informs them that he has passed several rafts, which will soon arrive with other nice people on board. He insures the town people that they are going to have a good laugh

K. The rafts are coming and people holler "*ho-hei.*" Crow makes the rafts fall apart again with his brain-power.

L. People are furious; they break crow's beak off, and hide it away. Crow stays around to get his beak back. The people want to give him as a husband to an old woman.

M. People see new rafts coming downriver with people on board. These are crow's last rafts, which had been made to wait upstream thus far. However, people are convinced that these are real and go to the shore to welcome the visitors on board. Meanwhile crow finds the old woman that has his beak. She promises to give it back if he pays her with sex. Crow agrees, has a good time with her and gets his beak back. Crow puts it back on his face and runs away with his canoe.

N. As the rafts are getting very close to the people, crow makes them break apart again and only driftwood is seen floating around.

O. The people run after crow but he is gone.

Here the differences between the two versions are more stunning than is the case with the two foggy woman versions. The 1984 version focuses on crow's ravenous appetite and his stealing of people's winter food stock. In it, the breaking off of his bill is a punishment for having stolen food, and while a raft with moss mannequins is made and "*ho-hei*", is hollered toward the end (5), the event plays absolutely no crucial apparent role in this plot. In contrast, the 1991 version starts with "*ho-hei,*" and centers around crow being intrigued by the arbitrariness with which sounds are selected to mean things and in the present case to institute a social relation by themselves without having any precise referent (*ho-hei,* as hello and as instituting a welcoming relationship as it is uttered) and being amused by people who are unaware of it as is revealed by his raft-and-moss-mannequin trick. He finds it so amusing that he repeats the ploy twice (indicated in the summary as *first* and *second sub-stories*). In the end, his bill is taken away from him as a punishment for making fun of people. Nevertheless, there are also overlaps between the two versions. In the 1991 transcript, a very oblique reference is made at the very beginning of the first sub-story to crow's appetite but in this case the people are simply said to be feeding him well (B). Furthermore, in both cases crow his punished by losing his bill (in 1984 "chin" is used by Mr. McGinty who told me later on that he meant *u dye* but did not know the English word for it) and by having to have sex with an old widow to get it back.

Should the two versions have been kept separate? For research purposes certainly and this is why an account of the differences is being given here. However, if the aim is to keep the episode flowing as well as to highlight its potential and its complexity as revealed by the existence of its two different versions, probably not. For this reason (I shall come back to this point of indeterminacy below), I chose to select the 1991 version with its two sub-stories as the reference text. However, not to miss the fish grease motif, I added, to the all too brief mention of crow being well fed in the 1991 first sub-story, the 1984 theme of hiding under a bear skin to subsequently steal more food. Placed in this particular sub-story the fish grease motif is thus preceded by an evocation of the *"ho-hei"* theme, which Mr. McGinty put at the very beginning of his first sub-story in 1991. In consequence, the apparent meaninglessness of the reference to *"ho-hei"* at the end of the 1984 version disappears.

Notwithstanding, this solution was not without difficulties. In the 1991 version the breaking off of crow's bill is located in the second sub-story as a punishment for making fun of people hollering *"ho-hei."* I chose to have this sub-theme used only once in the written version. However, to keep it at the end of the written version would have made the stealing of the fish grease go unpunished, and would have made the important connection made in the 1984 version between crow recommending people to hit the bear on its nose with a small stick and him loosing his own chin/beak because of his own stupid recommendation, to disappear from the account. To avoid missing the weaving together of these two motifs, I therefore located the beak theme and subsequent sex with the old woman into the first sub-story. On a formal level, the composition of the final written version of the episode then is as follows:

$$(1+A), (2 \Leftrightarrow B), 3, (4 \Leftrightarrow L), [C \Leftrightarrow M \Leftrightarrow (5+6)], (7 \Leftrightarrow G) \mathbin{/\!/} H, I, J, [(D+E+F) \Leftrightarrow (K+N)], O.$$

In this formula, numbers are segments from the 1984 version; letters are segments from the 1991 transcript as summarized above; commas indicate the changes of segments in the episode; the double-slash the separation between the two sub-stories -- (1+A) means that the first segment is made from the *addition* of A to 1; (2 $\Leftrightarrow$ B), indicates that the second segment is made by *fusing* 2 with B, etc.).

Therefore, the written version is still divided into two sub-stories. The first one opens with the *"ho-hei"* theme but soon drops it for the "craving for food" motif followed by the sex for beak theme. Finally, it ends by having crow at last fully noticing the matter of the meaning of *"ho-hei."* In a way, the new first sub-story focuses on the gist of the 1984 version while preparing the reader for the *"ho-hei"* theme of the 1991 version. The latter is then fully developed in the second sub-story, which is exclusively devoted to this *"ho-hei"* question.

Other arrangements were possible. One of them could have consisted of treating the 1984 version as a first sub-story to which could have been appended the two sub-stories of the 1991 version. The repetition the beak/sex punishment motif in two different sub-stories and contexts (stealing fish grease vs. mocking people's *"ho-hei"*) separated by only the brief first *"ho-hei"* sub-stories of the 1991 version (where the beak/sex motif is absent) would have looked strange but would not have been uncommon for a religious text. For example, in traditional Christian translations of the biblical *Genesis* (Société Biblique Française, 1987), God first makes male and female human beings at the same time (Gn 1. 27-28). Then, a few verses later, the theme of the creation of the first human beings is picked up again but to say that God first makes one man out of dust, and, second, one woman out of one of the ribs of the first male (Gn 2, 7, 18, 21-22). Similarly, in *Exodus* the same incident is repeated in different parts of the narrative. Why was this option not selected? We have seen that it was a question of flow for the written version of the story, but the stylistic choice made also served to embody into a written text, which is necessarily fixed once completed, an index of the possible greater malleableness of a "text" up to now kept exclusively oral -- an index which could not have been provided if there had been no problems between the two versions of this particular episode, no need for making choices, and no need to have to explain the decisions taken in the present postscript.

6. TRANSUBTANTIATING THE WRITTEN BACK INTO THE ORAL

Which brings to the fore a central problem: should readers of a fixed written version narrate *The Story of Crow* to new audiences exactly as they read it, or, stated in another way, how could future narrators detach themselves from the written and go back to the oral? The question is essential in that Mr. McGinty seems to have regarded the writing down of his narration as providing only a mere firebrand on which generations to come should have to blow if and when they should want to rekindle and keep the memory of crow's doings alive. Walter Benjamin, already quoted in the introduction, has written that stories are not meant to be read but told and retold to *listeners* in whose memory the telling and retelling takes the standing of a personal experience, which makes the listeners feel inhabited by the will to become narrators themselves in turn. For, storytelling is always the art of repeating stories, and the art is lost if the stories are no longer retained. It is lost because there is no more weaving and spinning to go on while they are being listened to (cf. Benjamin, [1955], 1969: 91). Would Mr. McGinty have agreed? Most certainly!

For the difference between thoughts communicated in and through writing/reading and thoughts passed on in and through speaking/ listening is indeed profound. In short, thoughts that are born out in our brains cannot be expressed or even formulated without the mediation of language whereas this very mediation corrupts the very thoughts one had wished to express. This point has been beautifully conveyed in *Madame Bovary,* where Flaubert despairs at language for being ultimately nothing more than:

> ...A broken tin kettle on which one hammers out tunes to make bears dance, when one longs to move the stars (quoted from memory).

To be certain, thoughts orally expressed are also necessarily mediated by language but speech does not make it apparent to either speaker or listeners. When one hears or emits the sounds "egZEMpluhFYE" one does not hear "egZEMpluhFYE" and then understand "exemplify." The material *signifier* (the series of sounds "egZEMpluhFYE") and the meaning or *signified* (exemplify) present themselves as a single whole. In fact, here, the difference between sound (signifier) and meaning (signified) can be made tangible only through the possibility of the conversion of the sounds into two different visual marking systems ("*egZEMpluhFYE*" versus "*exemplify*"). To borrow from Jonathan Culler (1982: 107), hearing and understanding my speech as I speak is the same thing -- I do not hear first and then understand. Furthermore, in speaking one's thoughts (and not writing them), the signifiers (the sounds) disappear as soon as they are uttered. As they do not obtrude, the speaker can explain any ambiguities to insure that the thoughts have been conveyed or alternatively the listener may fill in the gaps with his imagination as when invited to *see* or to *know* what he, the speaker, means ("You see what I mean?" or "you know what I mean!" are the usual interjections). Some of the speaker's supplemental "explanations" are also communicated by his body language; others by his variations in tone, the manner in which some words are stressed, pauses taken. This is nowhere more evident than when speech is 'transcripted' *verbatim* and thus almost totally deprived of the never "fully scriptable" accompanying means with which communication is completed. For instance, in the 1984 version after crow has made love to the foggy woman, Mr. McGinty makes our "birdman-hero" utter the English sound patterns:

> [And he said,] next time I do that to you, you're gonna go after me, you're gonna love me real hard.

The reader of this sentence who has not *heard and seen* the way it was articulated and physically projected by Mr. McGinty cannot hope to discern in it any more (but no less) than a blind and tone-deaf person to whom it had been read in a flat tone. Any *verbatim* transcription of an audio-tape necessarily omits many indications, verbal and non verbal, which an oral narration always provides. In the present case, the exact length and intensity of a pause begging for the listener's attention located where the script is interrupted by a first comma {,} sign; a middle finger pointing upward instead of the second {,} mark; an understanding or conniving smile instead of the third {,}; both hands used to designate who is talking to whom, which is nowhere indicated by any mark of any kind in the script, and laughter instead of a {.} at the very end. And yet it is thanks to these "omitted non verbal signifiers" that the orally emitted signifiers selected for script could truly acquire the particular meanings they were given by Mr. McGinty at the precise time they were orally delivered. This is why I slightly modified the written corresponding phrases and made them read:

You'll see, next time I do that *again* to you, you're going to go after me *for more*. You're going to love me real hard *then*."

"You'll see," is used to call the reader to attention. It replaces "And he said," which was used two sentences earlier to the same end. Here, the aim is simply to avoid repetition while keeping Mr. McGinty's pause. "I do that *again* to you" (versus the original "I *do that* to you"), is an attempt to incorporate into the "I do that to you," the unblushing middle finger gesture. "You are going to go after me *for more*" (instead of "you're gonna go after me"), together with "You are going to love me real hard *then*" (instead of "you're gonna love me real hard") is meant to make males readers smile as indicated by Mr. McGinty own laughter. This, in as much as male readers (listeners) are supposed to feel above those males who (like crow) believe that they make their female companions dependent solely through the corporeality of sex (and needless to add, through their own supposed physical prowess in this supposedly simple-minded body-game) without seeing that, from a female viewpoint, male/female permanent bonding comes from something a lot more complex, as the foggy woman episode clearly demonstrates).

Oral narration is furthermore syntactically less exacting than written communication. For instance, it is the storyteller's own laughter (and its timing) that makes the listener laugh, and the oral wording is made humorous from without so to speak. In contrast, written texts have to be more explicit with words and make the wording humorous from within, often through a reworking or chiseling of the speech syntax. However, this scriptural reworking only limits the greater indeterminacy of the written. Writing always appears as physical marks (the words are not in sounds which disappear as soon as they have been uttered but in series of indelible letters, or ideograms like in Chinese), which the reader must always animate in order to interpret. In the process, he commits himself to an unchanging and unchangeable version, which he will never feel as his own story; as a story that he has himself heard from someone else and is just passing along; and because of the latter point, as a story that he has committed to memory because as the story was not yet committed to writing, he felt the urge to retell it.

Moreover, as the marks operate in the absence of the writer, the reader can never be absolutely certain that he has rightfully interpreted the clusters of signs left for him to decipher from the paper on which they have been inked. Thus, while a written story may easily be acted out, it is much more hazardous to recount it as a personal experience with someone who had heard it from someone else, who had in turn heard it from a person who was there. As Goody (1987: 85) observed, indeed, the oral tradition is characterized by continual creation; it is the written that encourages repetition. If so, how do we re-enact *The Story of Crow* using its written version only as a firebrand? How do we recapture in it the permanent personal re-creation and recreation the oral fostered?

Mr. McGinty's own narrating practices may offer a key.

We have seen that he disliked translating *verbatim* from Tutchone into English and preferred to tape directly an adaptation he had already made for English speaking monolingual Tutchone. He was aware, that in his indigenous language version, plays on words were wittier than in his English adaptation. Yet, he must have realized that a linear translation (word for word, phrase for phrase) would have been terribly tedious. So many Tutchone terms and plays on words would have required explanations that the telling of the story would not have been a story told but an introduction to Athapaskan prosody, which, no matter how interesting, was not what he felt important or feasible for him to pass on. However, readers will have noticed that he never felt embarrassed to make full use of his acquaintance with the English language and certain traits of Anglo-Canadian culture to introduce new dimensions into the story.

The most impressive of these supplements occur in the episode dealing with the creation of the first women out of already existing men. One remembers that some males wanted to be turned into females. Crow brought back vaginas from a damp, half-flooded, and dark cave, which had so far forbidden its entrance to men. To place the vaginas in between these men's crotches to make them female, crow slid their penises through the vulva openings making their penises drop by themselves. He thus created, as Mr. McGinty has it in English now, the first "*free*-males." Obviously, this cultivated slip of the tongue based on the assonance between *fe*male and *free*-male was not and could not be made in Tutchone language. Yet this pun is more than simply amusing. It resonates with the beginning of the episode as the last movement of a symphony usually replies to the overture. Were not all males in this story said to be homosexuals before the creation of the first "*free*-males?"

Is it to say that males are not born free? That to be turned into female is for them the way to develop their full potential? Mr. McGinty does not say and even pretends to ignore why he always says "*free*-male" instead of "*fe*male." In fact, as any born storyteller he keeps his formulation compact, foregoing any psychological shading, probably because as Benjamin once observed ([1955], 1969: 91), there is nothing that commends a story to memory more effectively than the absence of the explanation the listener wants and expects and should be deliberately kept longing for. Talking too much as dogs do at the end of this episode condemns one to lose forever the capacity to speak! True enough, dogs will recover this ability if made too angry by human brutality. Yet there is nowhere in this an actual remedy! A dog too enraged to be trapped into having to argue back with words with a too callous master makes the latter pass away within -- a fact that has been undeniably witnessed by Tutchone in a few rare but enlightening instances (*scribitur ad narrandum, non ad probandum*).

Mr. McGinty's stage-whisper on the word "cunt" in the same episode is of a same nature. It could never have occurred in the Tutchone version in which *u druu* (her "cunt") cannot be fairly translated by either her "*cunt*" or, more reasonably, by her *vagina* or her *vulva* (Can a healthy excitement over this body part be really conveyed through gynecological terminology?). *U druu* is something closer to "her own endowments" -- the word *druu* having a charming import rather than importing the truly dark insinuations it has in English, or worse, in French, where *con* does not mean *druu* anymore to any contemporary French speaker but merely a stupid or unintelligent or absurd person. (This change of meaning in French seems to have taken place as early as the 1200's (See Robert, 1981, supplément)). Thus, *cunnus* in Latin, *coño* in Spanish, *con* in French, *cunt* in English, are restored to their probable original and descent meaning by a Tutchone who knew nothing of these root words and who did not know how to read or write.

The point for storytellers to come? Unlike Mr. McGinty they may have lost or never acquired a full command of Tutchone. However, after Mr. McGinty's opening of the path, these new storytellers could keep the Tutchone story alive in English if they are so inclined. And if they do so, their greater command of the idiom could be used to make the English tongue truly wag if put by them in crow's mouth. This could add further supplements to the story making it speak anew. Often innovations on the basis of new linguistic constraints consists in treating "accidental" or "external" relationships between new signifiers (sounds) as conceptual relationships in the old story (*fe*males as *free*-males, or *his* story as *his*tory). Better than explicit and straightforward cultural criticism, such puns command an emotional recognition of both overlaps and spacing between meanings, between cultures, and commit unforgettably to memory initially unwanted admissions of meaningful crisscrossing -- through the selection of signifiers with sounds so closely alike that their material similitude nearly cancel out their semantic (meaning) differences. Mr. McGinty's *freemale* oral pun is, in storytelling, equivalent to Derrida's graphical but neverthe-less meaningful pun on *différance* and *différence* in philosophy (Der-rida, 1986, 1968) and, ironically, supports Derrida's seemingly outra-geous *dictum* according to which the written "precedes" the oral (Der-rida, 1967: 65-95). So much for Marshall McLuhan who, in his world-famous *Gutenberg Galaxy* (1962), postulated a fundamental and irre-mediable difference between the *perception capacities* of "the illiterate oral primitive individual" and that of the "contemporary literate, typo-graphical and reading/writing man" when the actual difference was only between the oral and the written as distinct *systems* of communi-cation with the oral remaining dominant in the case of any individual even when the written competes for pre-eminence. Rereading McLuhan's text some 35 years after it has been published, one cannot help being struck by how much its generalizations on the "primitive" are "mostly unwarranted" (I choose these words out of politeness). Not only does McLuhan rely on writings which, as was usual in the fifties and earlier, denied coevalness between the then colonized and coloniz-ers, but he also stacks the cards so as to come up with what he wants his book to demonstrate. Had he lived and been able to truly socialize with such "unread 'primitive' persons"," say in Canada, in his own country, would he have changed his mind? If he had met with a per-sonality such as Mr. McGinty, one of his fellow citizens, would he have been so unconsciously ethnocentric?

Following in Mr. McGinty's footsteps, contemporary narrators should feel free to develop the connections they find between the con-cepts crow put forward at the dawn of time and how his seminal ideas have been evolved in the West -- existing bridges that Mr. McGinty and his own elders may have missed. New storytellers may also spin threads of some curious materials left over by crow to be woven again or rather anew. Why did he break the mother-in-law taboo? Why are laws constantly breached today? Why should there be taboos for Indi-ans and none for Whites? Or should there be some imposed on Whites and none on Indians? Or should there be none at all? The significant difficulty for today's narrators, and it is a challenging one, will be to structure the new critical observations they may want to make into true storytelling patterns -- lessons do not make stories; cutting a story fragment short from the moral it seems to imply does make a story.

Mr. McGinty's own narration patterns also indicate that his successors could see themselves as equally unfettered by the particular turns taken by events in this or that episode of this or that version. Consider his own 1984 and 1991 accounts of the foggy woman installment. In the first one, he underscores crow's lust for sex and downplays the bird's ravenous appetite for food to a point that the food theme is barely audible. In the second, he reverses the relative importance of the two motifs: crow's concern for eating is paramount whereas the idea of having sex scarcely comes into play. One should also ponder over the liberties this old narrator grants himself with the *"ho-hei"* section. In the 1984 rendering the central element is crow masquerading as a bear to steal fish grease, crow being punished for it by getting his bill stolen away and having "to sex" an old woman to get it back -- in it, the *"ho-hei"* motif appears as a very secondary and somehow disconnected frill, with no consequences for crow. In contrast, in the 1991 rendition, there is no bear, and no fish grease. The main theme is crow using phoney raft-men to mock people for using a signifier (*"ho-hei"*) with a signified which cannot be truly reworded through other signifiers/signifieds and whose meaning can only be deciphered through an *a contrario* experiment: the deceitful rafts. As a reward, crow gets his bill torn out of his face and has "to sex" the same old woman for it to be returned.

Another episode provides possibilities for a different kind of play within the same episode. In the segment dealing with the stealing of the sun from the trout, there is the presence of a muskrat woman. In the 1984 version, crow meets this woman at the very beginning of the story. He shows her what roots to eat and they happily live together. Then, the trout, which keeps the sun under water, steals crow's wife and makes her a slave. A frog woman lifts the water to show crow where his wife is. Crow discovers that she now lives under water. Similarly, he also uncovers the existence of the sun and of light. At the very end, after the woman is freed from the trout and the sun is stolen away, crow tells his wife that from now on there will be summer and winter and that she will have to dig burrows with underwater entrances for summer time, and mud and wood lodges on ice for winter. In contrast, in the 1991 variant crow first meets the frog woman. She shows crow what goes on under water. Crow sees a nice woman (his muskrat wife of the 1984 rendition) and the sun. He decides to free both. After he has done so, he instructs the rat woman what will constitute good food for her sort, but he does not tell anything about the two kinds of dwelling the rat will have to build every year. He then leaves for further travelling through his world.

Obviously, Mr. McGinty felt that there existed broad margins for telling this or that story. Will a written version now restrict the freedom he granted himself? It could but need not.

One should keep in mind that when an anthropologist commits several oral deliveries of the same story to paper, this medium imposed on him or her, the making of certain stylistic editorial choices between the various ways of phrasing offered by the narrator. For the written version, I elected to treat differences as complementary. As it is in the nature of a book to be written only once, it was for me the only way to pass along in one single written episode *all* the various themes which I knew surrounded this episode thanks to a plurality of oral versions given at different times by the same storyteller. However, as it is in the nature of storytellers to repeat stories, there is no need for them to weave together in each single narration all its various possible motifs. One day they may make such or such a theme pre-eminent and at another time reverse the order, or even modify the focuses, as Mr. McGinty did. Other options existed for the scribe I have been for Mr. McGinty. The two versions could have been published side by side, *verbatim*, with some editing to facilitate comprehension; but this would not have been the exercise in written storytelling Mr. McGinty and I intended the book to be. At any rate, the very existence of the possibility of having several different written versions should suggest, to those whom print keeps in awe, that, yes, there could be as many distinctive renditions of *The Story of Crow* as there are occasions to re-tell it to various audiences of listeners. Mr. McGinty's flexible narrative practice certainly makes this a viable option.

The written, which in the eyes of readers necessarily confers to a story a fixed beginning, middle and end, and which maintain this order for each reader, also hides the fact that oral communication need not follow this pattern. In my experience, a Tutchone storyteller almost never narrates *The Story of Crow* in its entirety. Most often story time is limited to one or two episodes picked from anywhere in the so-called cycle. Sometimes, but more rarely, it is expanded to three or four, without the narrator explaining his selection. In addition, even on the very unusual occasion of a full narration the story may be started at almost any point. This, I both witnessed and had confirmed by Mr. McGinty. The following *verbatim* transcript of a dialogue between the narrator and me, bears witness. The tape-recorder was switched on after a long conversation (not-taped) on how the episodes should follow each other in the book. The title refers to the tape. In the first entry, for recording purpose, I briefly dictate in the microphone what we had been talking about earlier.

T. McGINTY - LEGROS. JAN 10TH, 1991. # 1/3. CROW STORY. *SIDE A: T. McGINTY -- LEGROS JAN 10, 1991. CROW STORY*

LEGROS: January nine, nineteen ninety-one. Tommy McGinty and Dominique. Tommy was telling me not the whole story, but how it worked that story.

McGINTY: Yeah.

LEGROS: So you say, when does it start that story with crow?

McGINTY: Huh?

LEGROS: Crow story, where you want to make it start? Where? When the old timers they tell that story where they start then?

McGINTY: They start from any place: from the middle.

LEGROS: Uh-huh.

McGINTY: And after some other time he, he all, they all join em up [them episodes].

LEGROS: Ah, O.K. But you O.K. [with] that, now you would like to start it when he [crow] got his [fancy and colorful] blanket there, you told me, huh? [This refers to the fifth episode in his 1984 version and in the written one: *Crow throws his old blanket away*]

McGINTY: Yeah, from that blanket, something like that, can start from there.

LEGROS: O.K. so, O.K. Go ahead start as you just told me. What happened with this blanket first?

McGINTY: Where he killed that fish? [Refers to the "sucker-fish," episode 8 in the 1984 and the written version].

LEGROS: Uh-huh.

McGINTY: And from there then you [we] gonna start all over again.

LEGROS: He go inside that FISH? [Legros' reaction of surprise, a bit late, to Mr. McGinty placing the "suckerfish" segment right after the "blanket" section]

McGINTY: [pondering] He go inside the fish... [Change topic and starting the whole story with the blanket episode] Crow there he he walkin along on the shore.. on.. around ocean. (And [that was] after, ah, after he made everything; [after] he made ah, he made, he made the river, and made everything fish, everything I guess [the whole aside in regular parenthesis refers to the first four episodes in the written version: (1) *The world is flooded but crow saves his life*; (2) *Crow builds the world anew*; (3) *An osprey does not want to share water*; (4) *A second flood comes*]). [Crow] he walk, he walk on-on along there, he found, he found a blanket [Mr. McGinty then proceeds with the narration of the episode of crow's blanket].

Naturally, this led Mr. McGinty into a special sequencing in his 1991 version. Next page, a table indicates the result. The left-hand column is a list of all the known episodes of the story in the order they appear in the written version. Except for two special episodes, which have not been included in the present book deliberately but for reasons to be explained a few pages below, the list order was based on the two taped versions and of further information provided by Mr. McGinty. The second column gives the order in which the episodes were narrated in the 1984 rendition; the third, the episodes told in the 1991 version and in what progression; the fourth, the episodes as they follow each other in the written version. This table highlights several interesting aspects of storytelling.

A narrator may truly start in the middle of a given story. In such a case, its beginning may be told at the end as Mr. McGinty does

VARIOUS SEQUENCING

MR. McGINTY'S CROW STORY

Episodes	1984	1991	Written
The world is flooded, but crow saves his life	1	18*	1
Crow rebuilds the world anew	2	19*	2
An osprey does not want to share water	3	20*	3
A second flood comes	absent	21*	4
Crow throws his old blanket away	5	1	5
Crow wishes something he doesn't want	6	5**	6
Crow marries a good woman	7	3	7
Inside a suckerfish	8	2	8
Crow meets the otter people	9	4	9
Crow steals the sun from the lake trout	10	6	10
The first matches	11	7***	11
The birds get painted by crow	absent	8***	12
Eyeball, watchman and playing ball	13	9	13
Ho-hei, ho-hei, ho-hei, ho-hei	14	10	14
A jealous gopher	15	11	15
Who's the oldest one in the world?	16	absent	16
A cannibal horsefly-man	17	13	17
Crow makes the first women	18	14	18
Moose, caribou, sheep and goat	19	15	19
Crow's mother-in-law	absent	16	20
Indians get to be too many for crow	absent	17	21
Crow makes mosquitoes to keep people busy	absent	absent	?
Crow kills the devil (always treated as a separate story, not belonging to the so-called cycle)			

* Narrated at the end of the story with Mr. McGinty clearly stating that it is the beginning of the sequence of crow's stories.

** Narrated in position 5 but with narrator indicating that he made a mistake and that this episode should come right after the "sucker" episode.

*** Narrated one day after the end of the story because Mr. McGinty remembered that he missed this episode. *Post-facto* insert in the sequence as indicated by Mr. McGinty.

in the 1991 column (episodes 1,2,3 in 1984 are told in position 18,19,20 in 1991). The storyteller simply informs his audience that what he tells at the end occurred before the event with which he started the narration. Is it to say that there is a known fixed chronological order for crow's deeds, irrespective of how these feats succeed each other in each actual narration? Not quite. A close look at the differences between the 1984 and 1991 versions reveals that a storyteller allows himself not only to start anywhere in the story but also to rearrange the chronological order of crow's deeds.

This becomes evident when the succession of the first five episodes of the 1991 version is compared to the progression of the same episodes in the 1984 rendition.

EPISODES	1984	1991
Crow throws his old blanket away	5=1	1 =1
Crow wishes something he doesn't want	6=2	5* =3
Crow marries a good woman	7=3	3 =4
Inside a suckerfish	8=4	2 =2
Crow meets the otter people	9=5	4 =5
* Narrated in position 5 but with narrator indicating that he made a mistake and that this episode should come right after the "suckerfish" episode which in 1991 was in position 2		

In the table, for each of the versions the left-hand number is the actual position in the cycle and the right-hand number the order in which the episodes would have been told if both versions had begun with the blanket segment. From top to bottom, the 1984 right-hand column reads 1, 2, 3, 4, 5. Each number represents one of crow's stories and the sequence 1➔ 2➔ 3➔ 4➔ 5, the chronological order in which the events corresponding to these stories are supposed to have occurred in crow's time. Now, when we read from top to bottom the corresponding 1991 right-hand column (1➔ 3➔ 4➔ 2➔ 5) we see that a storyteller of Mr. McGinty's stature has no qualms about re-ordering, from narration to narration, the chronological sequence of crow's feats. In the 1991 chronology of crow's doings, event 3 comes in second position; event 4, in third position; event 2, in fourth position. Deeds 1 and 5 are the only ones remaining in the same locations as in 1984.

For discussion purposes, the 1984 sequence might tend to appear as the norm. This is reinforced by the order given in the written rendition. However, all this is artificial. For the narrative order of the written version, I chose the chronological order given in the 1984 version. Had I heard the 1991 version first, its narrative order -- 1, 3, 4, 2, 5 (1991 right-hand column) -- would have been assigned the chronological numbers 1➔ 2➔ 3➔ 4➔ 5, and as a result the 1984 version's chronological order, the sequence 1➔ 4➔ 2➔ 3➔ 5. Other data confirm the possibility of such rearrangement. For instance, Stanley Jonathan, another great storyteller from Pelly, tells the *Birds painted by crow* episode before the *First matches* whereas Mr. McGinty, when he does not omit these two sections (see above the *** note and no. 12 absent in 1984 in VARIOUS SEQUENCING IN MR. McGINTY'S CROW STORY), narrates them in Mr. Jonathan's reverse order.

The consequence for today's storytellers is clear. The exact narrative order given to the episodes in the written version should not be regarded as a fixed chronological norm. In fact, this version presents a danger for them. Ink marks stay forever, cannot truly be erased, and will tend to confer to the sequencing of the episodes in the written version, the allure of a standard chronology, whereas the practice of a traditional storyteller shows that no such precisely fixed order should exist.

Perhaps this is related to the nature of the oral medium? Sounds disappear as soon as they are emitted and may be forgotten. Precise sequencing disappears too. Orally transmitted stories long to be retold, less they disappear altogether. Perhaps is it better to re-iterate them, in whichever manner, than to be paralyzed by the belief in a past strict norm and the will to recapture this "perfect" version before speaking up.

Which brings up the question of whether there may ever have been a perfect version? In this respect, the table of Mr. McGinty's various ways of sequencing of the full story is enlightening. In each oral narration he omitted one or several episodes. To the listener that

I was, it did not feel as if he was forgetting something, but rather that some of crow's deeds did not call upon him to be told and to be given an outside life by his lips on the particular day he offered this or that narration. Given that other storytellers do the same, it seems safe to assume that any actual narration is always incomplete and has always been so in the past. If we shift focus from the number of events in each actual narration to the total number of crow's distinct doings as represented by the sum of all the instances this story was narrated, it seems that there should logically exist a finite number of distinct episodes and that their addition should constitute the "final version." Perhaps, but it is not so simple.

To start with, in Pelly Crossing several narrators know and tell a long episode describing how crow killed an evil being (*tsekänzraw*), whose teeth can now be found in the skull of any salmon. However, they always tell this story as a separate episode and never seek to integrate this segment into the main cycle. For this reason, it has not been included in the present written rendition of the narrative but reserved for subsequent publications of other Tutchone stories.[6] This editing choice is also an attempt to reproduce within the written universe, the separation that the oral makes between the main story and this particular feat. Second, one may believe that after hearing several different narrations of the story, one has heard all crow's original deeds. But surprises still may occur. For example, years after Mr. McGinty's 1984 version and months after his 1991 rendition, I was walking alone in the bush with the narrator. At one point I complained about the presence of too many mosquitoes eating us up alive. Instead of empathy I was asked to shut up:

"Crow has made mosquitoes for our own good!"

"What do you mean, uncle?" I asked.

---

[6] *This episode does not seem to be a recent elaboration made in reaction to the motif of the devil among Christians. On the contrary, its details strongly suggest an Athapaskan origin -- or at least a non-Christian origin.*

"Well, at some point people were getting very lazy; crow saw that and made mosquitoes to keep men and women exercising, hitting one bug here with this hand and this other one there with that hand, and so on -- ever since, it sure has kept people busy when summertime comes."

Is this singular "crow story" ancient? Did Mr. McGinty make it up? Thus far, it is impossible to answer for this is all I ever heard of it. Should future storytellers recapture its details from other narrators? In case Mr. McGinty put the broad outline of this story forward only as a seminal idea to be further developed, should they project themselves back into the past to elucidate its possible plot? Either way... Why not? The little Mr. McGinty said about it hints at what crow could very well have done.

Let us assume that this admittedly arguable strategy provides a convincing solution for the "mosquitoes" episode. Would it put an end to the question of whether a given version is finally exhaustive? Most likely not, for it is by definition in the nature of oral cultures never to commit the knowledge of each of its individuals to a common repository. Thus, having heard many storytellers will neither guarantee that all storytellers have been heard nor that each has been fully heard; that there is not close by, or further away, in another village, a woman or a man who is tortured by some yet untold components of crow's saga begging to be heard at last too. And should all possible episodes of the story be discovered through some miracle, there would remain the question of where the singular events thus far unknown to oneself fit into one's habitual sequencing of the story.

Ann Chowning (1962) who has studied many versions of the so-called "crow cycle" states that in fact this story is not a real cycle. The Tutchone rendition, which was unknown to her, certainly supports her contention. We have seen that the same narrator may invert elements within the same episode as well as re-arrange the succession of the episodes from narration to narration. Furthermore, the same narrator may omit some episodes in one narration and re-insert them in the next. He or she may also start anywhere in the story and disclose its beginning only at the end of his narration. Finally, whatever his version of the "whole story" may be, he will almost never expose his listeners to it entirely in one single narration.

To some, this may be the result of acculturation. In this perspective, Mr. McGinty could simply never have been confronted by a full and exhaustive narrative, which must have existed in the past. Yet again nothing is so certain. In the 1920's, during his youth, long versions definitely existed. Thus, the single archival document I know of which discusses storytelling reports the following for the year 1927:

> Their story of the creation is both weird and lengthy. It took four long evenings in front of a flickering campfire before an old man finished telling the story (Stringer, 1928).

This is reported by an Anglican missionary. The event occurred at Dalton Post among the Southern Tutchone. But there is no reason to believe that Copper Joe, the old man who raised Mr. McGinty and who was born in the 1850's knew any less. And if Mr. McGinty felt free to vary his own account of the story, who is to assume that his grandpa Copper Joe did not do the same thing in relation to the various versions he got from his own elders? In fact, the family context of storytelling-time among these hunters invites storytellers to constantly adjust and readjust the narrative, rather than to repeat it *verbatim*, as one heard it from someone else. And this is so for the single reason that one always hears and learns it from different narrators rather than from one single source. As Mr. Stanley Jonathan, another very knowledgeable narrator, explained to me once:

> Marriage makes men move around quite a bit [residence is matrilocal]. So in any camp there are some men who come from different places and tell the same story in different ways. To know the true story you have to listen to everybody and put the pieces back together. This is what I did when I was young. I always sat by old stumps [old men] and listened to all of them and that is why I now know how to tell their stories the right way.

Mr. Stanley Jonathan is the man who narrates the painting of the birds (no. 11) before the making of the first matches (no. 10). And there is no reason to assume that in 1900, in 1870, in 1850, in 1830, etc., the situation was any different. Then, like in the 1920's, several individual renditions must have been in circulation. Then, men like Copper Joe (one of the sons of the White River Copper Chief of the 19th century) or Chief Big Jonathan (Stanley Jonathan's father) must have been exposed to the same story in different ways and must have put it back together for themselves, each one doing it slightly differently from the other one, just like Mr. McGinty and Mr. Jonathan have done in their own generation, modifying in different directions either Copper Joe's or Big Jonathan's own personal renditions and resolving in their own way apparent contradictions between the various versions they have heard.

In a way, Mr. McGinty and Mr. Jonathan faced a situation not entirely different from that of contemporary students of the Bible. Earlier, we have noted that modern Christian scholars translate *Genesis* as containing two different stories of the creation of the first human beings. First both male and female are said to have been created at the same time. In the second story a male is first created and then a woman is made out of one of his ribs. Yet, Everett Fox's reading of the Hebrew wording (1983: 18-19) makes it possible to suggest that the first being created may have been androgynous, each individual being both male and female, and that the second story of creation may have been about dividing maleness and femaleness between two different individuals. As Fox indicates, the Hebrew word usually translated as rib might also be read as "side."

For us the point is not to decide which translation is best but to realize the quandary we would be left with should the two translations be regarded as equally authoritative. We would then be in a dilemma similar to that faced by Mr. McGinty and Mr. Jonathan during their own sacred text apprenticeship, in which different narrations like Mr. Copper Joe's and Mr. Big Jonathan's, told different renditions of the same story

At this juncture, a modest aside is in order. If an oral text may be and is regularly transformed in such a manner, it might be illusory to attempt to derive its deeper meaning for the people it belongs to, from the precise sequence of its episodes *at a given time among a given people* -- a thought entertained by the structuralist school of thought. The problem with deriving the meaning of a myth from a written version giving a fixed sequence to its episodes is manifold. First, the best narrators do not seem to attach too much importance to a fixed sequence and may change the order of some of the episodes from one narration to the next. Second, at any given time, one narrator exposes his/her audience to only short portions of the whole story without necessarily indicating how the various portions told at various times fit with each other. Third and last, different narrators *in the same culture at the same time* may somehow order episodes in different ways, skip some in one version, collapse two in one single different story at another. The main point is that the audience is never receiving a whole script, or the same partial scripts from the same narrator and, even more so from different narrators. Thus, the meaning the audience derives from the variety of what the audience *hears* must be different from what it would conclude were it compelled to *read* a single fixed written version over and over again, from a fixed beginning, an immovable ending, and a stable middle part.

When there is no print communication whatsoever, the oral keeps its audiences exposed to gaps between all existing versions. It thus invites listeners to re-create what must have been "the true original story." In this game, what matters is not whether there ever was "a single true account," but that the unavoidable divergence between narrators gives listeners good grounds for believing each narrator is at least a little wrong. In itself this is sufficient to encourage each future narrator to "restore the truth," and, ultimately, to re-create and thus create by increments. And as each new "restoration" may diverge in its details from the last, there are always enough differences left at any given time to keep the process of creating and re-creating going on forever. In contrast, when the oral coexists with the written, the printed "performance" remains, is allowed to grow old and to be transformed into a canon against which every oral "text" must measure itself. When such a time comes, the search for an original but lost truth loses its *raison d'être* and stultified becomes the desire to re-create the story from memory so as to recreate an audience. Storytelling gives way to acting out set written stories or visible performable texts as Dennis Tedlock (1983) calls his transcriptions of the ephemeral oral performances he has heard and seen.

Now this does not mean that I have no feelings of admiration for this brilliant writer and poet. In fact I like his performable texts very much. But I do not think that this kind of literary product would be a better means to keep the art of storytelling from memory alive and fun among a people like the Tutchone. In fact, and I hope he will forgive me for being so critical on this score (but on this score alone), my hunch is that it might kill it for reasons which must now be clear to everybody. Tedlock might become a towering figure of twentieth century literature, but for different reasons. He worked very hard and took native American oral literature so seriously that as a poet he has been able to transpose most of its way of structuring the audible telling of stories into a written literary product that previously existed neither in the Western world nor among the people who produce only a variety of audible performances. In effect he has successfully created a new literary genre as other writers did, a few centuries earlier, when they invented a new way of telling a story which has come to be called the novel -- and this new genre is the performable text. But the performable text as a genre is independent from the native audible performances that have allowed its inception as a new writing/reading genre. For example, Tedlock's own scholarly conferences, such as the one on Derrida and logocentrism, have been written, read and published as performable texts (Tedlock, 1983: 247-260). Tedlock is quite aware of his breaking away from the Western written tradition, "from the established trajectory, of the whole dictation era... all the way back to the making of the Homeric texts" and he is thankful to his First Nation friends who have helped him make the move. But to perform in writing for audible reading and in audible reading for writing is not to perform in telling from memory, as Benjamin rightly points out. Tedlock knows this and recommends that future storytellers depart from his written performances (1978: xii) and work with tapes of audible performance (1983: 5-6) rather than with his written performable versions. To fully grasp the inevitable authorship of the one signing a performable text an analogy might be useful. Short of attendance at performances, a videotape of a Tutchone elder's narration would probably be the best medium for learning how to tell stories in a certain style -- a video is much more informative on non-linguistic signs than Tedlock's audio-tapes. Now watching one continuous tape of such a narrator is normally extremely boring, even when some of the shots are focused on the audience. The live-group context is gone, and you are not where and when the story was told. To make such a video interesting to look at on a VCR and worth buying one would have to edit the footage in a radical way so as to make it swing, so to speak. Well, when Tedlock writes a performable text, this is exactly what he does inflict to the oral performance he has previously taped, and he does so with such great talent that one is charmed into taking the written for the oral. But gone is the narrator taking a full minute to spit out a mouthful of black tobacco juice and debris into his tin can spittoon while deliberately making you wait for what is coming up in the story. No matter what, when you transform an audible text (a tape or a video) from a man like Mr. McGinty into some visible written text or some sort of palatable audio-visual medium, whatever the kind or genre of text or video, you ineluctably have to make of this live narrator's material means of communication a different means of communing or you'll never sell.

Is this to admit that Mr. McGinty's and my own writing project might forever kill the kind of creativity which was bound to oral storytelling when no other means of communication existed? There is this danger, but it certainly can be averted. One should keep in mind that the form given to the written story of crow is not the product of a Tutchone but that of an anthropologist from France, who had to put pieces of the story back together to make it a single whole, who, to do so, chose certain options, and who in the process must have made some inadequate choices here and there, or at least some editorial decisions a Tutchone elder might not have made. Thus, between Mr. McGinty's various oral versions, Mr. Stanley Jonathan's existing account, between Copper Joe's and Chief Big Jonathan's renditions, and finally the written version, there must remain enough question marks to keep storytellers spinning and weaving the truth back into the story.

To keep this old oral art going on, I deliberately want the reader to feel off balance with the written, not convinced by its seeming completeness and neat ordering.

My synthetic written version is as much a new telling of the story as Mr. McGinty's, Mr. Jonathan's, Mr. Copper Joe's, and Mr. Big Jonathan's various ones. And if these versions from the Central Yukon Territory were found to be too homogeneous in spite of their differences, would-be storytellers might remember that crow's deeds have been chronicled by other aboriginal peoples, by various peoples from Eastern Siberia, Alaska, the Northwest Territories and the northern parts of the Western Canadian provinces. What these peoples have retained from crow's dealings in the early world diverges sufficiently for them to experience the same riddles and challenge Mr. Stanley Jonathan or Mr. McGinty felt at hearing their elders' departing versions in the 1920's, in and around Fort Selkirk.

Let us give an example. There exists another interesting version of the Tutchone *"ho-hei"* episode, which was published by the *Journal of American Folk-Lore* in 1900. Unfortunately, my source (Erdoes and Ortiz (Eds.), 1984: 346) does not indicate from what precise Northern Athapaskan group it came from and I have been unable to locate a copy of the issue of the journal it comes from. Yet it is worth quoting in detail to show how themes are maintained over time and space as well as how thematic fragments can be reshuffled between episodes when the whole narrative is told by different peoples. Here follows the 1900 version provided by Erdoes and Ortiz – a version coming from the North but I do not know yet where from.

> Raven was always cheating the people, so they finally took his beak away from him. After a time he went up the river and made a raft, which he loaded with moss. Floating down to the camps on it, he told the people that his head was sore where his beak had been torn off, and that he was lying in the moss to cool it. Then he went back upriver and made several more rafts. When the people saw these floating down toward them, they thought that a large group of warriors was coming to help Raven regain his beak. They held a council and decided to send a young girl to take the beak to an old woman who lived alone at some distance from the camp. Raven, who had concealed himself among them and heard the council's plan, waited until the girl came back. Then he went to the old woman and told her that the girl wanted

her to return the beak to him. Suspecting nothing, the old woman gave him his beak. He put it on and flew away, cawing with pleasure at his success. The warriors who had been on the rafts proved to be nothing but the tufts or hummocks of bog moss which are commonly known as *têtes de femmes* (women's heads).

By this example I do mean to concur with T. S. Eliot:

Tradition cannot be inherited, and if you want it you must obtain it by great labour.

Searching for other accounts of crow's deeds from beyond the Central Yukon Territory should be part of it.

7. Mr. McGINTY'S LIFE: IN BETWEEN AGENCY AND CONTINGENCY

This is my refusal to bring about any appearance of closure, and much less closure itself! Because this brings me to who Mr. McGinty was -- not a hunter turned into a rationalist or enlightened scholar, nor a shaman turned into a Christian or a Christian with some shamanistic inclinations, but rather, simultaneously and equally, a family man, a hunter and trapper, an inventive tinker, a faithful thinker, and an inclusive visionary. I know most of what follows from what Mr. McGinty told me and some of it from others.

Some twenty years before his birth in the late 1910's, there was one old man named Copper Joe. He was a powerful shaman born in the 1850's. This old man had been born to Copper Chief, head of the 19th century *Tzän* (muskrat) Northern Tutchone, in the surroundings of upper White River. After a dispute with one of his four brothers, Copper Joe moved to Aishihik Lake where he married. After his first wife died, he moved from Aishihik to Fort Selkirk where he married his second wife, Alice. Alice was Mr. McGinty's maternal grandmother.

Earlier than that, our storyteller's family history has to remain shrouded in mystery. Tutchone had individual Athapaskan names. When people were alive, these were known to everyone. But they were never used to address people or to refer to them. It was "bad luck" to do so -- "bad luck" for the individual voicing the name and for the bearer of the name uttered. Where upon, when death took away Mr. McGinty's older ancestors, men and women, it also took along their knowledge of the names of who was who in the early days. With this information lost, also gone are the traces of who, among the 19th century Tutchone, eventually branched off into Mr. McGinty, and later into his own family.

After the Klondike gold rush period (1898), all Tutchone took an English name in addition to their secret Indian names -- usually the name of White neighbor or friend. Voicing English names not being dangerous, these have been passed along openly ever since, matrilineally very early on (this is why there has been for example an Indian named Peter *Alice* in the Yukon) and later on patrilineally. So, neither Mr. McGinty's grandmother's Indian name, nor who brought her into this world, will ever be known. The only story that can be told is what comes after English names *trivialized naming* like many other things and relations.

Copper Joe met this Alice when he may have been in his fifties. Alice already had one grown up daughter named Suzie and maybe some other children. Some years after the marriage, Alice died. Mr. Copper Joe who survived her was given to his stepdaughter Suzie as a husband for her to "upkeep" and also to "learn from." Suzie was already the mother of a girl who, eventually, was to become the Ellen Silverfox I met in the 1970's and Johnny Mack's last wife. The memory of who Ellen Silverfox's father was has been either lost or kept secret.

Ellen's mother, Suzie, was in her twenties at the time Mr. Copper Joe was given to her. She was then about forty years younger than her husband was. Full of life, she took a Whiteman as a second and additional husband. Some say that this Whiteman was an Northwest Mounted Police local officer; others remember him as the local trading-post keeper. Could he have been in the police before retiring as a store manager?

Whatever the case, Suzie was pregnant twice between 1918 and the 1920's, first with Mr. Tommy McGinty, second with Harry

McGinty. Mr. Copper Joe saw that Suzie's children could not be his. He even nicknamed the second one with an Indian expression meaning "the fake one." But he accepted them anyway. The same cannot be said of his White co-husband. Polyandry, the marriage of one woman to several men, was beyond this Whiteman's understanding. He neither recognized Tommy nor Harry, never provided for them, and eventually left the Yukon when both children were still young, never to see them again nor to seek to know what had become of them. Hence, who were Mr. McGinty's earlier White ancestors on his father side will never be known either, but for somewhat different and darker reasons.

After some time, Peter McGinty was given to Suzie as a new and younger husband. Peter McGinty was the head of the wolf side for the Fort Selkirk group. His English last name was passed on to Tommy. As at this time Mr. Copper Joe was to find himself without a wife, he was given in marriage to his step granddaughter Ellen. The two of them had two children who died as infants. Later on, Ellen would take Pelly Jim, also known as Jimmy Silverfox, as a new husband and thus became Mrs. Ellen Silverfox. Mr. Copper Joe never remarried and lived alone to a very old age; some swear up to one hundred year old. He died in the late forties' or early fifties'.

Suzie and Peter McGinty who were still young found the young Tommy McGinty too difficult a child to handle. Mr. Copper Joe offered to take the child from the police officer (or was it from the store keeper) over, back with him. Suzie and her new McGinty husband agreed.

According to Mr. McGinty, Old man Copper was full of all kinds of tricks. He even knew ways to raise dogs which would never touch meat, even if left unattended to protect a moose carcass from grizzlies, even if terribly hungry. Old Copper Joe had answers in the form of stories for nearly every question the young Tommy asked and he told unasked stories to make the eager little boy think and raise more questions. With him, young Tommy slowly quieted down... And the animals roaming the bush around Grayling Lake -- Old man Copper Joe's hunting ground -- saw a young Tommy McGinty growing up into a Tutchone hunter. The animals readily saw that he was raised, trained, and thoroughly educated by one of the oldest elders living around Fort

Selkirk; he was raised into a Tutchone who learned from this old, old man, what it meant to animals to be respected. In return, they, the animals, kept showing themselves to him as food-animal to kill and eat, and he kept his killings respectful, shooting only what he and Copper Joe needed. The old man even taught him the "high Tutchone language" that pleased animals. At the time of his death, Mr. McGinty was the last one to know it and to have mastered the rhetoric of euphemism it rested on. But English, the language of his male genitor, he never spoke before his twenties', working as a deck-hand on Yukon River steamboats, and he never quite mastered it. What would it have been like for him, if the trading post manager (or was it a police officer?) had recognized him and taken him away to be raised down South? Would he have become a Whiteman? Sure! Yes! And would it have been the happiest of all possible options?

For he certainly was turned into a Tutchone. Old Copper Joe had him go through the ordeal of the old puberty rite of passage for boys. At the time, this ritual had been abandoned a long time ago by everyone. No one still had the guts to impose on any young male Tutchone the physical and mental prowess it called for. It was an exacting preparation for both war and hunting. But it was a preparation for war first, even though the last one heard of was a faraway First World War fought somewhere in the "Old Countries."

Early on, young Tommy McGinty's dreams were also visited by unasked visitors: the *zhäak*, the special poise or aplomb of many animals. And, on many occasions these spirits woke him up, made him tremble and he even entered into trances. Yet he came to expect these unannounced visitors. They were not harmful. Through his throat and lips they blew songs he had never heard and never learned -- songs which healed the lame, the crippled, and the sick. Even the mind-spirit of Jesus, his *zhäak*, came unasked to visit him in between those of his animal would-be helpers. Why these came to him and not to others? He never found out. But he kept the secret and because he did, secretly they kept visiting his dreams, giving him the power to be.

When Mr. McGinty was at rest with himself, stories came to him to be told and he told them to amuse you for a day. But if you happened to madden him like I did a few times, you felt as if you were under the gaze of an eagle musing about how to snatch you away in one single stroke. Yet... yet... he only circled above you -- making seemingly vicious, long, never-ending arcs within arcs. He never had to dive. Well before, you understood where he stood, against your kind of thinking, and why. Where did his aptitude come from? Old Copper Joe never told.

Mr. McGinty's adult life started on a bad note. He married a Little Salmon Indian woman. Soon it had to be over. Some witchcraft man made her wither away, as well as the wolf child Mr. McGinty had given her...(obviously she was a wolf and her child had to be so). Mr. McGinty dug a grave with a shovel and buried both himself. He cried, he cried, he did not understand. He searched through his own mind... He searched and found out who the jealous "witchcraft man" was. But when he did, he simply left to return to Fort Selkirk, never to tell who did the awful deed. Back in his home-village, soon enough he met Annie, a very young McMillan River wolf woman. He suddenly wanted to be given to her in marriage. He had seen her before, when she was a child and him already a young man. He had seen her every spring when her parents rafted down the McMillan and Pelly rivers to come to Fort Selkirk to sell their furs and buy some tea, sugar, flour, and ammunition with the money they made. He had seen her but he had never paid attention. Now she was a beauty, acted as a beauty. To this day, she still knows she commands what beauty inspires. And him, the circling eagle, for once dived. Her old folks gave him to their daughter and in return he gave her, her mother and her mother's brothers four wolf children for their side. Four children to whom he became very much attached!

And this was a soft side in this strong man or rather the proof that real strength goes together with sensitivity "Wait!" he was telling me when my daughter Leïla was on the way in 1991.

Wait... and you'll see, you'll lose your mind over the baby. Me, I got crazy with my first-born. I would go moose hunting, and not an hour had passed that I was already being missing my little girl, my Lucy. I would run back to camp to kiss her... smell her all over. Then, I would go back in the bush to kill something to eat for the family. Wait... and see what happens to you. Girls are worth ten times as much as boys. Girls help you all your life; boys get married away to help their wives' old folks...

And Eva Billy (a crow woman from the Northern Tutchone Little Salmon First Nation, a member of my own crow side, and the widow of an old wolf moiety friend and ethnographic collaborator from the 1970's), who visited us in Pelly Crossing gave to Leïla, my unborn wolf moiety daughter, the name of *Tsäntch'ia*, "the cute one." Before Leïla, *Tsäntch'ia* had lived in the Little Salmon area. She had died from tuberculosis in the 1930's. But there, sixty years later, on the side of a hill near Little Salmon village, her grave-house was still very well maintained. It was a small house all right -- a bit more than the width and the length of a coffin and about five feet high. But through the grave-house small glass windows, you could still see resting on the ground under which she was lying a small bottle of "Chanel" perfume she had bought through a catalogue before she died -- a bottle that her relatives had placed there in the 30's for her to keep enjoying in her future life after death.

In 1991, after Leïla's birth, it took three attempts and as many complaints to get Leïla's *Tsäntch'ia* Indian name correctly typed in her Yukon Government birth certificate. Even with sophisticated computers, print technology keeps denying coevalness in naming one's own children. As a result, in the mid 1980's, only half of the Northern Tutchone had an Indian name (mainly the older people) and even this one half did not have it as their legal name (Anonymous Report, no date: 30).

Mr. McGinty never could understand Canadian hunting laws. How could you and your family live on bull moose alone as the law used to be and not kill some moose cows too? Moreover, how could you feed your people on *one single* bull moose a year as the Federal Government tried to impose it in the 1950's? Once, he argued the point with a game warden:

> You, Whiteman, know about farm animals fine. One bull and forty or fifty cows and it works. All them damned cows want to be fucked by that one bull. But you know nothing about wild animals. They are like people. And you, game warden you may be, but if you want to fuck tonight, you think the first Indian or

White woman you gonna ask to, you gonna get her. Forget it! And wild moose cows are the same as people's women. Me here, I have seen it myself with my own eyes. When a cow moose wants this guy she takes him. When she does not like him, she runs away into thick bush and the bull get stuck; his horns are so wide that there is no way for him to follow her inside there. So, if I always kill bull moose, some moose women are gonna find no man to fuck them. So when I see a cow moose with no husband I kill her, and if I kill her, I kill her calf too, because he can't live without her. To kill just bull moose and on top of that just on single bull moose a year is good but just for the White hunter. He's got cows to back him up. Indians have got nothing like that.

And Mr. McGinty was a butcher too, a fast one. He had killed so many animals in his life that the inside pouches, glands, muscles, tissues, and bone structures had no secret for him. He could finish the gutting and quartering of a big moose in less than an hour, way before the muscles of the dead animal had stopped trembling and jiggling by themselves, on their own, agitated by the uncontrollable spasms that linger on after death.

Mr. McGinty and Annie, his wife, came to hate Canadian schooling laws. But in the end they had no choice, and lost their children's education to the missionaries of the Anglican Church. This was the most trying moment of their lives. They often cried. But they also survived. They learned to numb their pain into dead-drunkenness. Ten years before his death, before the *zhäak* of Jesus visited his dreams again, but unasked for, Mr. McGinty was still washing down a bottle of whisky a day, when the money was there, that is. Had not it been for Jesus' *zhäak*, a word best translated as animal poise or aplomb, which came to him one night while he was "night-thinking," he would have kept drinking until his very end.

Still, there were not many things this old storyteller could not do. For he was born an inventor. After seeing his first water planes in the thirties, he revolutionized Tutchone water transportation. He observed the planes' floating technique and used it to construct a faster raft, which he called an airplane raft. Instead of the traditional 15 to 20 logs side by side, he constructed a single big log with two other parallel logs used as floats and mounted on a cross-piece to keep the center log steady. He also invented a special mechanism for catching wolverines, an animal notoriously known to be almost impossible to capture. Caught in a steel trap, it chews its trapped leg off and walks away on three feet. Wolverines are also known to torment people. They eat their food caches. What they cannot eat or take away, they pee on. It smells so bad that no one, not even a wolverine, can ever eat it. Once a mean wolverine came, unasked, into Mr. McGinty's life. For three years, it spoiled all his catches. For three years, he set more and more ingenious traps. All in vain! The few times the wolverine was fooled, it got away, once abandoning a whole foot, at another time a foot and the lower part of its leg, once a half a foot. Finally, Tommy thought through a more complicated plot. The wolverine would be baited into crawling inside a steel stove-pipe out of which it would be impossible to backtrack. One night, the stove-pipe-trap caught something. In the morning, Mr. McGinty looked inside. It was a wolverine all right and it had frozen to death. He pulled the corpse out. It was missing three of its feet. Mr. McGinty had seen one-foot-three-stump tracks for two winters in a row and right then he knew that he had caught the right beast. His hunting and trapping miseries ended.

Was Mr. McGinty living in the same world as other Canadians? From his life story we have to concede that he probably did not... Surely not!

For all kinds of stories from a different space kept coming to be told through his mouth:

Crow's story, but also the beaver man's;

The story of a giant man a hundred feet high;

Stories from the time huge snakes lived in the North;

Stories from the time cannibals came to the Yukon to eat Tutchone;

Stories of girls stolen by Beaver Indians and made slaves;

Stories of Beaver Indian slave girls escaping back to the Tutchone;

Women stolen from beyond the sky;

Innumerable stories of cannibal bushmen;

The mother-of-the-plants story;
Giant wolverine stories;
The man on the moon story;
The story of how wolves came to eat dogs;
The story of why beavers fought with porcupines;
The four-husband-woman story;
The crane story;
The swan story;
All kinds of squirrels', gophers', groundhogs' and muskrats' stories;
Tatlaman Lake war stories;
Chief Kwanatak's stories;
Chief Skalai's stories;
Chief Lane's awful stories;
The mesmerizing story of his grandpa Copper Joe's single-handed war with the Han Indians;
The trade stories with the Tlingit Indians;
The story of a trip to the Inuit at the mouth of the Yukon River, 2,000 miles away;
Copper chief's stories;
Old shaman Abraham's stories;
How old shaman Susay got kidnapped by caribou;
All kinds of different animal stories -- lynx's; fox's; wolf's; wolves as pets; bear's; bears as pets;
Another kind of bear eating men's penises or women's breasts (females doing the first and males the second);
Wolverines' stories; moose's; caribou's; mountain sheep's; mountain goat's;
White men's stories with Indian women;
The story telling how Tutchone men used to wrestle;
The story of the old marriage ceremonies;
Stories of how moieties' chiefs used to share power;
Stick gambling stories;
How the old potlatches used to be run;
Zozo's last potlatch;
Why there is no potlatch if the body of a drowned person cannot

be found.
The story of the peace ceremony;
How women used to give birth;
The story of the old yearly round;
How children used to be fixed up with animal spirits...

He told all the stories that kept banging on his door to be given life by his lips because he had never learned to read and write, or, one could say, to lay down his burden, as writing or re-writing would have allowed.

Tl'aku! Here in the Tutchone intense manner must end my own modern day Tutchone story of the story of Mr. Tommy McGinty wanting to have a book made out of the Northern Tutchone story of crow.

REFERENCES

Abu-Lughod, Lila
1991 Writing against Culture. In Richard G. Fox (Ed.) *Recapturing Anthropology: Working in the Present.* Santa Fe, New Mexico: School of American Research Press.

Angulo, Jaime de
1953 *Indian Tales* (Written and Illustrated by Jaime de Angulo with a Foreword by Carl Carmer). New York: Hill and Wang (Farrar, Strauss and Giroux).

1973 *Coyote Man and Old Doctor Loon* (Edited with and Introduction by Bob Callahan). San Francisco: Turtle Island Foundation.

1976a *Shabegok* (Edited, with notes, by Bob Callahan). San Francisco: Turtle Island Foundation.

1976b *How the World Was Made* (Edited, with notes, by Bob Callahan). San Francisco: Turtle Island Foundation.

Anonymous Report,
(No date) *A Reader's Guide to a Profile of Aboriginal Languages (Sponsored by the Canada-Yukon Funding Agreement on the Preservation, Development and Enhancement of Aboriginal Languages)*. Whitehorse (Yukon): Yukon Executive Council Office, Aboriginal Language Services.

Benjamin, Walter
1969 The Storyteller: Reflections on the Works of Nikolai Leskov. In Walter Benjamin, *Illuminations.* [1955]. Edited and with an Intro-

duction by Hannah Arendt, Translated by Harry Zohn. New York: Schocken Books.

Bettelheim, Bruno
1975 *The Uses of Enchantment: The Meaning and Importance of Fairy Tales*. New York: Vintage Books.

Brettell, Caroline B. (Ed.)
1993 *When They Read What We Write: The Politics of Ethnography.* Westport (Conn.) and London: Bergin and Garvey.

Charnes, Linda
1992 Comment on Jan Zita Grover. In Lawrence Crossberg *et al.* (Eds.), *Cultural Studies*. New York: Routledge.

Chowning, Ann
1962 Raven Myths in Northwestern North America and Northeast Asia. *Arctic Anthropology* 1(1): 1-5.

Clark, D. and R. Morlan
1982 Western Subarctic Prehistory: Twenty Years Later. *Canadian Journal of Archaeology* 6: 70-94.

Clastres, Pierre
1974 De quoi rient les Indiens. In P. Clastres, *La société contre l'état*. Paris: Editions de Minuit. Pages 113-132.

Cruikshank, Julie
1990 *Life Lived Like a Story: Life Stories of Three Yukon Native Elders (In collaboration with Angela Sidney, Kitty Smith, and Annie Ned)*. University of Nebraska Press and Vancouver: University of British Columbia Press.

Culler, Jonathan
1982 *On Deconstruction: Theory and Criticism after Structuralism.* Ithaca: Cornell University Press.

Dauenhauer, Nora Marks and Richard (Eds.)
1987 Haa Shuká, Our Ancestors: Tlingit Oral Narratives. In Dauenhauer, Nora Marks and Richard (eds.), *Classics of Tlingit Oral Literature*, Vol. 1. Seattle and London: University of Washington Press and Sealaska Heritage Foundation, Juneau, Alaska.

Derrida, Jacques
1967 *De la grammatologie*. Paris: Les Éditions de Minuit.
1986 Différance. In Hazard Adams and Leroy Searle, (eds), *Critical Theory Since 1965*. Tallahassee: University Press of Florida (Original in French, 1968)

Dyen, Isidore and David F. Aberle
1974 *Lexical Reconstruction: The Case of the Proto-Athapaskan Kinship System.* London: Cambridge University Press.

Erdoes Richard and Alfonso Ortiz (Eds.)
1984 *American Indian Myths and Legends, Selected and Edited by Richard Erdoes and Alfonso Ortiz.* Pantheon Fairy Tale and Folklore Library. New York: Pantheon Books. [For a book on Indian religious texts, notice the ethnocentricity of "myths and legends," and of "Pantheon Fairy Tale and Folklore Library"].

Fabian, Johannes
1983 *Time and the Other: How Anthropology Makes its Object*. New York: Columbia University Press

Fox Everett (Ed.)
1983 *Genesis and Exodus: A new English Rendition*. New York: Schocken Books.

Freeman, Derek
1983 *Margaret Mead and Samoa: The Making and Unmaking of an Anthropological Myth.* Cambridge and London: Harvard University Press.

Goody, Jack
1987 *The Interface between the Written and the Oral (Studies in Literacy, Family, Culture and the State).* Cambridge: Cambridge University Press.

Gotthardt, Ruth
1987 *Selkirk Indian Band: Culture and Land Use Study.* Whitehorse (Yukon): Yukon Renewable Resources

Greenfeld, Liah
1992 *Nationalism: Five Roads to Modernity.* Cambridge: Harvard University Press.

Grover, Jan Zita
1992 AIDS, Keywords, and Cultural Work. In Lawrence Crossberg *et al.* (Eds.), *Cultural Studies*. New York: Routledge. Pp. 227-239.

Hurston, Zora Neale
1991 *Moses, Man of the Mountain*. New York: Harper Perennial (Originally published 1939 by J.B. Lippincott Inc.).

Jameson, Fredric
1972 *The Prison-House of Language: A Critical Account of Structuralism and Russian Formalism*. Princeton: Princeton University Press.

Krauss, Michael E.

1988 Many Tongues -- Ancient Tales. In William W Fitzhugh and Aron Crowell (Eds.), *Crossroads of Continents: Cultures of Siberia and Alaska*. Washington D.C., and London: The Smithsonian Institution Press.

Krauss, M. E. and Golla Victor K.
1981 Northern Athapaskan Languages. In J. Helm (ed.) Subarctic. In W. C. Sturtevant (ed.), *Handbook of North American Indians*. Volume 6. 67-85. Washington D. C.: The Smithsonian Institution.

Laguna, Frederica de
1972 Under Mount Saint Elias: The History and Culture of the Yakutat Tlingit. *Smithsonian Contribution to Anthropology*, vol. 7 (in three parts). Washington D.C.: The Smithsonian Institution Press.

Legros Dominique
1981 *Structure socio-culturelle et rapports de domination chez les In- diens tutchone septentrionaux du Yukon au dix-neuvième siècle.* Ph.D. Thesis: University of British Columbia. Pp.1098 (On microfilm at U.M.I. Ann Arbor, Michigan, and la Bibliothèque Nationale du Canada, Ottawa, Ont. (No. C.T. 56751 ISBN 0-315-08834-6)).

1982 Réflexions sur l'origine des inégalités sociales à partir du cas des Athapaskan tutchone. *Culture* II(3): 65-84.

1984 Commerce entre Tlingits et Athapaskans tutchones au XIXe siècle. *Recherches Amérindiennes au Québec* 14(2): 11-24.

1985 Wealth, Poverty, and Slavery Among 19th Century Tutchone Athapaskan. *Research in Economic Anthropology,* VII: 37-64.

1987 Communautés amérindiennes contemporaines: structure et dynamique autochtones ou coloniales. *Recherches Amérindiennes au Québec* XVI(4): 47-68

1988 A propos des bandes patrilocales: illusions théoriques et réalités ethnographiques. *Journal de la Société des Américanistes (Paris).* *V*ol. 74: 125-161.

Lévi-Strauss, Claude
1958 *Anthropologie structurale.* Paris: Plon.

Lyotard, Jean-François
1971 *Discours, figure.* Paris: Klincksieck

McClellan, Catharine
1975 My Old People Say: An Ethnographic Survey Of Southern Yukon Territory, 2 vols. *Publications in Ethnology 6 (1 & 2).* Ottawa: National Museums of Canada.

McLuhan, Marshall
1962 *The Guntemberg Galaxy.* Toronto: University of Toronto Press.

Ong, Walter J.
1981 *Fighting for Life: Contest, Sexuality, and Consciousness.* Ithaca and London: Cornell University Press.

Pouillon, Jean
1991 Tradition. In Pierre Bonte et Michel Izard, *Dictionnaire de l'ethnologie et de l'anthropologie.* Paris: Presses Universitaires de France.

Reid, Bill
1984 The Anthropologist and the Article. *Culture* IV (2), 63-65.

Richardson, John
1851 *Arctic Searching Expedition: A Journal of a Boat Voyage Through Rupert"s Land and the Arctic Sea, etc.* (2. Vols.). London

Robert, Paul
1981 *Le Robert: Dictionnaire alphabétique et analogique de la langue française.* Edition corrigée en 6 volumes et un supplément. Paris: Société du Nouveau Littré, Le Robert.

Rosaldo, Renato
1989 *Culture and Truth: The Remaking of Social Analysis*. Boston, Mass: Beacon Press.

Sahlins, Marshall
1994 Goodbye to Tristes Tropes: Ethnography in the Context of Modern World History. In Robert Borofsky, (ed.) *Assessing Cultural Anthropology*. New York: McGraw-Hill. Pp. 377-395.

Sioui, George E.
1992 *For an Amerindian Autohistory: An Essay on the Foundations of a Social Ethic*. Montréal: McGill-Qeen's University Press.

Société Biblique Française
1987 *La Bible: traduction oecuménique, texte intégral*. Paris: Livre de Poche. 3 volumes

Stringer A.
1928 Missionary Report from Champagne. In *Report of the Synod of the Diocese Yukon, Sixth Synod, Diocese of Yukon, July 31, 1928, Pp. 39-40*.

Tedlock, Dennis
1978 *Finding the Center: Narrative Poetry of the Zuni Indians* (translated by Dennis Tedlock). University of Nebraska Press (Bison Book Edition).

1983 *The Spoken Word and the Work of Interpretation.* Philadelphia: University of Pennsylvania Press.

Thomas, Nicholas
1994 *Colonialism's Culture: Anthropology, Travel and Government*. Princeton: Princeton University Press.

Trigger, Bruce
1995 Conflicts and Blind Spots: Can Non-Native Scholars Write a History of the Native Peoples of North America? Paper presented at the *McGill Institute for the Study of Canada, Sixth Seminar*, Montréal, March 28, 1995

Wilson, Clifford
1970 *Campbell of the Yukon*. Toronto: Macmillan.